90%

attendance across term

DYNAMIC class lectures connect content to *real world* applications

25 ... less

... r tutorial ... timate ... ent in the **LARGEST** course on campus

A critical consumer of **INFORMATION**

Ready to Tackle the World

40,000+

GRADUATES
since 2007

MAC IntroPsych

Personalized Learning Through Discovery

4.54 out of 5

highly trained TAs facilitate **PBL** tutorials with *campus-leading* evaluations

225

OFFICE HOURS
(in class or online) per term give you *personal* attention when you **NEED IT**

Blended Learning

provides students with the *best* of online & face-to-face learning

4.65 out of 5

highly rated web modules
provide students with **INTERACTIVE** *on demand* access to course materials

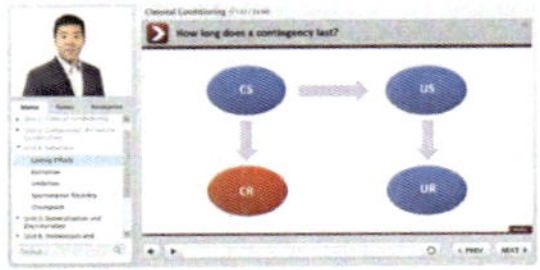

TERM 1

MAC IntroPsych

Psychology 1X03/1N03/1F03

Official Course Handbook 2020/2021

MACINTROPSYCH.COM

Your one-stop course companion website.
Includes:

- Important links
- Academic advice
- Departmental information
- And more!

NOTICE:
These learning materials are to be used as a guide to assist you with understanding the module material - they are not a replacement to viewing the online modules, attending your tutorials, or taking your own notes. Your grade will be determined by your full participation in all aspects of this course.

If you find any errors or omissions within this document, please feel free to email us (intropsych@mcmaster.ca) and we will be sure to have the issue rectified for the next release of this handbook.

This handbook was made possible by the tireless efforts of our handbook team, consisting of:
Dr. Joe Kim: Primary Instructor
Dr. Michelle Cadieux: Course Coordinator & Instructor
Veesta Mavandadi: Special Contributor
Kristal Cerga & Thomas Samson-Williams: Head TAs
The Science Media Team

1280 Main Street West • Psychology Building
Hamilton, Ontario L8S 4K1
Phone 905.525.9140 x 24428
Email: intropsych@mcmaster.ca
Web: macintropsych.com

Contents

Quick Start Guide

Are you in Psych 1F03? An updated syllabus is available on Avenue.

Before your First Class

1. Read the **<u>ENTIRE</u>** course outline.
2. Write the important dates in your calendar (last page of syllabus has a great table!).
3. Make a checklist of the course features and check out each one!

During the Semester

1. Watch the weekly web modules **BEFORE** your lecture and tutorial. Take <u>effective</u> notes using the outline and slides provided in this handbook as a guide.
2. Use a separate notebook for additional notes and write down any questions you have or concepts that were not clear. Bring these questions to your tutorial to get help from your TA.
3. For weekly web modules, look up unfamiliar words in the glossary and review them to build a solid foundation. As with most university courses, the psychology knowledge base you are expected to understand is cumulative and small gaps in understanding can become large gaps over time.
4. Complete the assigned readings (textbook/journal articles) to gain context, background, and additional examples to consolidate your knowledge.
5. Join one or start a study group with tutorial members or other peers on Avenue.
6. Complete the weekly activities and questions in this handbook. These can be a great starting point for your study group.
7. After completing each week's Pre-Quiz and Quiz, be sure to review the feedback on your results to see where you went wrong and right. Feedback for the Pre-Quizzes is available immediately, and feedback for the Quizzes is released on Tuesday mornings.

McMaster Student Absence Form (MSAF)

What is it?
The MSAF is a self-reporting tool that allows you to report absences for up to 3 days due to illness. You are limited to 1 total per semester so use it wisely. The MSAF form should be filled out within 3 days of the missed work and it is *your* responsibility to follow up with your instructor to discuss the nature of the accommodations. If you miss more than 3 days or exceed 1 request per semester, you must contact your Associate Dean's Office (Faculty Office). At this point, you may be required to provide additional supporting documentation.

Please use intropsych@mcmaster.ca as the contact email on any submitted MSAF, including for tutorials.

<u>NOTE:</u> It is *your* responsibility to catch up on missed work! It is a good idea to get peer contacts during the first week of classes so you can share notes and catch each other up.

Where do I go to fill this out?
The MSAF is available in the MOSAIC Student Center in the drop down menu under Academics. You can also go to the McMaster website and either search MSAF or type in http://www.mcmaster.ca/msaf/ in the search bar. At this point, read the page and click agree. From there you will be guided through the process in filling out the form.

Absences/Missed Quiz/Tutorial/Exam
If you must miss a quiz or tutorial due to illness or other situations and you have already used your MSAF, the

Course Coordinator requires the permission of your Associate Dean's office to excuse your absence. You may require documentation (e.g. doctor's note, wedding invitation). The Associate Dean's office will make a decision and forward the dates of any excused absence to the Course Coordinator without details of your illness/situation.

How to Use this Handbook

What Is Your Handbook?

Your handbook is the official courseware compiled by the Introductory Psychology instructional team and is designed to facilitate your academic experience in Psych 1X03/1N03/1F03. This handbook is continually revised to ensure that students have effective study aids and up-to-date information for the course. Your handbook is not a textbook. It does not contain mandatory readings that are required for you to pass the course. However, it does have a wealth of resources to help you reach your academic goals in Psych 1X03/1N03/1F03.

How To Use Your Handbook Effectively with the Rest of the Course Components

1. Read the week's intro and preview the key slides.

2. Watch the web module before reading the textbook, using the key slides as a guide to taking notes.

3. Carefully answer the checkpoint questions in the web module (note: these are basic level Qs to make sure you are paying attention). If you get these wrong, you should review the preceding unit.

4. Complete activities, questions and exercises in the handbook to apply and test your knowledge. Don't forget to make use of the flashcards!

5. Check out the challenging question (with a full explanation) from a previous Avenue Quiz in the handbook, which tests understanding rather than ability to memorize. Often, first-year students fall into the pattern of studying to gain a superficial factual knowledge, rather than a complex understanding, of the concept. If evaluations then simply asked you to regurgitate everything you had memorized, you would do fine. However, if you study like this, you're studying for the wrong type of test! The challenging questions demonstrate how you will be tested in this course. A hallmark of superior understanding is the ability to transfer knowledge to new contexts (Marsh). In these questions, you can't simply regurgitate terms you memorized. You really need to understand and apply. The best way to do this is to test yourself. Force yourself to explain concepts in your own words and better yet, try teaching them to a peer and drawing on personal examples to make your point. When you're ready, take the Pre-Quiz for the week. The questions on it are drawn from the same test bank as the actual Quiz on Friday. It doesn't count, but it will give you a good idea of the level of challenge you should expect from the Quiz. It's graded immediately, and provides detailed explanatory feedback on your chosen option. Many students do not take advantage of the Pre-Quiz. Don't be one of these students!

6. Read the textbook to give you additional context and details to fill in the framework provided by the web modules. Complete the practice exercises at the end of each section in the handbook to consolidate your knowledge.

Handbook Sections

Taking Notes: The inclusion of important graphics is meant to facilitate your learning so that you do not have to recopy all of the information from the web modules. In addition, ample space has been provided beside each key slide for you to take notes in your own words. Furthermore, the skeleton notes are ordered sequentially, providing some additional structure to your note-taking. Copying down the script from the web modules word for word is not an effective way of studying. Instead, watch the web modules once, reflect on the material you've just viewed, and then go back to re-watch the modules while taking notes on the concepts you're struggling with.

Activities and Practice Questions: Completing the activities and practice questions at the end of each module and checking your answers against the answer key at the end of the handbook is an effective way to learn and assess your understanding of important concepts. We encourage you to review the answers in the back of the handbook after finishing the questions to see if you're on the right track. Even if you have selected the correct answer, make sure to read through the explanations provided to ensure that your logic is accurate and to have trickier concepts explained again using different words.

Bottleneck Concepts: This section compares and contrasts concepts and terminology that students often get confused. One of the pairs is given a full explanation. You should practice by completing the others yourself!

Concept Maps: The concept maps are designed to help students see the "big picture". You can use concept maps as a quick pre-quiz review or to check if you have accurately understood all of the connections between the different elements in the module. As you begin studying for your final exam, you may also wish to use your concept maps to check if you have forgotten a key concept in the course.

Sample Quiz Question Explained: Make sure you answer the question yourself and write this answer down before reading the explanation provided. This way you can accurately assess whether or not you know the material before doing your pre-quiz or Avenue quiz. Additionally, if you've selected an incorrect answer, you may be able to identify why you did not choose the correct answer and how to avoid making the same mistake on future quizzes using the feedback provided. By critically evaluating your approach and performance on multiple-choice questions, you will find it easier to reach your desired level of performance on our quizzes and in the course. This may also be very helpful for your tests in other courses.

Glossary: Use the glossary as a quick reference for the key terms without having to re-watch modules to obtain definitions. The glossary clearly defines the key terms and even provides you with new examples. You can test your knowledge of these terms by covering the definitions, writing down your answers to a specific term, and then checking to see if you are correct. Conversely, you could cover the terms, read the definition and see if you can accurately match the definition with its corresponding term.

Flash Cards: All glossary terms have also been made into cue cards that you can cut out to help you learn all of the important vocabulary. Remember to fill in the blank example section for each card. Coming up with your own example is the best way to learn new terms.

Course Staff	Location	Office Hours
Dr. Joe Kim Instructor	PC/106 - Online	Posted weekly on Avenue
Dr. Michelle Cadieux Course Coordinator & Instructor	MacIntroPsych Office PC/110 - Online	Posted weekly on Avenue
Kristal Cerga & Thomas Samson-Williams Head TAs	Online	
TA drop-in hours	Online	Tuesday - Thursday 11:00am - 1:00pm

All correspondence regarding this course should be sent to: ***intropsych@mcmaster.ca*** using your McMaster email and **NOT** your Avenue account. If you have additional questions regarding course material, you have several options:

- Ask the course coordinator or TAs during Office and TA drop-in hours, posted weekly on Avenue
- Ask your personal TA during tutorial
- Join the active discussions on Avenue forums.

You may also call the MacIntroPsych office at X24428 during office hours. Please note that **phone messages will not be returned.** If you have a request, please during office hours or send an email to intropsych@mcmaster.ca. Note that during busy periods, it may take up to 48 hours to return your email. Please be patient!

In addition to the course staff, you have been assigned to a tutorial section with your personal **Teaching Assistant (TA)** who will lead your group through weekly discussions, activities, and questions.

Course Description

This course introduces a scientific framework to explore important questions in psychology, neuroscience, and behaviour. Using psychological research methods to understand learning, cognition, and social psychology, this course helps learners to develop skills to integrate, evaluate, and examine information that is useful in applied settings. The intended learning outcomes are to:

- Integrate knowledge from research design, learning, cognition, and social psychology
- Apply the language of psychology in real-world settings and connect with current events
- Critically evaluate scientific information, data, and research methodologies
- Discover how psychological theories help assess, predict, or change human behaviour

Evaluation

Your final grade in Psychology 1X03 will be determined by the following measures:

Tutorial Participation	10%
Avenue Quizzes	30%
Avenue QuizTerm	7%
Final Examination	53%
PeerWise Multiple Choice Questions (optional)	3% reweight of final exam
Sona Research Participation (optional)	5% - 6.5% reweight of final exam

Tutorial Participation (10%)

Weekly tutorials are an important part of the course and contribute to 10% of your final grade. Your TA will expect **active** participation to create a dynamic learning environment. If you have specific issues with this process, you must speak to the course coordinator as soon as possible.

Tutorials will be live-streamed throughout the term. Specifics are still being determined, but information will be posted on Avenue as it becomes available. Tutorials will not be recorded for student privacy reasons.

Your TA will assign you a grade out of 10 every three tutorials based on your participation in one tutorial (5 points), and your attendance in the other two (2.5 points each). To encourage participation during all tutorials, you will not be aware of which tutorial you are being marked for participation. You will be assessed on the elements of participation using the rubric below.

PARTICIPATION	Points	Description
Excellent	4-5	Consistently exemplifies all three elements of participation
Satisfactory	3	Occasionally exemplifies some elements of participation
Poor	1-2	Rarely exemplifies elements of participation
Absent	0	Does not attend tutorial

Element	Description
Knowledge	Demonstrates knowledge of course material
Insightfulness	Demonstrates insightful and critical thinking
Synergy	Demonstrates positive and constructive interactions with peers

Your TA will also post a content-related question onto your tutorial's Avenue discussion board. Students who choose to answer all three discussion board posts within a marking period will receive a bonus mark (*i.e.* a mark of 8/10 would become 9/10).

Note: students who regularly attend tutorials but make no contribution to class discussions cannot receive a grade higher than 5 out of 10. Therefore, it is essential that you **actively participate** if you wish to earn a high participation grade. Your TA can help you with suggestions for demonstrating active participation.

Avenue Quizzes (30%)

There are 10 weekly online Avenue Quizzes during the semester which will cover material from the web modules, in-person lectures, and assigned readings. For example, Quiz 1 will contain material covered in the Research Methods 1 & 2 web modules and online lecture, as well as Chapter 2 from the textbook. Each Quiz is "open book" and you may collaborate with your peers but you may NOT post questions online. Avenue Quizzes are an opportunity to assess and consolidate your knowledge of the week's content in preparation for the Final Exam, where you will be working independently and without access to supporting resources.

The weekly quizzes are not cumulative. Each Quiz will consist of 10 multiple-choice questions. Avenue Quizzes will be made available online every Friday at 6AM and will promptly close on Saturday at 6AM. You will have 20 minutes to complete each quiz once you open it. After closing on Saturday, the Quiz will be reviewed, and grades will be released on the following Tuesday.

Quiz questions are designed to go beyond mere recall and challenge you to apply and demonstrate your comprehension. In other words, simply memorizing terms will not lead to a favourable grade. To help you prepare and assess your studying, you will have a **Pre-Quiz** each week (released on Monday) that will be graded immediately and will provide you with feedback on why your chosen option was correct/incorrect. You can review the completed Pre-Quiz under the Quizzes tab on Avenue. The Pre-Quiz serves as an excellent learning tool as it is drawn from the same question bank as your actual Friday Quiz, but does not count for grades. Note that the Pre-Quiz **MUST** be completed to gain access to the weekly Avenue Quiz.

Internet Problems

Internet issues can happen. We always recommend that you complete your quizzes where a reliable Internet connection is guaranteed. While we do not accommodate for individual Internet issues, we can grade your quiz manually if you take screen shots. Please make sure that all photos have your name in the shot.

Quiz Review

Quiz scores are released on Avenue Tuesday mornings. They can be found in the Grades section under the Assessments tab. Feedback on your quizzes is available once the grades are released. To see the feedback, go to the quiz page and scroll down to the bottom. You will see all of your past quizzes. Click on the small triangle next to the quiz and select "submissions". This will bring you to a new page with your attempt on that quiz. Click on this attempt and you will be able to see your quiz. After each question you can also expand the feedback to get a more detailed reason why your answer was right or wrong. Students have one week after the quiz grades have been released to bring up any concerns related to a specific question. Please email a screenshot of the question to intropsych@mcmaster.ca. Don't forget to provide a detailed explanation of your concern.

Weekly Lectures

Lectures will be live-streamed each week. Each session will be recorded and posted to Avenue to Learn. Details will be posted on Avenue regarding how to access the live-stream. If you wish to earn the iclicker bonus points mentioned in the next section, you will need to attend your registered lecture section during the live-stream.

Lecture iclicker Bonus Points

During your weekly lectures you will be given the opportunity to earn iclicker bonus points. Each week, you will have a short quiz during class. Each question will be worth a maximum of 2 points. You will receive 1 bonus point for simply answering the question and a second point if you answer it correctly.

All lecture bonus quizzes require a subscription to Reef. Reef allows you to participate in iclicker polls online using your smartphone or computer. These can be purchased at the Campus Store. We do not recommend purchasing the Reef subscription online as it is much cheaper from the Campus Store. You can only earn iclicker bonus points in your registered lecture section. At the end of the term, your total number of points will earn you the following rewards:

Points	Reward
20 and above	Drop lowest participation grade
30 and above	Drop lowest participation grade + lowest quiz grade
40 and above	Drop lowest participation grade + 2 lowest quiz grades

Register your iclicker Reef Account

To register please go to https://app.reef-education.com

You will need to create an account if this is your first time using iclicker. You MUST use your MacID in the student ID section during your registration. This is what you use to login to Avenue/Mosaic. It is also the first part of your McMaster email address. Do NOT use your student number for this section.

Once you have created an account, you will need to add the course. You can search using Psych 1X03. **You need to select the correct core section for your course**. Failure to register correctly may result in a zero being assigned.

You will also need to add your reef subscription to your profile. This can be done by clicking the menu button in the top left corner and selecting subscriptions. You will then see the option to enter the access code you purchased from the bookstore.

iclicker Trouble Shooting
iclicker points are updated weekly on Avenue. Only points that appear on Avenue are counted. If your points are not appearing on Avenue you have most likely made an error somewhere. The two most common mistakes are:

1) You have entered your student number in your iclicker profile. You need to enter your MacID (NOT your student number). Your MacID is your login for Avenue/Mosaic. To update this information, login to the iclicker website and click the menu button in the top left and select Profile. Once this is corrected, your points will appear on Avenue during the next weekly refresh.

2) You are attending a lecture section that you are not registered in. You can only earn points in the lecture section you are registered in on Mosaic.

If all of the above appears to be in order and you did not receive your points. Please take a screenshot of your iclicker profile and email it to intropsych@mcmaster.ca (using your McMaster email address). Please also include your lecture core section.

Avenue QuizTerm (7%)

The QuizTerm will take the form of a longer Avenue Quiz. It will be 30 multiple choice questions and you will be given 60 minutes to complete it. The QuizTerm will open on Friday October 30th at 6am and will close on Saturday October 31st at 6am. This is a cumulative assessment. It will contain information from Research Methods, Classical and Instrumental Conditioning, Problem Solving & Intelligence, Language, and The Science of Learning. It will cover material presented in the web modules, lectures, tutorials, and assigned readings.

Final Exam (53%)

A cumulative online Final Exam will be written in December as scheduled by the Registrar's Office. If you choose to complete both the optional multiple-choice question writing and 3 credits of optional research participation (see below), the weight of your final examination will be reduced from 53% to 43.5%. The Final Exam covers material presented in web modules, lectures, tutorials, and assigned readings from the entire term.

NOTE: This course may use proctoring software for the final exam. This software may require you to own a video camera, present identification, and may turn on your video camera, monitor and record your computer activities, and lockdown your browser during the exam. This software may require installation before the exam begins. A final decision has not be made on which software will be used. Information will be updated as it becomes available. If you have questions about whether this software will be used, or concerns about the use of this software, please contact the course coordinator at intropsych@mcmaster.ca.

Multiple-Choice Questions – PeerWise

You have the option to reduce the weight of your Final Exam by 3% by creating and answering multiple-choice questions on PeerWise (https://peerwise.cs.auckland.ac.nz/at/?mcmaster_ca). There are two deadlines for this assignment, and you must meet both to earn the bonus. You must write 10 multiple choice questions and answer 10 questions created by your peers before the QuizTerm. You must also write and answer 10 more questions between the QuizTerm and the Final Exam.

Before QuizTerm	Between QuizTerm and Final Exam
Write 10 Questions Answer 10 Questions	Write 10 Questions Answer 10 Questions

This is an all-or-none assignment. You will not receive partial points if you complete or answer less than the required number of questions or if you complete them after the deadlines. The deadline for the first half of the assignment is the **start** of the QuizTerm at 6am on Friday October 30th. The second deadline is the start of the final exam.

Creating multiple-choice questions is a great way to study for the weekly quizzes and for the final exam. Writing questions requires you to reflect on what you have learned in the course and explaining each option in the feedback section helps you to fully understand the concept. Writing plausible distractors is also trickier than you might think. You need to consider all the potential misconceptions and interpretations of a concept. Answering other students' questions may help you identify areas of weakness in your knowledge or view a topic from a perspective you hadn't thought about before. We recommend completing questions every week as a way to help study for the quizzes, instead of waiting to do it at the last minute before the deadline.

To participate on PeerWise you must first create an account. You can do this by clicking the registration button in the bottom left corner of the website. You will need 2 things to complete your registration: The course ID and your identifier. **The course ID is: 21701 and your identifier is your MacID (NOT your student number).** Your MacID is your login for Avenue. It is also the first part of your McMaster email address.

Writing Questions

Once you have logged in, under the "Your Questions" section click on "View Questions" and you should be directed to a new page. When writing multiple-choice questions you will need to provide the question text as well as 4 response options for each question. Make sure your question is very clear and not likely to be ambiguous. Use professional language and avoid slang or spelling mistakes. You will also be asked to provide "tags" for your question. Please use this feature to indicate the relevant web module(s).

You will also need to provide an explanation for your question. This is one of the criteria for how your question is rated by your fellow students. For this section you should create a list and provide an explanation corresponding to each of the options. Indicate why each answer is right or wrong. This is the same format as the feedback on your weekly quizzes, where you receive a specific explanation for your answer and not just a reason why one answer is correct.

Answering Questions

Once you have answered a question, you will be given feedback on the response you selected, and you will be shown an explanation of the answer. You will also be able to see how other students answered. You will then be given an opportunity to select the difficulty level you think best matches the question and to give the question a rating, which you should think about very carefully.

When rating a question, you should be judging two things:

- Whether you think the question is of a high enough quality that it could appear on an Avenue quiz.

- Whether you think the explanation provided with the question is sufficient so that if someone answered the question incorrectly the explanation would help them to understand what they had done wrong.

Other things to keep in mind:

- You should not rate questions differently based on their difficulty – an easy question can be just as useful as a hard question. Everyone is at different levels of understanding.
- Be fair with your ratings – you should justify a poor rating with a comment to the author of the question, or by agreement with a previously written comment.
- Make sure any comments you provide are constructive – you are rating questions written by your peers so provide the kind of feedback that you would find useful and encouraging yourself.
- To encourage everyone to participate equally, all activity on PeerWise is anonymous (however your instructor is able to track contributions).

Research Participation – Sona

You have the option to reduce the weight of your Final Exam from 53% to 48% by completing and attaining **two credits** of research participation with the Department of Psychology, Neuroscience, and Behaviour. If you complete **three credits** you will reduce the weight of your final exam by 6.5%, making your exam worth 46.5%. In addition to providing you with extra credit, the research participation option allows you to take part in some exciting research taking place right here at McMaster and observe how psychologists conduct their studies.

Given the current COVID-19 pandemic, we are unsure at this time if in-person research opportunities will be available in the fall semester. However, there will be online options to complete your Sona credits.

Please remember that your Sona participation is voluntary and that you can withdraw at any time. If you do not wish to participate as a research subject for any reason, you may still earn your research participation credit by *observing* experiments. If you would like to observe studies instead of participating, please email the course coordinator at intropsych@mcmaster.ca or visit during office hours. Observations are more difficult because of the pandemic so we encourage you to participate if possible. If you would like to sign up as a participant, please follow the instructions below.

The system that the department uses to track research participation is called Sona and it can be accessed at **mcmaster.sona-systems.com**. To access Sona for the first time, select the "Request Account" option on the right of your screen and enter your name, student number, and McMaster email address. You will also be asked to pick your courses. Please select Psych 1X03 from the list. After a short delay, you will receive an email from Sona with a username and temporary password that you can use to access the website. You should change your password to something more memorable by selecting "My Profile". Make sure your student number is entered correctly! **Note: You must activate your McMaster ID before you can create a Sona account. To activate your ID, please go to www.mcmaster.ca/uts/macid**

Completing Your Research Participation Credit

When you login to Sona for the first time, you will be asked to fill out a short survey. This information is used to filter out any experiments for which you are not eligible.

To register for an experiment, select "Study Sign-Up" from the main Sona page. You will be presented with a list of currently available experiments, with a short description given about each. Before selecting an experiment, be sure to read the description carefully, making special note of any specific criteria for participation (for example, some experiments only allow females to participate, while others may require subjects who speak a second language). When you have found an experiment that you would like to participate in, select "View Time Slots for this Study" to view available timeslots, then select "Sign-Up" to register for a time that fits your schedule. You will receive a confirmation email with the details of your selection. Be sure to write down the Study number, experimenter name, location, and telephone extension from this email.

In-Person studies: After you have completed an experiment, you will be given a paper slip verifying your participation. This slip is for your records only—in the event that an experiment is not credited to your Sona account, this slip is your proof of participation. Shortly after completing an experiment, you should notice that your Sona account has been credited by the experimenter.

Online studies: We recommend you take a screenshot of the final completion screen as proof of your participation. You do not need to send this to anyone, it's just good to have in case something goes wrong with your credit. Credits for online studies are generally uploaded sometime after the study deadline so it may take a while for the credit to show up on Sona.

Important Notes

- You must complete two credits on Sona, and no less, if you wish to earn the 5% exam reweight.
- If you fail to show up for two experiments, you will lose your option to complete the research participation credit. If you know in advance that you will be unable to attend a scheduled experiment, please contact the experimenter as soon as possible. You can access their email by clicking on the envelope next to their name on the study information page.
- All credits must be completed by the day of the final exam (end of day).

Welcome to Psychology 1X03/1N03/1F03

Welcome to PSYCH 1X03: Introduction to Psychology, Neuroscience & Behaviour, one of two MacIntroPsych courses offered at McMaster University (PSYCH 1XX3 is offered in Term 2). Your IntroPsych course follows in the tradition of McMaster University's long-standing reputation of excellence in innovative teaching and learning. In this course, you will experience a unique blended learning model that combines online learning technology with traditional face-to-face instruction. On your way to the weekly Quizzes and Final Exam, there are several resources available to help you master the curriculum:

Course Handbook: Your course handbook contains valuable information regarding course structure, outlines, and guides for web modules and tutorials.

Course Textbook: Your course textbook can be purchased at the McMaster Campus Store. It contains required readings with testable material for the course.

MacIntroPsych.com: There are many supplementary resources that have been specially developed to complement the handbook at MacIntroPsych.com including practice tests, study aids, important links, information about course events, university services, and tips for academic success.

Avenue to Learn: Your primary course content will be delivered through the Avenue learning management system located at **http://avenue.mcmaster.ca**. Avenue allows you access to weekly web modules, course announcements, discussion forums, and grade records. To access Avenue, use your MacID and password. Below are some of the features of Avenue.

Web Modules: The most unique feature of MacIntroPsych is the way you receive your primary course content—it's all online! You can access the web modules from the library, your room, or anywhere you have an internet connection. The interactive web modules feature audio, video animations, and vivid graphics. Check out the many advanced features that allow you to interact with the content according to your personal learning preferences. Use the navigation tools and integrated search function to move about the module. You can test your knowledge with checkpoints, participate in class polls, learn more about faculty related research, and check out interesting links in our media+ section. Be sure to view the assigned web modules **before** you attend your weekly lecture and tutorial to stay on schedule, get points on the bonus quizzes, and actively participate.

Discussion Boards: More extended topic discussions are available on the Avenue Discussion Board. Join an existing discussion or start a new thread. Our discussion boards are consistently the most active in comparison to any other course on campus, so jump right in with your opinion!

Tutorials: You will join a small tutorial section (capped at 26 students) led by a Teaching Assistant (TA) who is enrolled in or has completed PSYCH 3TT3: Applied Educational Psychology, a course designed specifically to help TAs lead effective tutorials and guide you through MacIntroPsych. Each year, our TAs receive top ratings from students across campus so don't be shy to ask questions. If you think your TA is especially amazing, consider nominating them for the Kathy Steele Award, which honours the top TA of the year. Your TA will guide discussions, lead activities and demonstrations, and answer any questions you might have. Tutorials are updated each year by feedback from students and TAs.

Lobby Hours: Have a question? Still confused about a specific concept? Need some one-on-one time? Drop by during our online office hours to speak with your TA. The times are posted on Avenue. If you have administrative questions please visit Dr. Michelle Cadieux, the course coordinator, or send her an email. Her office hours are updated on Avenue weekly.

How to Use Google Scholar

Google scholar is a great tool to find peer-reviewed journal articles (a few of which will be assigned as your weekly reading). It is quick and simple. Below, we have outlined a few tips to make it even simpler.

How do I get there?

Easy! Type in http://scholar.google.ca, or just type "scholar" into Google.

I can't seem to access any articles, what do I do?

Most journals require you to purchase an article before you can access it. Luckily, McMaster has purchased these articles for us! All you have to do is click on "scholar preferences" at the top right of the window. Where it says "Library Links" enter "McMaster" then scroll to the bottom and save preferences. Simple!

I am trying to find articles about a general topic, what do I do?

Use the search box to search articles by their journal, author(s), title, or topic. Another search option is to click on "advanced scholar search" beside the search box. This will allow you to search for specific journals, authors, and titles. You can even search for articles about a particular topic published within a particular time frame and published in a particular journal. Play around with it and get used to this tool. It will come in handy not just this semester, but for much of your university career.

Privacy and Conduct

We will be using Avenue for the online portions of this course. Students should be aware that when they access the electronic components of this course, private information such as first and last names, MacIDs, and program affiliation may become apparent to all other students in the same course. The available information is dependent on the technology used. Continuation in this course will be deemed as consent to this disclosure. If you have any questions or concerns about such disclosure, please discuss this with the Course Coordinator.

All posts on discussion forums should be polite and refrain from derogatory and unacceptable language.

Changes During the Term

The instructor and university reserve the right to modify elements of the course during the term. The university may change the dates and deadlines for any or all courses in extreme circumstances. If either type of modification becomes necessary, reasonable notice and communication with the students will be given with explanation and the opportunity to comment on changes. It is the responsibility of the student to check their McMaster email and course websites weekly during the term and to note any changes.

A Note About Note Taking

Students often wonder (and worry) about how extensive their notes should be. This handbook provides outlines with key points and slides reproduced from the web modules to guide your own note taking. There really is no substitute for doing this yourself to learn the material. If, however, you can refer to your notes and answer the practice questions that follow the handbook outlines, you should find yourself in good shape for the weekly quizzes and the exam to come.

A Note About Tests

With practice questions in this handbook, iclicker bonus point questions, Pre-Quizzes and Quizzes, you might be wondering "why are there so many tests?!". The simple answer is that testing has been shown to be the most effective way to learn information in the long term.

Retrieval-Enhanced Learning

Many students likely view testing as a negative necessity of their courses and would prefer to have as few tests as possible. Thinking about testing this way is due to years of experiencing tests as a high-stakes assessment of learning. This is unfortunate given the fact that testing improves learning. Over the past hundred years, research on the characteristics of human learning and memory has demonstrated that practice testing enhances learning and retention of information (e.g., Dunlosky et al., 2013; Roediger & Karpicke, 2006a). Practice testing can take many forms. It can refer to practicing your recall of information by using flashcards, completing practice problems or questions in a textbook, or completing low-stakes tests as part of a course requirement. This principle was the primary motivation for redesigning the MacIntroPsych course to have weekly, low stakes quizzes.

An excellent example of the power of testing memory comes from a study by Roediger and Karpicke (2006b), wherein undergraduate students were presented with short, educationally relevant texts for initial study. Following initial study, students either studied the material again or took a practice test. A final test was taken after a short retention interval (5 minutes) or long retention interval (2 days). After a short retention interval, restudying produced better recall than testing (81% vs. 75%). However, with the long retention interval, testing produced significantly better recall than restudying (68% vs. 54%). Thus, after two days, performance declined 27% for students who restudied the material, but only 7% for students who practiced recall.

Interestingly, providing students with the correct answer feedback after a test enhances the positive effect of testing. With feedback, learners are able to correct errors, and maintain their correct responses. Moreover, taking a test and reviewing feedback can enhance future study sessions. Research shows that when a student takes a test before restudying material, they learn **more** from the restudying session than if they restudy without taking a test beforehand (e.g., Karpicke, 2009). This is called test-potentiated learning.

Why does testing improve retention of information and how can I use it?

Explanations for the positive effects of testing focus on how the act of retrieval affects memory. Specifically, it is suggested that retrieving information leads to an elaboration of memory traces and the creation of additional retrieval paths. Together these changes to memory systems make it more likely that the information will be successfully retrieved again in the future. This suggests that testing is not just an assessment tool, but also an effective learning tool.

As a student in this course you can take advantage of retrieval enhanced learning each week in preparation for your weekly Quiz. This begins with studying web module content early in the week (e.g., Sunday or Monday). You can then engage in retrieval practice as a form of review after your initial study session. At this point you should be ready to complete the Pre-quiz and review the feedback (by Wednesday or Thursday). This gives you the opportunity to take advantage of test-potentiated learning when you review content again before completing your Quiz on Friday. This suggested schedule of studying, and incorporation of retrieval practice will help you learn and retain the course content. Engaging in this process each week enhances your long-term memory for course content and therefore advances your preparations for the final exam!

Suggested further reading:

1. Dunlosky, et al., (2013). *Psychological Science in the Public Interest, 14*(1), 4-58.
2. Karpicke, J. D. (2009). *Journal of Experimental Psychology: General, 138*, 469–486.
3. Roediger, H. L., & Karpicke, J. D. (2006a). *Psychological Science, 17*, 249–255.
4. Roediger, H. L., & Karpicke, J. D. (2006b). *Perspectives on Psychological Science, 1*, 181–210.

A Note About Multiple Choice Questions and Flashcards

Test questions can challenge you to demonstrate your mastery of course content through 3 levels of increasing difficulty:

1. To *remember* psychological terms, concepts, theories, and methods.
2. To *understand* information that has been remembered.
3. To *apply* understood information to novel situations (this is called *transfer* and demonstrates true mastery of learned material).

Let's take a look at an example of a psychological concept you will learn:

Confounding Variable: An extraneous variable whose presence affects the variables being studied so that the results do not reflect the actual relationship between the variables.

Here is a simple question that challenges your ability to *remember* the term:

1. Which of the following best describes a confounding variable?
   a. A dependent variable whose absence affects the variables being studied so that the results do reflect the actual relationship between variables.
   b. An independent variable whose absence affects the variables being studied so that the results do not reflect the actual relationship between variables.
   c. An extraneous variable whose presence affects the variables being studied so that the results do reflect the actual relationship between variables.
   d. An extraneous variable whose presence affects the variables being studied so that the results do not reflect the actual relationship between variables.

The correct answer is D, and knowing this requires the ability to *remember* (or look up) a word-for-word definition of confounding variable taken directly from the course material

2. If a confounding variable is unnoticed, it can lead a researcher to:
   a. Make a more accurate connection between an independent and dependent variable.
   b. Make a more accurate connection between two independent variables.
   c. Make an erroneous association between an independent and dependent variable.
   d. Make an erroneous association between several confounding variables.

The correct answer is C, and knowing this requires the ability to *understand* information that has been accurately remembered, because you must be able to recognize a definition of confounding variable that is composed of different words than the original definition.

3. A researcher gives the same IQ test questions to a group of children and discovers that arm length is positively correlated with number of correct responses. He concludes that longer arms lead to increased intelligence. What confounding variable may account for this finding to weaken this conclusion?
   a. Some children may have been purposely answering test questions incorrectly.
   b. Arm length increases with age, so this study may demonstrate that older children outperform younger children.
   c. IQ is a hypothetical construct that may not accurately reflect intelligence.
   d. IQ test questions may lack validity and reliability.

The correct answer is B, and knowing this requires the ability to *apply* understood information in a novel situation.

Using flashcards effectively can be a solid method for efficiently building your knowledge to prepare for the three types of test questions. On the back of each flashcard is a ready-prepared definition for the term to help you *remember*. When studying, you should try to rework this definition into your own words to help you *understand*. Finally, create an original example that illustrates the term to help you learn to *apply*.

To provide some additional help for effective use of the flashcards, we have included an additional set of cards on the following page. These flashcards will require you to go deeper with the concepts thus increasing your understanding and retention.

Bonus tip: One of the most robust findings in research on the science of learning is the distributed practice effect, which shows the benefits of spreading out study sessions over time. Let's say Claire and Elger both spend 4 hours studying the same material for a test. Claire distributes his practice by studying 1 hour a day for 4 days and Elger crams all 4 of her study hours in one long study marathon the night before the test. Even with time-on-task equated, Claire will show significantly improved long-term benefits.

Describe a movie/television scene that depicts this concept

MAC IntroPsych

Pick two cards and make a connection between the concepts

MAC IntroPsych

Describe this concept without using any of the key words written on the flashcard

MAC IntroPsych

Draw this concept

MAC IntroPsych

How would you explain this concept to a child?

MAC IntroPsych

What is the opposite of this concept?

MAC IntroPsych

What situation in your life has depicted this concept?

MAC IntroPsych

Create a concept map with all of the cards from a module

MAC IntroPsych

Campus Resources

The following are some of the resources available to McMaster University students. Read over each description and familiarize yourself with what is available!

Student Accessibility Services

Student Accessibility Services offers various supports for students with disabilities. They work with full-time, part-time, and prospective students. SAS assists with academic and disability-related needs, including learning strategies, note-taking, assistive technologies, test & exam administration, accommodations for courses, groups, and events.

Website: http://sas.mcmaster.ca/
Phone: 905-525-9140 ext. 28652
Teletypewriter (TTY): 905-528-4307
Email: sas@mcmaster.ca
Office: McMaster University Student Centre (MUSC) - Basement, Room B107

Student Wellness Centre

The Student Wellness Centre offers medical & health services, personal counselling, and mental health services.
Medical & Health: The Student Wellness Centre provides a wide range of health services for students and will act as their personal health care provider throughout their studies at McMaster. Appointment bookings should be made ahead of time.
Personal Counselling & Mental Health: At some point, almost everyone experiences major concerns that may interfere with their success, happiness, and satisfaction at university. Common concerns are relationships, mood disorders, learning disabilities, body image, anxiety, and depression. The Student Wellness Centre provides experienced counsellors for bookings and emergency appointments.
Website: http://wellness.mcmaster.ca/
Phone: 905-525-9140 ext. 27700
Email: wellness@mcmaster.ca
Office: PGCLL 210/201

Emergency First Response Team (EFRT)

The McMaster Students Union Emergency First Response Team (EFRT) is a group of approximately 30 student volunteers who provide emergency medical services to the McMaster Campus, with an average response time of 2-3 minutes. All responders are certified Emergency Medical Responders, with more senior members being trained in International Trauma Life Support (ITLS), and Advanced Medical Life Support (AMLS). The EFRT is available 24/7 throughout the academic year except Thanksgiving, Easter, the Holiday Break, and both Reading Weeks.
Website: https://www.msumcmaster.ca/services-directory/7-emergency-first-response-team-efrt
Phone: "88" from any campus phone or 905-522-4135 on any cell phone

The MacPherson Institute for Leadership, Innovation and Excellence in Teaching

This institute is designed to enable success in teaching and learning. Their activities include both general and discipline-specific approaches to the promotion of successful learning in all its forms and contexts.
Website: mi.mcmaster.ca
Phone: 905-525-9140 ext. 24540
Office: Mills Library L504

Academic Advising in PNB

Ann Hollingshead is the academic advisor for anyone in the PNB department at McMaster. She has a lot of knowledge about upper-year courses and can help you make the best decisions about what courses to take. Ann is available Monday – Friday 9:00am-5:00pm for drop-in help or by appointment.

Email: hollings@mcmaster.ca
Phone: 905-525-9140 ext. 23005
Office: PC 109

Note: For academic advising for other departments, visit your faculty's website (Social Science, Science, Engineering, etc.) for more information.

Academic Integrity and Honesty

As a McMaster student, you are expected to exhibit honesty and ethical behaviour in all aspects of the learning process. The academic credentials that you earn are rooted in the principles of honesty and academic integrity.

Academic dishonesty is to knowingly act or fail to act in a way that results or could result in unearned academic credit or advantage. This behaviour can result in serious consequences, (e.g., the grade of zero on an assignment, loss of credit with a notation on the transcript which reads: "Grade of F assigned for academic dishonesty") and/or suspension of expulsion from the university).

It is your responsibility to understand what constitutes academic dishonesty. For information on the various types of academic dishonesty please refer to the Academic Integrity Policy:
https://www.mcmaster.ca/academicintegrity/index.html

Some helpful information can be found here: **https://sscm.mcmaster.ca**

The following illustrates only three forms of academic dishonesty:

- Plagiarism, e.g. the submission of work that is not one's own or for which other credit has been sought or obtained;
- Improper collaboration (which includes posting Avenue quiz questions or answers online); or,
- Copying or using unauthorized aids in tests or examinations.

Statement on Inclusivity and Academic Integrity

The University values integrity, inclusiveness and teamwork, and strives to support the personal and collective growth of the McMaster student community.

These values are foundational to ensuring campus environments – both in-person and virtual –are conducive to personal wellbeing and academic success.

Inclusivity and a Culture of Respect

As a McMaster student, you have the right to experience and the responsibility to demonstrate respectful and dignified interactions within all of our living, learning and working communities. Expectations are described in Code of Student Rights & Responsibilities: https://secretariat.mcmaster.ca/app/uploads/Code-of-Student-Rights-and-Responsibilities.pdf

It is essential that students be mindful of their interactions online, as the Code remains in effect in virtual learning environments. The Code applies to any interactions that adversely affect, disrupt, or interfere with reasonable participation in University activities. Student disruptions or behaviours that interfere with university functions on online platforms (e.g. use of Avenue 2 Learn, WebEx or Zoom for delivery), will be taken very seriously and will be investigated. Outcomes may include restriction or removal of the involved students' access to these platforms.

Additional information about the Code and netiquette can be found here: https://sscm.mcmaster.ca/the-code/the-code-virtual-communities/

A Note from Dr. Joe Kim

We have many talented and passionate members of the Instructional Staff and Development Team that work hard to bring you an outstanding course experience. MacIntroPsych was honoured with the 2010 President's Award for Excellence in Course and Resource Design. Our unique IntroPsych Program has been the topic of academic study and received widespread media attention in the Toronto Star, Globe and Mail, CHCH News, and Maclean's (not to mention Mac's own Daily News). Importantly, the continual development of the MacIntroPsych Blended Learning Environment model is supported by ongoing research. As the Director of the Education & Cognition Laboratory (EdCog Lab), I am actively interested in teaching, learning, and technology from both an academic and a practical perspective. For more information, visit https://edcog.ca or follow my twitter feed: @ProfJoeKim

University can sometimes seem like an impersonal and strange place, especially for Level 1 students who are dealing with many adjustments. I hope that in exploring the course resources, you will not forget that there is a real live faculty member responsible for the MacIntroPsych Program—me! I have regular office hours (posted weekly on Avenue) set aside solely to give me a chance to meet and talk with you. If you have a question, comment, complaint, concern, or just want to see and chat with a live faculty member, do come. Many students are reluctant to talk to a faculty member outside of class. Don't give in to the feeling! I have had many great conversations with students that have started off with a supposedly "silly" question.

As a Teaching Professor, my primary responsibilities are teaching and interacting with students; even my area of research interest concerns pedagogy—the formal study of teaching and learning. My goal is to help you understand and appreciate some of the really interesting and important things that we know (or think we know) about human thought and behaviour. In most fields—and as you will see, certainly in psychology—the simplest questions are often the most important and difficult to answer.

One last piece of advice—get involved in the course! MacIntroPsych is a fascinating world waiting to be explored by you! Keep up with the web modules, actively participate in tutorials, join the discussion forums, and attend the monthly Discover Psychology talks on Fridays. It really will make all the difference. Following each web module, I would also encourage you to participate in the feedback surveys. Many of the most popular interactive features were suggested by students just like you. I really do read every single comment and they have contributed enormously to minor and major changes made to all aspects of the course, and this includes the very course handbook you hold in your hands.

On behalf of all the wonderful people that work hard on the frontlines and behind the scenes, best of luck and have a great year!

Dr. Joe Kim

Course Content Schedule for Psychology 1X03/1N03 – Fall 2020

The general schedule for the course content is given below. Any changes to this structure will be announced on Avenue. It is your responsibility to keep up-to-date with any schedule changes.

Week of	Web Module	Chapter Reading	Notes
Sep 7			**No Lecture or Tutorial**
Sept 14	Research Methods 1 and 2	2	Quiz 1
Sept 21	Classical Conditioning	3	Quiz 2
Sept 28	Instrumental Conditioning	4	Quiz 3
Oct 5	Problem Solving and Intelligence	Journal Article	Quiz 4
Oct 12	**Midterm Recess**		**No Lecture or Tutorial**
Oct 19	Language	5	Quiz 5
Oct 26	The Science of Learning	Journal Article	QuizTerm
Nov 2	Categories & Concepts	Journal Article	Quiz 6
Nov 9	Attention	6	Quiz 7
Nov 16	Memory	7	Quiz 8
Nov 23	Forming Impressions	8	Quiz 9
Nov 30	Influence of Others 1 and 2	9	Quiz 10
Dec 7	---	---	**Final Lecture, No Tutorial**

Avenue Quizzes open each week on Friday at 6am and close promptly on Saturday at 6am

RESEARCH METHODS

"Extraordinary claims demand extraordinary proof."
- Carl Sagan, noted astronomer and science journalist

There's an extraordinary dog named Jaytee who lives in Ramsbottom, England. Over the years, he has developed a special bond with his owner Pam. Pam's parents noticed that Pam always seemed to arrive home shortly after Jaytee went out to the front porch to wait for her. This was true even when Pam returned home at unusual times. Intriguingly, it seemed that Jaytee could sense when Pam was starting her journey home. This special ability did not escape the attention of the media and Jaytee was featured on several television shows that celebrated his paranormal powers. Things got even more interesting when a study supporting the claim was published by Dr. Rupert Sheldrake, a researcher interested in 'psychic pet' phenomena. However, you might want to consider alternate explanations. Can Jaytee pick up his owner's scent at great distances? Are Pam's parents unknowingly giving cues that Jaytee detects? Do correct responses by Jaytee coincide with Pam's normal routine? The psychic dog underwent a series of experiments under the direction of Dr. Richard Wiseman, a paranormal sceptic who was critical of Sheldrake's study. Over a series of experiments, several factors were controlled: Pam's return time home was randomly selected; residents of the home were kept unaware of Pam's return time; and, Pam drove home in a different car (to eliminate characteristic car sounds). Before the experiment began, Wiseman operationally defined psychic ability as "a trip to the porch preceding Pam's return home within 10 minutes." As with many sensational claims, it turned out that the simplest explanation was correct—under these controlled conditions Jaytee turned out to be a normal dog. There were certainly a lot of resources dedicated to test an admittedly flimsy claim. However, think about the news reports, advertisements, and urban myths you hear making extraordinary claims in the absence of solid scientific research. It is often easier to passively accept these statements than to be a healthy sceptic. More than likely, a miracle pill is not so miraculous, a fortune is not waiting for you to claim, and pet dogs often lack psychic powers.

Sheldrake, R., & Smart, P. (1998). A dog that seems to know when his owner is returning: Preliminary investigations. *Journal-Society for Psychical Research, 62*, 220-232.

Wiseman, R., Smith, M., & Milton, J. (1998). Can animals detect when their owners are returning home? An experimental test of the 'psychic pet' phenomenon. *British Journal of Psychology, 89*(3), 453-9.

Weekly Checklist:

- ☐ **Web Modules to watch: Research Methods 1 and 2**
- ☐ **Readings: Chapter 2**
- ☐ **Avenue Quiz 1**

Upper Year Courses:

If you enjoyed the content in this week's module, consider taking the following upper year courses:

- PNB 2QQ3 Research Practicum
- PNB 2XE3 Descriptive Statistics
- PNB 3XE3 Inferential Statistics

Research Methods I – Outline

Unit 1: Introduction to Scientific Research

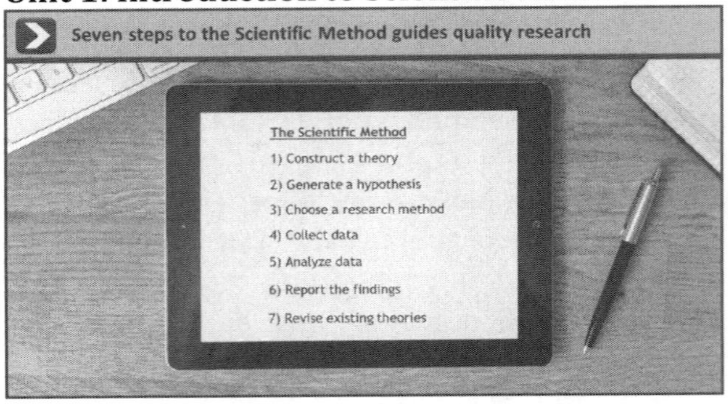

The scientific method provides a framework within which scientists conduct their research.

The Scientific Method:
1) Construct a theory
2) Generate a hypothesis
3) Choose a research method
4) Collect data
5) Analyze data
6) Report the findings
7) Revise existing theories

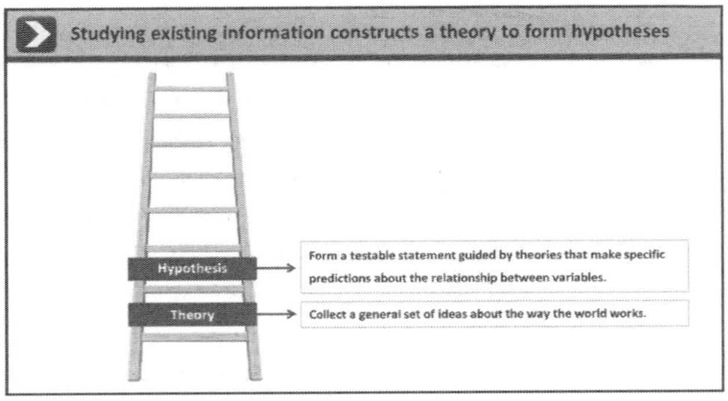

Theory: collect a general set of ideas about the way the world works

Hypothesis: form a testable statement guided by theories that make specific predictions about the relationship between variables

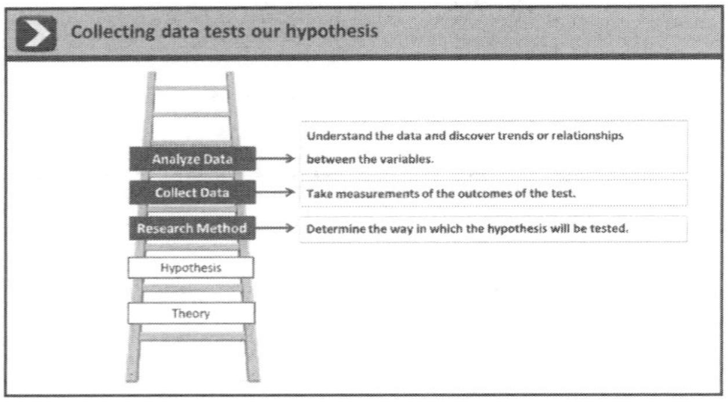

Research method: determine the way in which the hypothesis will be tested

Collect data: take measurements of the outcomes of the test

Analyze data: understand the data and discover trends or relationships between the variables

Report findings: publish articles in scholarly journals

Revise theories: incorporate new information into our understanding of the world

Unit 2: Conducting an Experiment

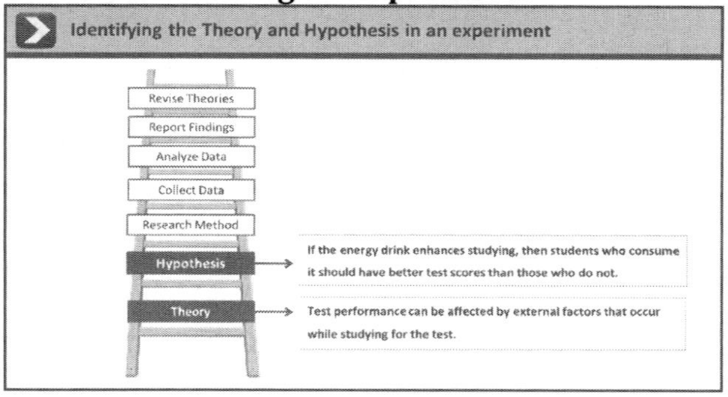

Case Study: Eric Tests the Mega Study Energy Drink

Eric's theory: test performance can be affected by external factors that occur while studying for the test

Eric's hypothesis: if the energy drink enhances studying, then students who consume it should have better test scores than those who don't

Anecdotal evidence: he might hear a story about a student who took an energy drink close to mega and then aced his psychology exam

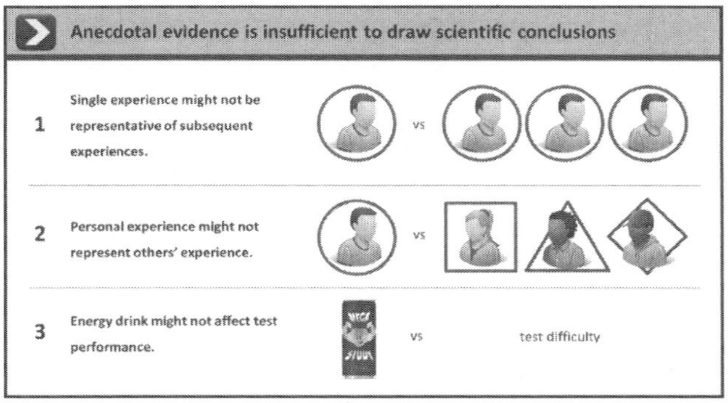

Without rigorous testing, it can be difficult to establish a cause and effect relationship.

1. You can not be sure that your single experience is representive of the general result that would occur if you drank it several times

2. you can't be sure that your experience is the same as what others experience under the same circumstances

3. you can't be sure that the change in test performance was due to the energy drink at all. The test may have been unusually easy or hard and that is what actually affected your performance

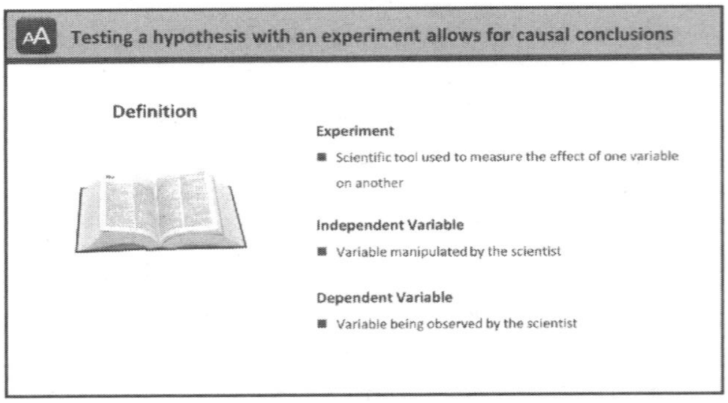

An experiment is one way with which scientists can begin to tackle complex research questions.

Experiment: scientific tool used to measure the effect of one variable on another

Independent variable: variable manipulated by the scientist

Dependent variable: variable being observed by the scientist

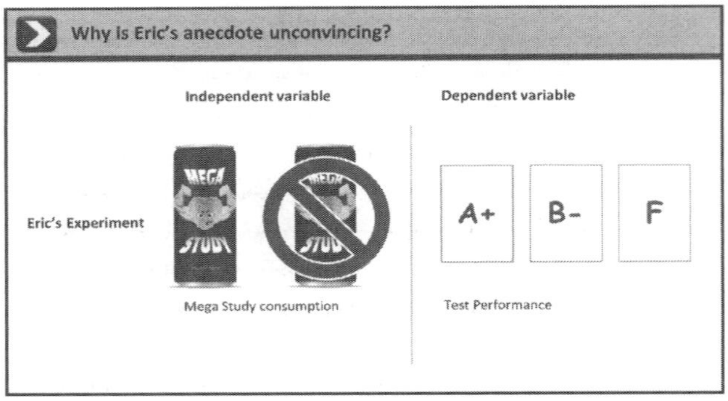

Eric's initial experimental methods contained several flaws.

- his single experience does not allow for him to properly measure the effects
- he needs to manipulate the independent variable while measuring the result on the dependent variable

Unit 3: Control Groups

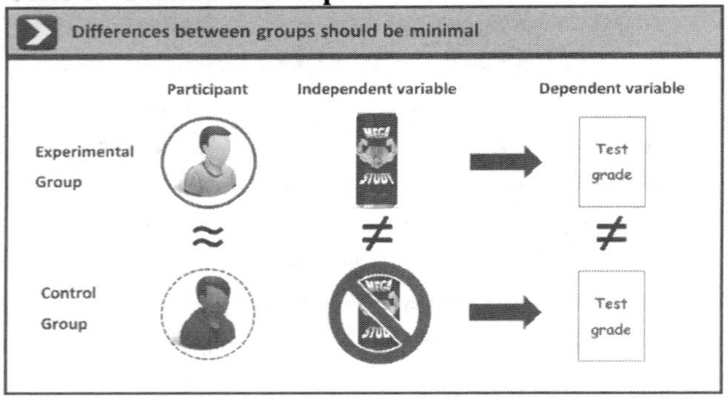

Control groups must be carefully selected to conduct an effective experiment.

- participants should be similar, minimizing the differences that exist between them
- if there is a difference in dependent variables found it is likely the manipulation of the independent variable that was the cause
- Eric will want to find someone with similar grades and study habits to him if he wants an accurate outcome

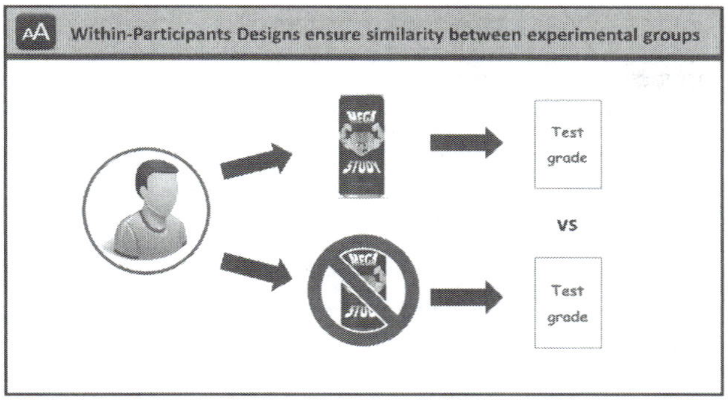

A within-subjects design allows experimenters to discount the effects of differences between groups.

- a "within participant" tests the same subject repeatedly while the independent variable is manipulated
- this design minimizes the effect of participant differences on the dependent measure innocence

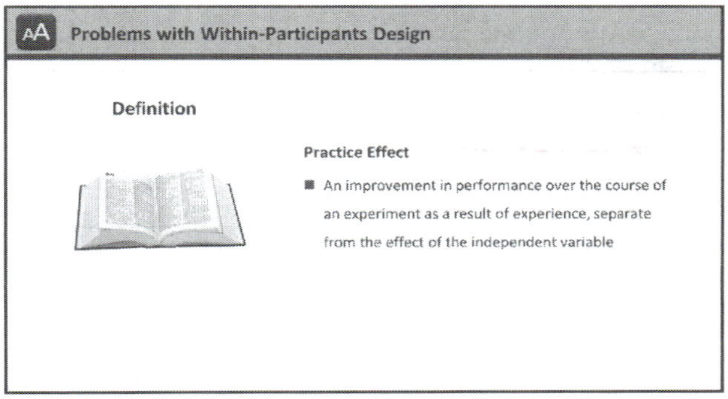

Nevertheless, a within-subjects design is prone to practice effects.

Practice effects:
an improvement in performance over the course of an experiment as a result of experience, separate from the effect of the independent variable

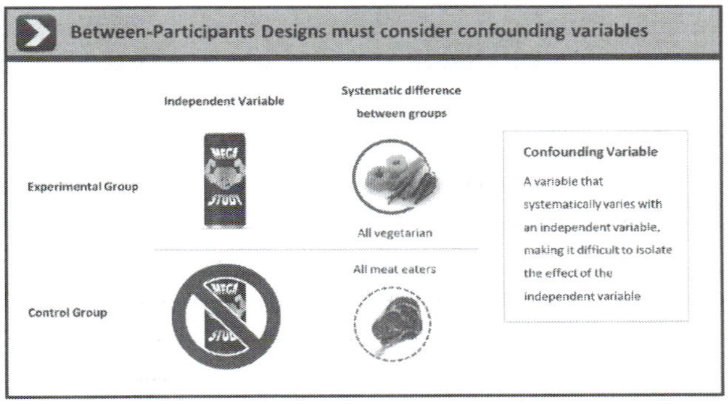

- any difference between the participants before manipulating the independent variable is called a confounding variable because it confounds our ability to determine the differences in the dependent variable

A between-subjects design compares the independent variable's effect on two groups.

- a "between participants" experiment is where one group of participants recieve the experimental manipulation while the others act as the control group
- this was Eric's experiment type
- it's important that in this experiment type individuals being compared are as similar as possible in every way except our manipulation of the independent variable

Unit 4: Sampling

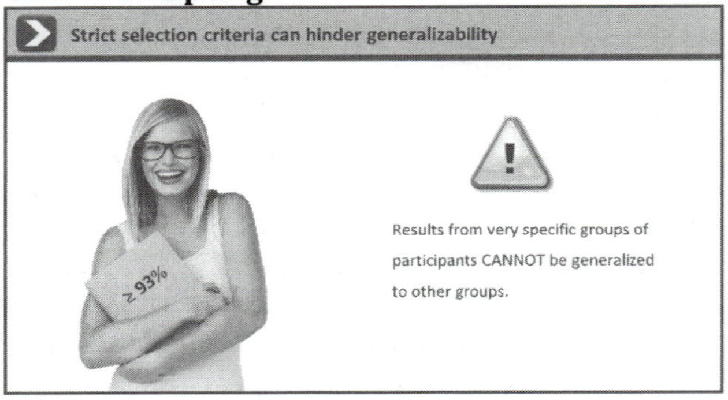

Participants must be carefully selected to allow researchers to accomplish the goals of their experiment.

- results from very specific groups in participants CANNOT be generalized to other groups
- by using such a specific group, he is limiting the scope of his conclusions
- the results may not hold true for everyone if groups are this specific

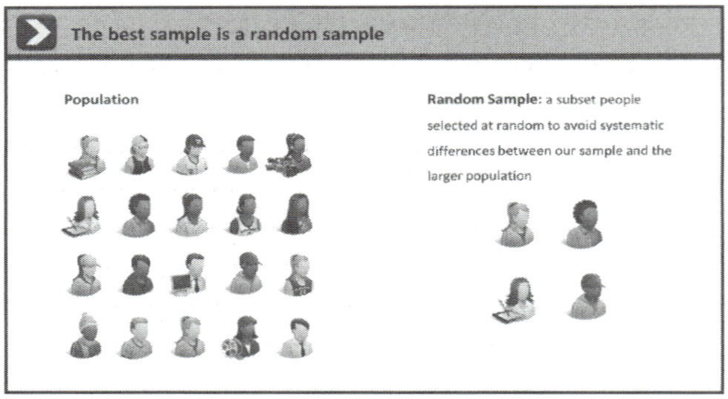

Random sampling is often used to ensure that participants accurately represent the population of interest.

population = general group of people
sample = selected members of population
random sample = a subset people selected at random to avoid systematic differences between our sample and the larger population (reduces bias)

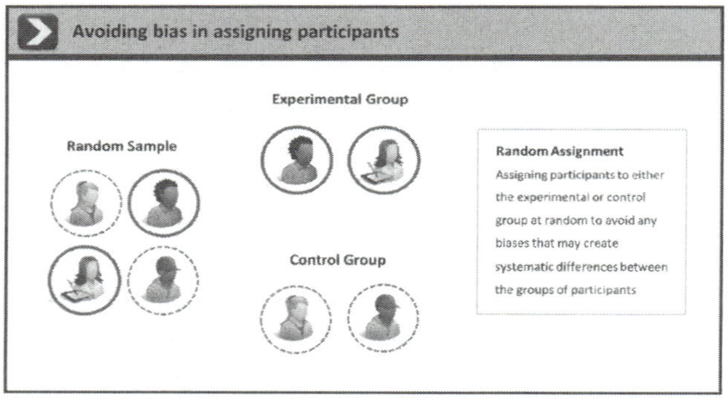

Random assignment further prevents systematic differences between the two groups.

- random assignment assigns participants to either the experimental or control group randomly to reduce bias that might cause differences between participants

Unit 5: Conducting an Experiment

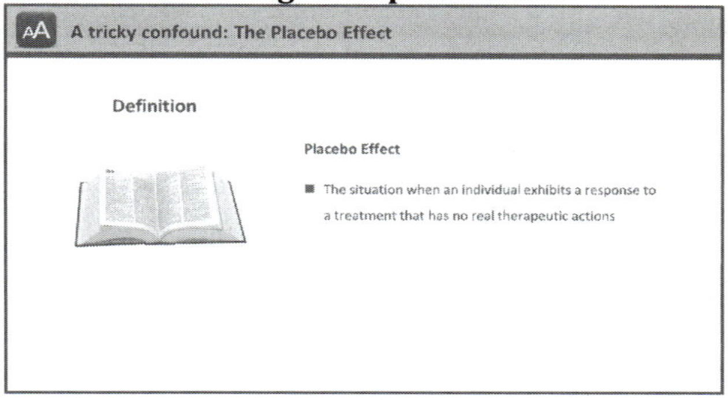

Placebo effects can have an undesirable influence on the experimental results.

placebo effect - occurs when an individual exhibits a response to treatment that in reality has no related therapeutic effect

- can be shown from when patients recover with drugs that were presented as miracle cures even when the drugs were known to have no effect
- the placebo effect can intentionally or unintentionally influence the results of the experiment

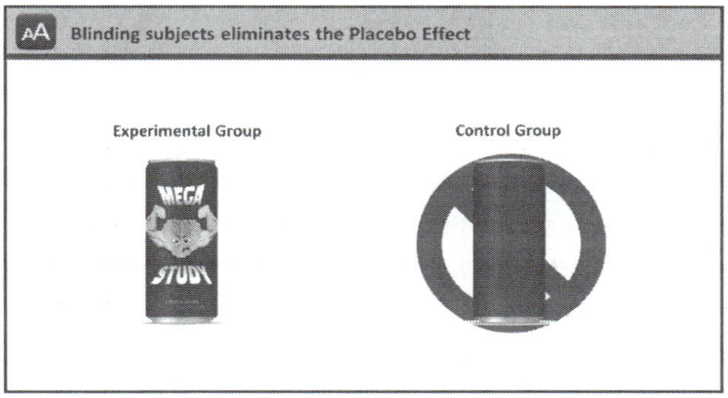

Researchers have devised several clever methods to remove unwanted effects on their experiments.

Participant bias: it's possible that the participants receiving energy drinks may be more motivated and show improved test performance solely because they want the drink to be effective

Blinding: when participants do not know whether they belong to the experimental or control group, or which treatment they are receiving

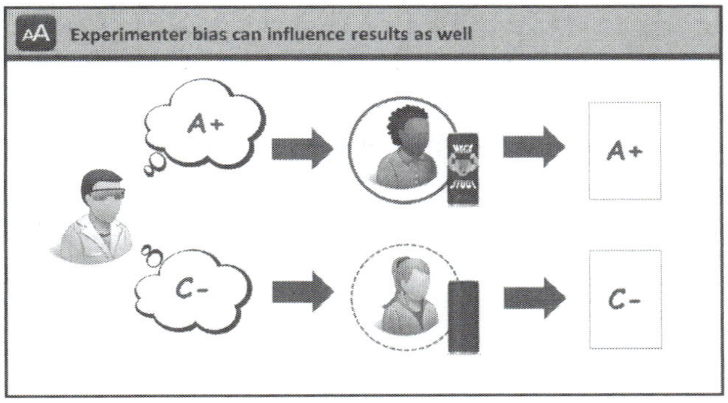

Experimenter bias: as experimenters know the hypothesis that they're attempting to test, it's possible that experiments may promote the result that they hope to achieve

Double-blind studies: experiments in which neither the experimenter nor the participants know which group each participant belong to

Research Methods I – Courseware Exercise

Now that you have a grasp on how to correctly design a scientific experiment, take a look at the following experiment and critique it to **find at least 5 problems** in the way that it is designed.

Lighting in Factories 1

The aim of this study is to explore conditions that lead to more efficient work environments. AMC, a small local factory, has volunteered to be the subject of our experiment. Every week, a condition across the factory will be changed, and performance of all workers will be observed by an experimenter.

1) ______________________________
2) ______________________________
3) ______________________________
4) ______________________________
5) ______________________________

Now take a look at the following corrected experimental design and find **at least 5 ways in which it improves** on the previous experimental design.

Lighting in Factories 2

The aim of this study is to determine whether brighter lighting increases production in factories that produce shoes. Forty factories in China, Mexico, and Canada have been randomly selected for study. Half of these factories will receive brighter lighting through the installation of desk lamps, while the other half of the factories will receive no manipulations. Differences between the average output of the two groups before the experiment are negligible. After two weeks, output numbers will be collected and a statistical analysis will be performed between the control group and the experimental group.

1) ______________________________
2) ______________________________
3) ______________________________
4) ______________________________
5) ______________________________

It is important to note that this second experiment is not perfect either! It is imperative to always be critical of any experimental method used in science in order to constantly improve and reduce errors and biases. As an added challenge, try to find two problems in the second experimental design, as well as solutions to solve each of these.

1) Problem: ______________________________

   Solution: ______________________________

2) Problem: ______________________________

   Solution: ______________________________

Research Methods I – Review Questions

1) Identify and describe the steps of the scientific method, with reference to the following social psychology experiment:

   Middlemist, R. D., Knowles, E. S., & Matter, C. F. (1976). Personal space invasions in the lavatory: Suggestive evidence for arousal. *Journal of personality and Social Psychology, 33*(5), 541-546.

   Step 1: Access Google Scholar at: http://scholar.google.ca
   Step 2: Type "Urinal Experiment" into the search box
   Step 3: Locate the article entitled "Personal space invasions in the lavatory: Suggestive evidence for arousal"

2) Describe the difference between a theory and a hypothesis.

3) Refer to the scenario below for questions a through d.

   Dr. Burns is conducting an experiment to study the effect of eating breakfast on the ability of university students to learn in lectures. In condition A, all students have breakfast prior to watching their psychology module. In condition B, the students are instructed to skip breakfast, and eat an early lunch after watching the module. One week later, all of the students are tested on the material learned from the module.

   a. What is the independent variable? What is the dependent variable?
   b. Is this a within-subjects or between-subjects design? Justify your answer. How could the experiment be manipulated to make it the other type of participant design?
   c. Why is random sampling necessary for a quality experiment?
   d. Referring to the above scenario, which of the following variables is **NOT** going to act as a potential confound?
      i. The time that passes before students eat lunch after watching the module
      ii. The amount of sleep students had the day prior to testing
      iii. The amount of time students take to review the module material

4) Which of the following experiments is a double blind study?
   a. To test the effects of a new psychotherapy technique, a clinical psychologist provides the new psychotherapy treatment for half of his clients, and provides the original treatment for his other clients. A month later, he evaluates all of his clients' progress.
   b. A neuropsychologist is conducting functional MRI studies to examine areas of the brain associated with humour. She asks a colleague to randomly assign half of her subject to be presented with a comedic sitcom while having the MRI scan and the other subjects to be presented with the weather forecast while having the scan. She then interprets the MRI images with the assistance of her colleagues.
   c. A social psychologist is studying how children handle conflict in the playground. He asked his research assistant to explain to half of the children that they will be exposed to a bully and have to behave aggressively, and to the other half of the children that they will have to behave passively. Not knowing which group is which condition, he observes the children on how they handle the conflict.
   d. To study the reaction time of toddlers, a psychology student asks a friend to present a group of 2-year-old children and another group of 3-year-olds with a toy, while the student is out of the room. All the children are required to press a red button as soon as they see the toy. The student then interprets the data on her own to determine which age group had a faster reaction time.

Research Methods II – Outline

Unit 1: Introdution to Scientific Research

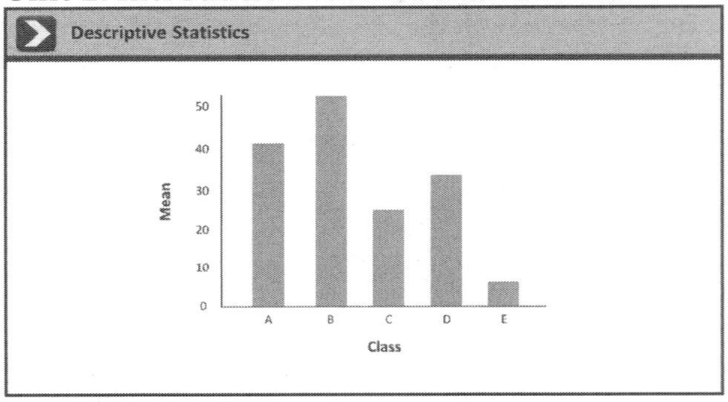

Raw data from an experiment can be converted into many easy-to-understand formats.

Descriptive statistics: presents information about data at a glance to give you an overall idea of the results of the experiment

• includes summary statistics; mean, median, mode

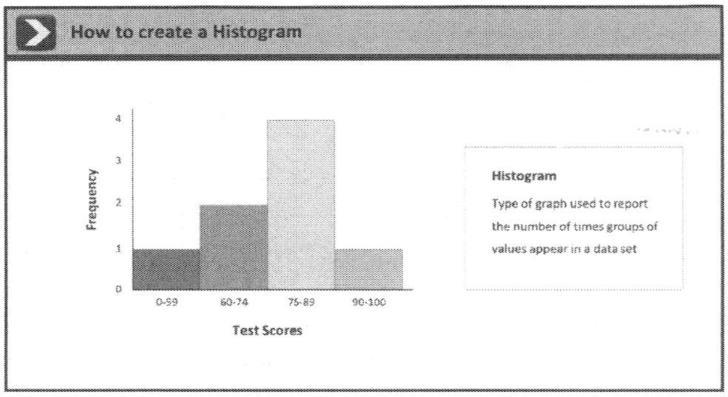

Histogram: type of graph used to report the number of times groups of values appear in a data set

• horizontal X axis is divided into groups of values called bins

• vertical Y axis measures the numbers in the data set that fall into a given called the frequency

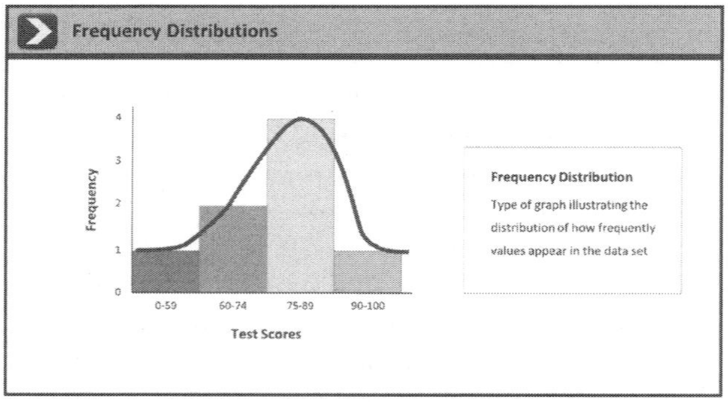

Frequency distribution: type of graph illustrating the distribution of how frequently values appear in the data set

• smooth curve that connects the peak of each bar in a histogram

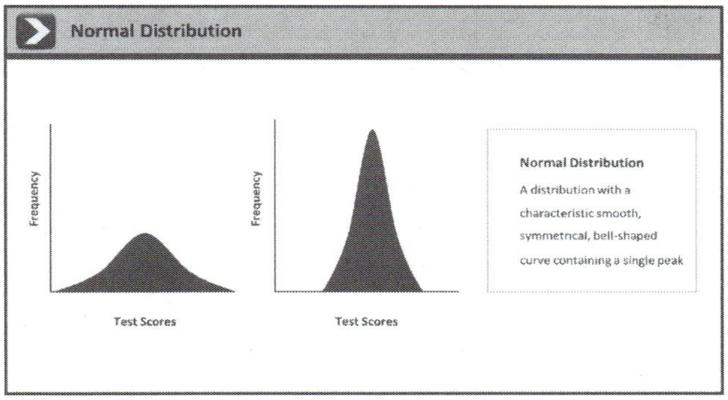

A normal distribution is a special kind of distribution.

normal distribution: a distribution with a characteristic smooth, symmetrical, bell-shaped curve containing a single peak

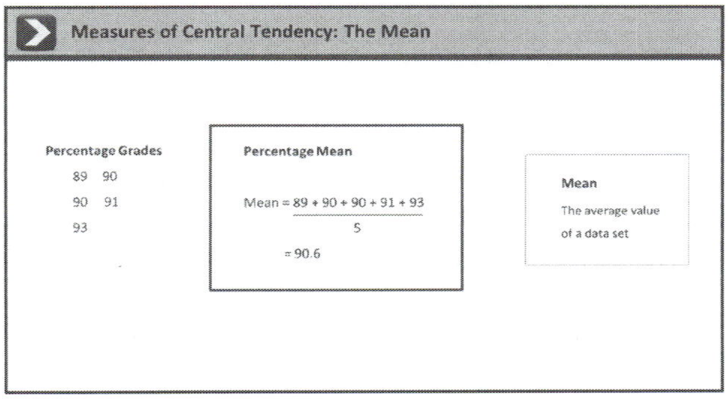

Measures of central tendency allow researchers to describe their data.

Mean: the average value of a data set

• adding all points in data set and dividing by # of items in a set

The effect of outliers: outliers are extreme points of distance from other data that may drop the data dramatically

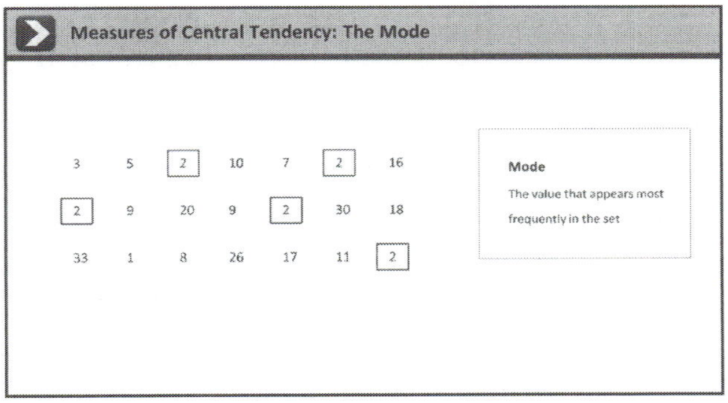

Mode: the value that appears most frequently in the set

Disadvantages of exclusively using measures of central tendency:

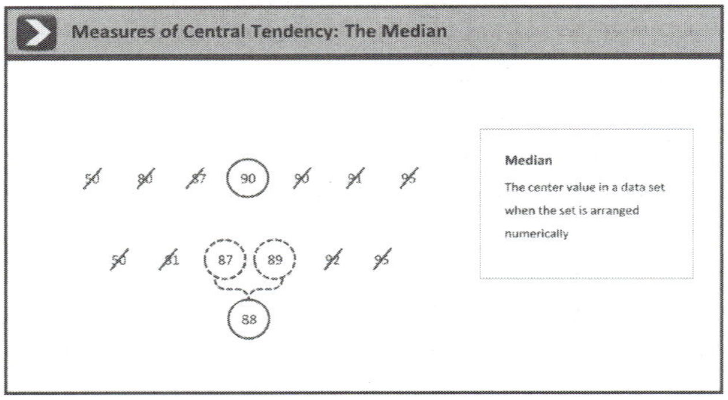

Median: center value in a data set when the set is arranged numerically
• if there is an even number of points the mean of ~~to~~ two center points is the median
• median tells us the middle of our data set but will not be pulled one way because of outliers like mean

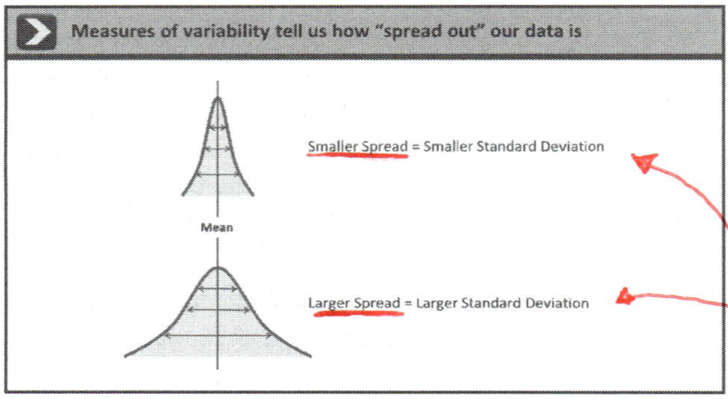

Measures of variability: a second group of descriptive statistic that review the spread and distribution of a data set

Standard deviation: is a measure of the average distance of each point from the mean
larger = spread out
Smaller = more compact

Unit 2: Inferential Statistics

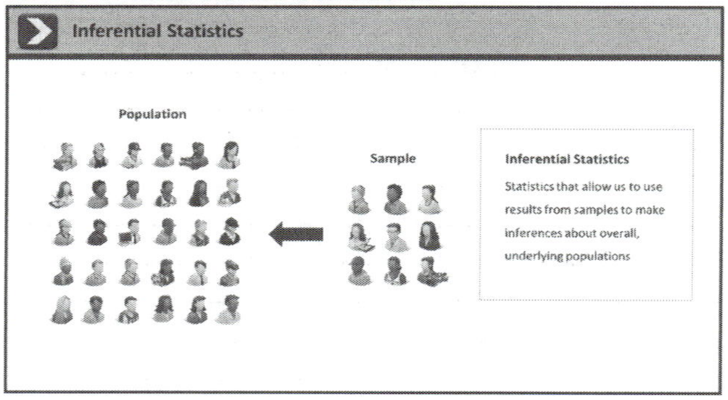

Inferential statistics allow researchers to make inferences about their population of interest.

inferential statistics - allow us to use results from samples to make inferences about overall underlying populations

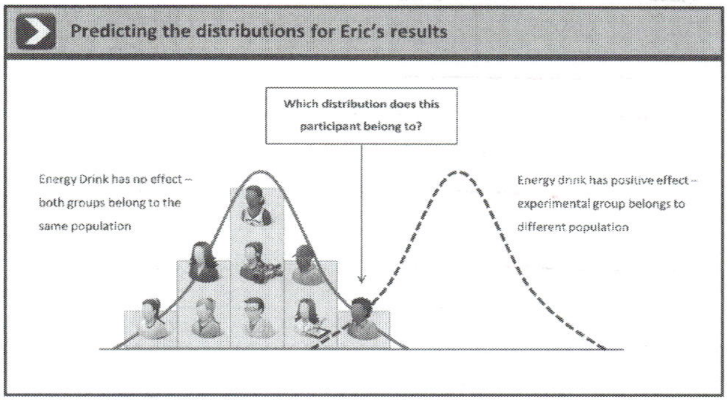

• without any experimental manipulation we would expect their test scores to naturally follow a similar distribution
• if Eric is correct the sample data he collects is drawn from 2 different distributions
• if Eric is incorrect the sample data is drawn from 1 distribution

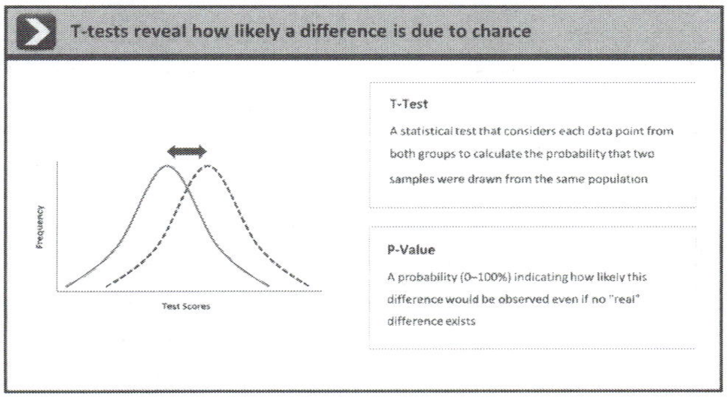

A t-test is a method of applying inferential statistics to your data set.

• T-test is used to compare the difference between the data from control and experimental groups
• the test considers each data point from both groups to calculate the probability that both samples were drawn from a single population
• produces a P-value which shows the probability

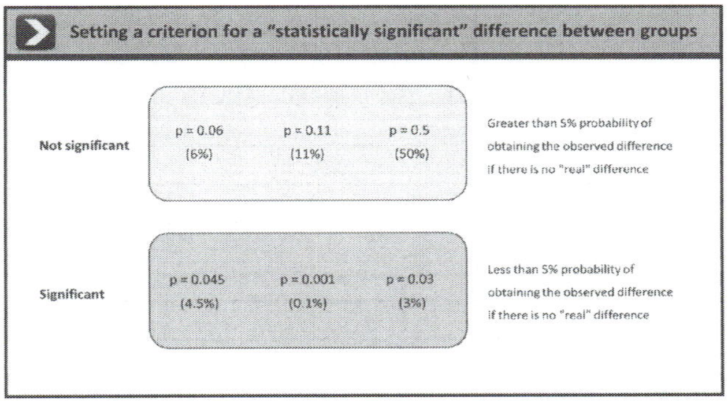

Statistical significance: it is possible that just by chance can cause a difference between groups which may not be there, so the scientists need very strong evidence
• require a T-test to show a P-value of less than 0.5, this means there is less than a 5% probability that they could have found the difference by chance, meaning the difference between the groups is true
• there is still chance for error but is an acceptable amount

statistical significance - when the difference between 2 groups is due to some true difference between the properties of the 2 groups and not simply due to random variables

Unit 3: Reviewing Experimental Design

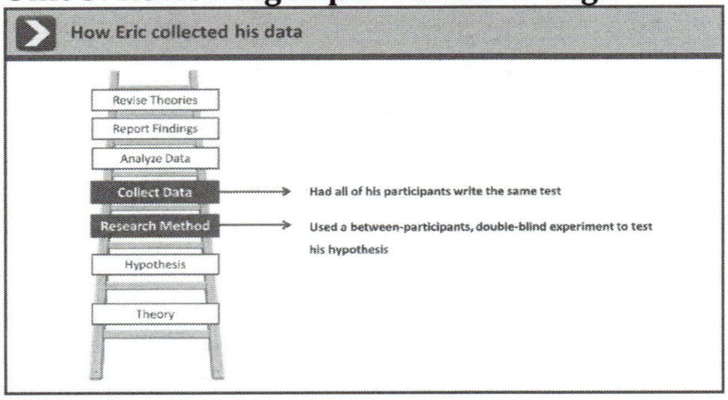

- independent variable - Mega study energy drink usage
- dependent variable - test scores
- hypothesis - students taking energy drinks will show improved test
- research method - between participant experimental design
- collect data - had all participants write the same test
- analyze data - using descriptive statistics like mean and standard deviation

Unit 4: Observational Research

Observational research can be an important tool for scientists in certain situations.

observational studies - observe the effect of variables they're interested in without performing any explicit manipulation

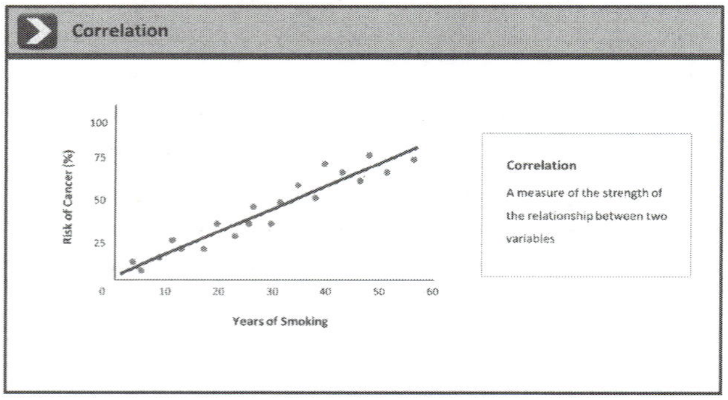

The relationship between two variables can be described by means of a correlation.

- if two variables are related to eachother they are considered as correlated
- correlation is a measure of strength of the relationship between two variables

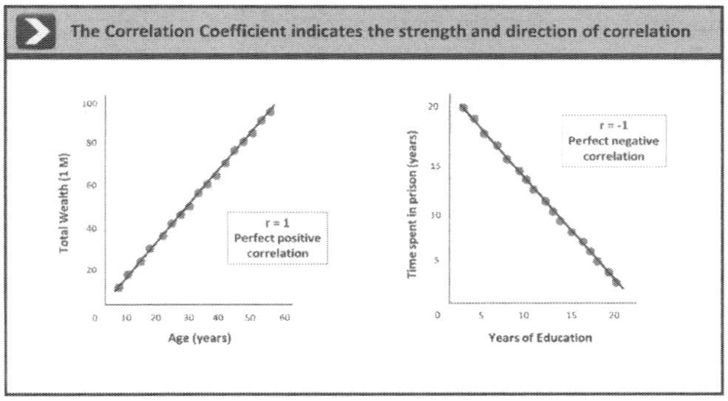

Describe how correlations can be measured:

- correlation coefficient = R
  - ↳ tells us both strength and direction of the correlation
- as one variable increases, the other variable also increases
- 0 = no relationship between 2 variables

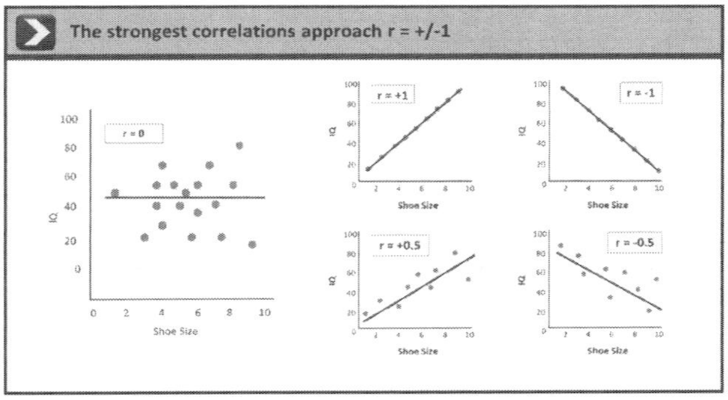

The correlation coefficient provides information about the strength and direction of the relationship between two variables.

- as one variable increases, the other variable also increases
- as the two variables become less alike they reach towards 0
- 0 = no relationship between 2 variables

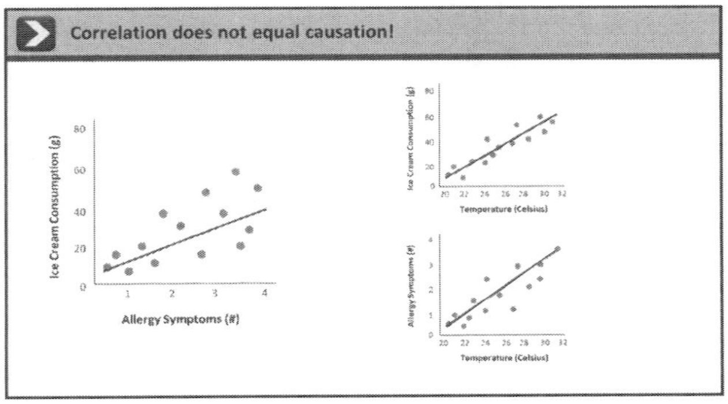

Correlations must NOT be used to determine a cause and effect relationship.

- there may be confounding variables that may affect the outcome of the experiment and may not give accurate results

Research Methods II – Courseware Exercise

On a recent test, Professor A's class had a fantastic average of 85%. Professor A, being a bit of a show-off, came gloating about his far superior average to Professor B, whose class had an average of 79%. However, upon examination of the class distribution, Professor B realized that Professor A may have been incorrect to assume that there was such a large difference between the two classes.

Here are the two distributions:

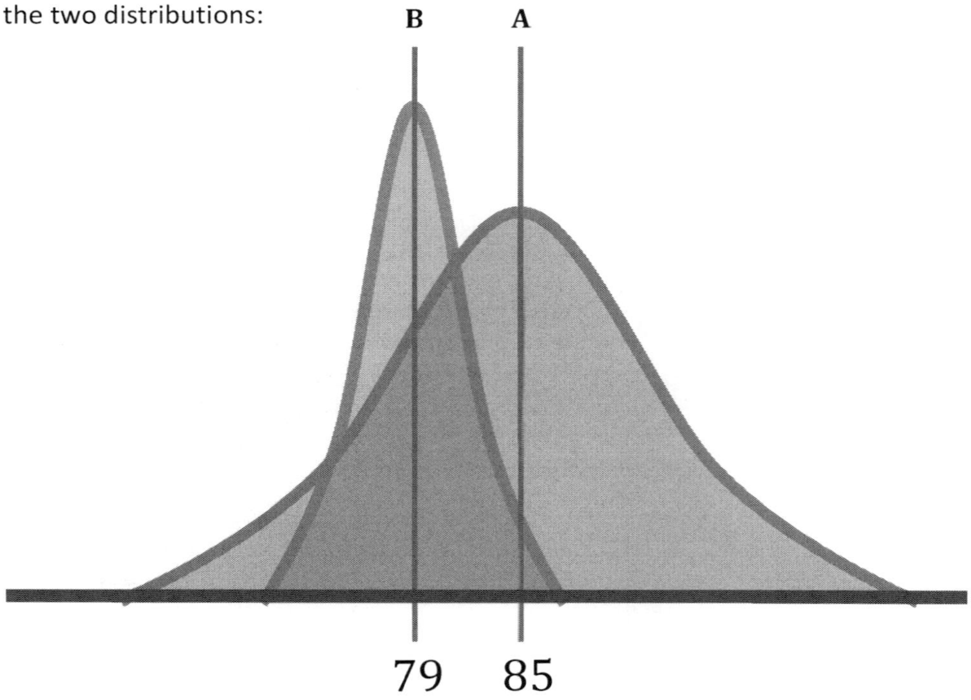

Using the graphic representation of the two distributions, can you think of one disadvantage of the spread of Professor A's class scores? Assuming that all else is equal, what could this inform you about how well students learn from Professor A?

____

____

____

____

____

Can you think of a way in which further statistical analysis may tell us more about how these distributions compare? What are the two possible outcomes of this statistical analysis?

____

____

____

____

Research Methods II – Review Questions

1) Using the following data set of scores, construct a histogram.

2	2	4	5	6	6	6	6	9	10

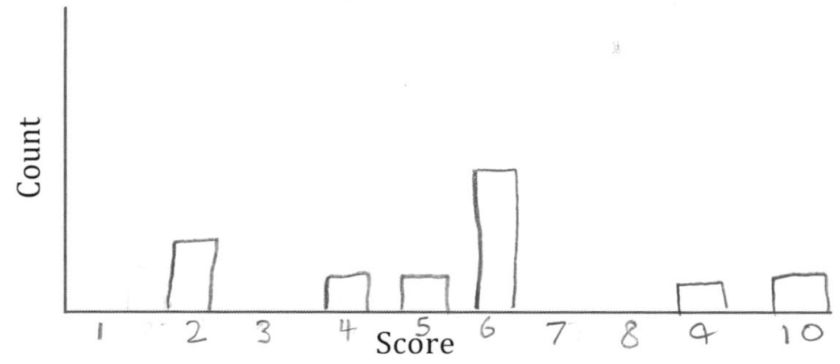

2) Based on the above data set, what is the Mean? Median? Mode?

Mean: 5.6 Median: 6 Mode: 6

3) What are the advantages and disadvantages of the three measures of central tendency?

	Advantage	Disadvantage
Mean		
Median		
Mode		

4) Which of the following curves has the greatest standard deviation? The smallest standard deviation?

a

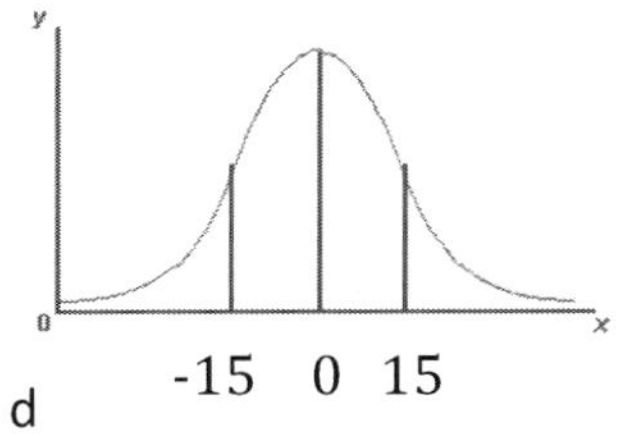

b

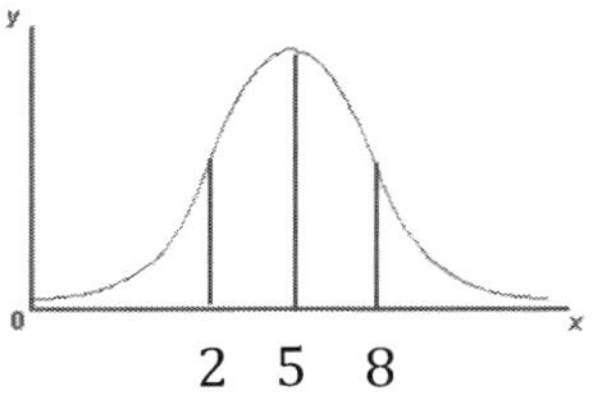

c

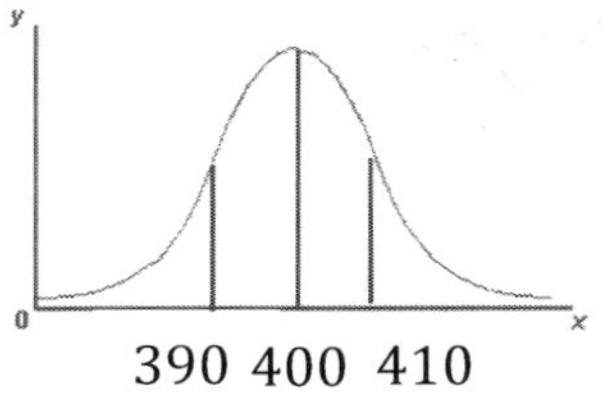

d

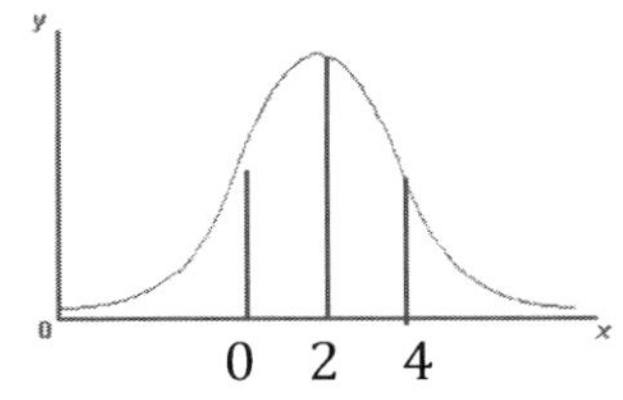

5) Define the concepts "sample" and "population". Would an experimenter prefer to conduct an experiment on a population or sample? Why? Explain the importance of samples in inferential statistics.
6) What do we mean when we say a result is statistically significant?
7) What are correlations? Why must we be careful when measuring correlations? Consider the example below. "*Men who are obese may have less brainpower than their trim counterparts, according to the research done at The University of Boston. The study found that men with a BMI of 30 or more scored an average of **23%** lower in tests of mental acuity. However, the study did not make clear whether lower IQ caused obesity or vice versa.*" Imagine the implications of this study if causation was implied (like it often is in the media).

Research Methods I & II – Quiz Question

Which of the following best characterizes the meaning of the **p-value**?

a. The result of a calculation of the probability that we would find a set of results by chance if our hypothesis was **correct** and all of our participants were from the **same population**. (24.39%)
b. The result of a calculation of the probability that we would find a set of results by chance if our hypothesis was **incorrect** and all of our participants were from the **same population**. (40.18%)
c. The result of a calculation of the probability that we would find a set of results by chance if our hypothesis was **correct** and all of our participants were from **different populations**. (20.53%)
d. The result of a calculation of the probability that we would find a set of results by chance if our hypothesis was **incorrect** and all of our participants were from **different populations**. (14.91%)

This is an actual question from a previous Research Methods Avenue Quiz that the majority of students struggled with. Again, we are going to go through this question together to identify what sort of errors students were making and how to avoid them in the future. To do so, we will look at each answer option individually and identify why it is correct or incorrect.

Before we begin to tackle this question, it is important that you actively attempt to understand the material presented in the web module. This question requires a solid understanding of the p-value concepts presented in the web module and serves as an example of how difficult the AVENUE tests can be if you only have a superficial understanding of the content. Explaining a concept to yourself in your own words is an effective alternative to simply scanning and rereading your notes. Try doing this with the p-value now. Come up with a description of what the p-value is and compare your description to those in the answer options. Here is an example of the description that you may come up with: the p-value is the probability that the difference found between two groups or the results of the experiment are merely due to chance and the two groups actually belong to the same greater population. Indeed, this is the probability that we would find the same results by chance even if our hypothesis was incorrect. Using your own description, let's move forward.

a. At first glance this option seems correct, but upon further examination, there is a small difference between this option and the description above. This option defines a p-value as, among other things, the probability that we find the same result if our hypothesis was correct. In fact, the p-value would be the probability that we obtain the same results even if our hypothesis was incorrect, i.e., groups are not actually different. Scratch this option—it is incorrect.
b. Again, this option seems correct at first and seems to be in line with my description of a p-value. Let's hold onto this option. (**Correct!**)
c. This option is talking about the probability that we find the same result if our hypothesis is correct. Scrap this option as well.
d. Ah, this option seems correct as well. It correctly defines a p-value as the probability of achieving the same result by chance even if the hypothesis is incorrect. However, it ends with a clause stating, "if the two groups are from different populations". A correct hypothesis would suggest the groups are from different populations, while an incorrect hypothesis would suggest the groups are from the same population.

After considering all the answer options, we are left with only **option B**. Remember, it is important to be able to understand the information in the web modules to the extent that you are able to explain and describe the content in your own words.

Key Terms

Between-Subjects Design	Hypothesis	Population
Blinding	Independent Variable	Practice Effect
Causation	Inferential Statistics	Random Assortment
Control Group	Mean	Research Method
Correlation	Measures of Central Tendency	Sampling
Correlation coefficient (r)	Measures of Variability	Scientific Method
Data	Median	Scatter-plot
Descriptive Statistics	Mode	Standard Deviation
Dependent Variable	Normal Distribution	Statistical Significance
Double-Blind Study	Observational Studies	Subject/Participant
Experimental Group	Outliers	T-test
Experimenter Bias	P-value	Theory
Frequency distribution	Participant Bias	Within-subjects Design
Histogram	Placebo Effect	

Research Methods I & II – Bottleneck Concepts

T-test vs. P-value
Single Blind vs. Double Blind
Causation vs. Correlation
Independent vs. Dependent Variable

T-test and p-value

When running an experiment, a researcher only tests a sample of the population. This is done to avoid spending excessive time and resources testing the entire population. An independent variable is manipulated and the investigators look for differences in the participants or their performance depending on the manipulation. However, to make their research relevant, experimenters must also ensure that the findings of their experiment reflect the general population. One way to do this is through a t-test. A t-test determines whether the manipulation of the independent variable had an effect or if the results could have been just because of chance.

As an example, pretend that the marks in a math class were 60, 65, 70, 70, 70, 75, 75, 75, 80, 85, 90, and 95. If you randomly split the marks into two groups, you could potentially end up with one group having students with the marks: 60, 65, 70, 70, 75 and 80, and the other group with 70, 70, 75, 75, 90, and 95. Their groups' average mark would be 70 and 79 respectively. However, did you notice that you did not do anything to manipulate students' marks and you found this difference simply by random chance? This same scenario could happen when a scientist runs an experiment. By chance, they could see a difference between their control and experimental groups! Running a t-test gives researchers a probability, known as the p-value, which states the likelihood that the experimenters obtained their results by chance. If the p-value is less than 0.05, then there is a less than 5% chance that the scientists obtained their results by luck and thus, greater than 95% chance that their manipulation of the variable caused the difference between the two groups. A p-value less than 0.05 is generally regarded as a significant result where the difference between the groups is likely due to the manipulation of the independent variable. (Note: You do not have to know the details of how to actually perform a t-test; you just need to know the meaning of the results.)

Test your Understanding

Brian wants to know if loud noises affect how well a person remembers. He gives a list of 50 words to 2 groups of 20 randomly selected people. They are to remember as many words as possible in 10 minutes. One of the groups is placed in a silent room while the other is placed in a room where construction noises are being played on loudspeakers. Brian then tests to see how many words each person remembered. He runs a t-test and is 90% confident that the noise reduced the people's ability to memorize words.

a) What p-value did he obtain? Are the results considered significant?

b) Brian suspects that there is an actual difference between the groups, but the data just haven't reached significance yet. What can he do in order to obtain significant results?

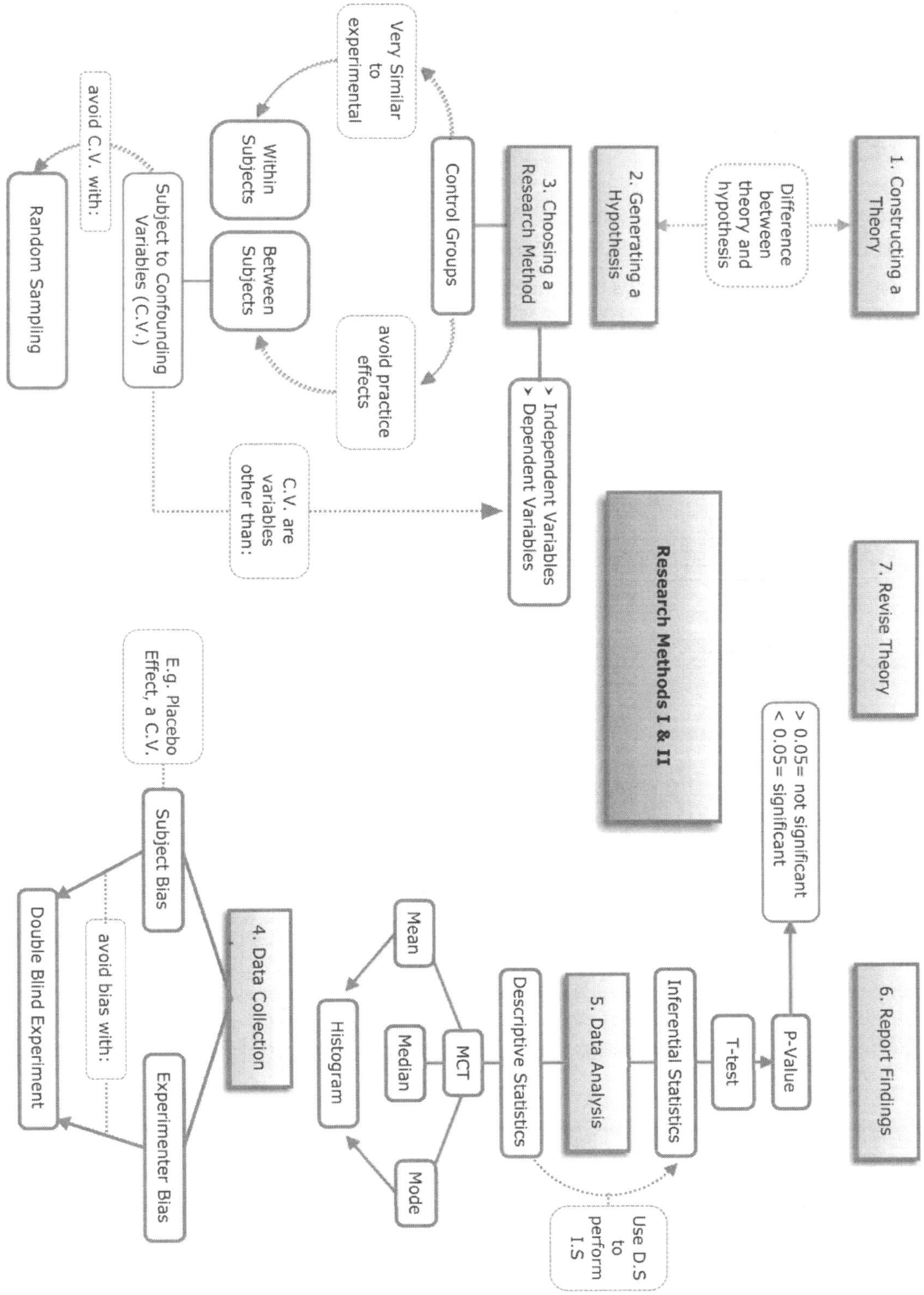
1. Constructing a Theory
Difference between theory and hypothesis
2. Generating a Hypothesis
3. Choosing a Research Method
Control Groups
Very Similar to experimental
avoid practice effects
Within Subjects
Between Subjects
Subject to Confounding Variables (C.V.)
avoid C.V. with:
Random Sampling
C.V. are variables other than:
> Independent Variables
> Dependent Variables
Research Methods I & II
7. Revise Theory
> 0.05= not significant
< 0.05= significant
6. Report Findings
P-Value
T-test
Inferential Statistics
5. Data Analysis
Descriptive Statistics
Use D.S to perform I.S
MCT
Mean
Median
Mode
Histogram
4. Data Collection
Subject Bias
Experimenter Bias
E.g. Placebo Effect, a C.V.
avoid bias with:
Double Blind Experiment

Between-Subjects Design
Research Methods

MAC IntroPsych

Blinding
Research Methods

MAC IntroPsych

Causation
Research Methods

MAC IntroPsych

Control Group
Research Methods

MAC IntroPsych

Correlation
Research Methods

MAC IntroPsych

Correlation Coefficient (r)
Research Methods

MAC IntroPsych

Data
Research Methods

MAC IntroPsych

Descriptive Statistic
Research Methods

MAC IntroPsych

When participants do not know whether they belong to the experimental or control group, or which treatment they are receiving.
Example: When comparing the effect of drinking caffeinated or decaffeinated coffee before bedtime, the participants do not know which type of coffee they are drinking.
Personal Example:

An experimental design in which an independent variable is manipulated across separate groups of participants. Each participant or group of participants will take part in only one of the conditions.
Example: When testing the effects of caffeine on alertness, researchers test ability to recall lecture information across different groups of students: those who drink coffee and those who don't.
Personal Example:

The group in an experiment that does not receive the experimental manipulation to the independent variable and, therefore, the group to whom the experimental group is compared.
Example: When testing the effects of caffeine before bedtime on sleep, the group that drank coffee is compared to the control group who did not drink coffee.
Personal Example:

The suggestion that one variable caused an effect to occur in another variable. A strong correlation alone is insufficient to determine whether or not causation exists occurred between two variables.
Example: A researcher may observe a positive correlation between hat sales and ice cream sales. However, hat sales do not cause more ice cream sales.
Personal Example:

Measures the degree to which two variables are correlated. Its value tells us the strength and direction of the correlation. Can be any value greater than or equal to -1, and less than or equal to +1.
Example: Age and height in children have a strong, positive correlation with a value close to r=+1 which means that as age increases, height increases.
Personal Example:

A measure of the strength of the relationship between two variables. Correlation does not equal causation.
Example: A positive correlation between hat sales and ice cream sales does not mean that hat sales cause more ice cream sales. Hat and ice cream sales both may be caused by a confounding variable, an increase in temperature due to warmer summer months.
Personal Example:

Describes data in a way that summarizes at a glance the overall results of an experiment. This includes summary statistics such as histograms, measures of central tendency (mean, median, and mode), and measures of variability (standard deviation).
Example: The mean time required for participants to fall asleep after caffeine consumption was 40 minutes.
Personal Example:

Quantifiable values which measure the outcome of a test.
Example: When testing the effects of caffeine on alertness, the data would be represented by the number of minutes that each participant required to fall asleep.
Personal Example:

Dependent Variable
Research Methods

MAC IntroPsych

Double-Blind Study
Research Methods

MAC IntroPsych

Experimental Group
Research Methods

MAC IntroPsych

Experimenter Bias
Research Methods

MAC IntroPsych

Frequency Distribution
Research Methods

MAC IntroPsych

Histogram
Research Methods

MAC IntroPsych

Hypothesis
Research Methods

MAC IntroPsych

Independent Variable
Research Methods

MAC IntroPsych

An experiment in which neither the experimenter nor the participants know which treatment a particular group of participants is receiving. **Example**: When comparing the effects of drinking caffeinated or decaffeinated coffee before bedtime, neither the participants nor the experimenter would know which type of coffee the participants are drinking. **Personal Example:**	The variable that researchers observe but do not change during an experiment. The researchers change the independent variable and measure the effects (if any) on the dependent variable. **Example:** When testing the effects of caffeine on alertness, the experimenter observes the amount of time required for each participant to fall asleep (dependent variable) by manipulating coffee consumption (independent variable) **Personal Example:**
Actions made by the experimenter, unintentionally or deliberately, to promote the result they hope to achieve. **Example:** When testing the effects of caffeine on alertness, the experimenter may spend more time talking to the experimental group than the control group, thus keeping them engaged and alert in ways not caused by drinking coffee. **Personal Example:**	A group of participants which receives the manipulation of the independent variable, in order to test the effect (if any) on the dependent variable. **Example:** When testing the effects of caffeine on alertness, the experimental group would receive regular caffeinated coffee and their alertness would be measured by the time it takes participants to fall asleep. **Personal Example:**
Type of graph used to report the number of times a group of values appear in a data set. It forms the basis of a frequency distribution. **Example:** A researcher may create a histogram that illustrates how many students have weights between 120 – 139 pounds, 140 – 159 pounds, 160 – 179 pounds, 180 – 199 pounds and 200+ pounds, respectively. **Personal Example:**	A type of graph illustrating the distribution of how frequently a given value or range of values appears in a data set. It is essentially a smooth curve that connects the peak of each bar in a histogram. **Example:** A researcher may create a frequency distribution that illustrates how many students have weights between 120 – 139 pounds, 140 – 159 pounds, 160 – 179 pounds, 180 – 199 pounds and 200+ pounds, respectively. **Personal Example:**
The variable manipulated by the scientist. **Example:** When testing the effects of caffeine on amount of time required to fall asleep (dependent variable), the experimenter can manipulate the amount or type of coffee the participants drink (independent variable). **Personal Example:**	A testable statement that makes specific predictions about the relationship between the variables in a theory. **Example:** When testing the effects of caffeine on alertness, researchers may hypothesize that drinking coffee keeps participants more alert and therefore take longer to fall asleep. **Personal Example:**

Inferential Statistics
Research Methods

MAC IntroPsych

Mean
Research Methods

MAC IntroPsych

Measures of Central Tendency
Research Methods

MAC IntroPsych

Measures of Variability
Research Methods

MAC IntroPsych

Median
Research Methods

MAC IntroPsych

Mode
Research Methods

MAC IntroPsych

Normal Distribution
Research Methods

MAC IntroPsych

Observational Studies
Research Methods

MAC IntroPsych

The average value of the data set, calculated by adding together all of the points in a data set and dividing by the number of items in the set.
Example: You can calculate your tutorial's mean age by adding up everybody's age and dividing by the number of students in your tutorial.
Personal Example:

Statistics that allow us to use results from samples to make inferences about overall, underlying populations.
Example: If you wanted to use your tutorial to determine the distribution of height of all undergraduate students at McMaster, you would make an inference using the distribution of height in your tutorial.
Personal Example:

Measures that tell us how other values within a data set fall around the centre of the data.
Example: Both you and your friend may have a mean grade in all university courses of B+ but you may have a larger standard deviation than your friend, meaning your grades are more spread out from the mean while your friend tends to consistently get grades around B+.
Personal Example:

Measures that tell us where a data set is centered, using the mean, median, and mode.
Example: To determine what value age is centered around in your tutorial, you collect all the ages in your tutorial and find that the mean is 18.4, median is 18 and mode is 18.
Personal Example:

The value that appears most frequently in a data set.
Example: If the majority of students in your tutorial are 18 years old, then the mode for this data set is 18.
Personal Example:

The centre value in a data set when the set is arranged numerically from smallest to largest.
Example: If there were 27 students in your tutorial, then the 14th student's age (after age is put in order) would represent the median. If there were 28 students, then the average of the 14 and 15th students' age represents the median.
Personal Example:

Studies in which researchers observe the effect of variables they are interested in without performing any manipulation, allowing them to infer correlational relationships but not causation.
Example: Researchers may compare the number of students who ride the bus and height of snow fallen in meters.
Personal Example:

A frequency distribution with a characteristic smooth, bell-shaped, and symmetrical-curve around a single peak. Many everyday measures are normally distributed.
Example: Height is normally distributed, with individuals of an average height being the most frequent (creating a central peak) and the shortest and tallest individuals being the least frequent.
Personal Example:

Outliers
Research Methods

MAC IntroPsych

P-Value
Research Methods

MAC IntroPsych

Participant Bias
Research Methods

MAC IntroPsych

Placebo Effect
Research Methods

MAC IntroPsych

Population
Research Methods

MAC IntroPsych

Practice Effect
Research Methods

MAC IntroPsych

Random Assortment
Research Methods

MAC IntroPsych

Research Method
Research Methods

MAC IntroPsych

The value resulting from a t-test used to determine statistical significance. If the p-value is below a 0.05, the data set is considered statistically significant. **Example:** If the p-value is 0.035, you can conclude that your results are statistically significant, meaning there is only a 3.5% chance that you obtained this result by chance. **Personal Example:**	Extreme points distant from others in a data set which easily influence the mean. **Example:** Nine out of ten of your first year grades are between B+ and A+; however, in Chemistry you got a D-. This D- is an outlier and will disproportionately bring down the mean of this data set. **Personal Example:**
An effect that occurs when an individual exhibits a response to a treatment that has no related therapeutic effect. **Example:** When testing the effects of caffeine on alertness, a group of participants may receive decaf coffee (which tastes, smells and looks like caffeinated coffee), but theoretically should not result in difficulties falling asleep; however, if they do experience difficulty, it may be due to the placebo effect. **Personal Example:**	When a participant's actions in an experiment influence the results apart from the experimental manipulations. **Example:** When testing the effects of caffeine on alertness, if the participant is aware of the purpose of the study, they may intentionally try to stay awake. **Personal Example:**
Improved performance over the course of an experiment due to participants becoming more experienced. **Example:** When testing the effects of caffeine on alertness, with repeated trials, participants may develop strategies to help them fall asleep, independent of what kind of coffee they are drinking. **Personal Example:**	The overall group of individuals that a researcher is seeking to study and that the results of an experiment apply to. **Example:** When testing the effects of caffeine on alertness, a select group of undergraduate students from diverse ethnic backgrounds in Toronto may be tested to represent the entire population of undergraduate coffee drinkers from universities in urban areas. **Personal Example:**
An experimental method used to test a hypothesis. **Example:** When testing the effects of caffeine on alertness, the research method would involve comparing the time required to fall asleep between a group of individuals drinking coffee and a group of individuals drinking decaf coffee. **Personal Example:**	Assigning participants to either the experimental or control group at random to avoid any biases that may cause differences between the groups of subjects. **Example:** When testing the effects of drinking coffee before bedtime compared to no coffee, the experimenter would randomly assign participants to either condition. **Personal Example:**

Sampling
Research Methods

MAC
IntroPsych

Scientific Method
Research Methods

MAC
IntroPsych

Scatter-Plot
Research Methods

MAC
IntroPsych

Standard Deviation
Research Methods

MAC
IntroPsych

Statistical Significance
Research Methods

MAC
IntroPsych

Subject/Participant
Research Methods

MAC
IntroPsych

T-Test
Research Methods

MAC
IntroPsych

Theory
Research Methods

MAC
IntroPsych

A series of steps used to design studies that allow researchers to objectively and consistently find answers to specific research questions. The steps are as follows: theory, hypothesis, selecting a research method, collecting data, analyzing data, reporting findings, and revising theories.
Personal Example:

Selecting a subgroup representative of the underlying population to study.
Example: When testing the effects of caffeine on alertness of all university students in urban areas, the experimenter selects a participant group of university students which is representative of as many ages, genders, and ethnicities as possible.
Personal Example:

A measure of the average variation of each data point from the mean. Data sets with a larger standard deviation are typically more "spread out" than data sets with a smaller standard deviation.
Example: A population of 30 whose minimum height is 4'8" and tallest height is 6'2" will have a larger standard deviation than one with a minimum height of 5'3" and maximum height of 5'11".
Personal Example:

A graph used to display the relationship between two variables in a data set. Scatter-plots are used to determine the correlation between two variables in a data set.
Example: If you wanted to illustrate the relationship between age and height, you would plot age on the x-axis and height on the y-axis.
Personal Example:

The individual taking part in an experiment. It may be a human or an animal, depending on the nature of the experiment.
Example: When testing the effects of caffeine on alertness, a participant will be required to drink either decaffeinated or caffeinated coffee and attempt to fall asleep.
Personal Example:

When the difference between two groups is due to some true difference and not due to random variation.
Example: When comparing mineral content in water found in Hamilton compared to water found in Vancouver, statistically significant data suggests there is actually a difference in the fluoride concentrations, rather than a difference found by random variation or chance.
Personal Example:

A general set of ideas about the way the world works.
Example: A researcher may theorize that certain substances may affect human cognitive abilities
Personal Example:

A statistical test that determines statistical significance. It considers each data point from both groups being tested to calculate the probability of obtaining differences by chance
Example: A t-test can calculate the probability of finding a difference in height between members of a basketball team and members of a general population. If results are not statistically significant, this would mean members of the basketball team are not significantly taller than the underlying population.
Personal Example:

Within-Subject Design

Research Methods

MAC IntroPsych

MAC IntroPsych

MAC IntroPsych

MAC IntroPsych

MAC IntroPsych

MAC IntroPsych

MAC IntroPsych

MAC IntroPsych

An experimental design where one group of subjects receives the manipulation of the independent variable to observe the effect on the dependent variable. In this design, one group acts as both the experimental and control groups.
Example: When testing the effects of caffeine on alertness, there would be two conditions, which involve drinking caffeinated coffee or decaffeinated coffee. One participant would take part in both conditions on separate days.
Personal Example:

CLASSICAL CONDITIONING

"We are thus confronted with two series of apparently entirely different phenomena. What now is the physiologist to do with the psychical phenomena?"
- Ivan Pavlov, 1904 Nobel Lecture address

In an episode of the television show The Office, lead character Jim describes learning in school about "this guy who trained dogs to salivate by feeding them whenever he rang a bell." For the next few weeks, Jim secretly conducts his own study using his hapless co-worker Dwight. Each time he shuts down his computer (playing the familiar Windows sound effect) Jim presents Dwight with a candy. In time, simply playing the Windows sound leads Dwight to reflexively reach for candy. The "guy who trained dogs" was a Russian physiologist named Ivan Pavlov. His experiments were known for their rigorous design and the use of objective and measurable behaviour. Pavlov's seminal work on the physiology of digestion laid the foundation for advances in theoretical and applied medicine. However, Pavlov is best known for his work on conditional reflexes conducted in the latter years of his career. In his study of the reflex regulation of the digestive glands, Pavlov paid special attention to a phenomenon that he initially called "psychic secretion." Pavlov observed that even food stimuli at a distance from the animal could elicit salivary secretions. A series of experiments led Pavlov to reject his initial subjective interpretation of psychic salivary secretion. He concluded that the psychic activity was actually a reflex. More specifically, it was a conditional reflex. This discovery was a model for how to study other so-called psychic activity through objective methods. Later experiments refined our understanding of complex interactions between an organism and its external environment. In 1904, he was awarded a Nobel Prize for Medicine/Physiology for his early work on digestive physiology. However, in his Nobel Lecture address, Pavlov chose to focus much of his speech on the conditional reflex as the first sure steps to a new line of investigation.

Pavlov, I. P. (1927). Conditioned Reflexes: An Investigation of the Physiological Activity of the Cerebral Cortex. (G. V. Anrep, Trans.). London: Oxford University Press.

Weekly Checklist:

- ☐ **Web Module to watch: Classical Conditioning**
- ☐ **Readings: Chapter 3**
- ☐ **Avenue Quiz 2**

Upper Year Courses:

If you enjoyed the content in this week's module, consider taking the following upper year course:

- PNB 2XC3: Animal Behaviour & Evolution

Classical Conditioning – Outline

Unit 1: Introduction to Learning

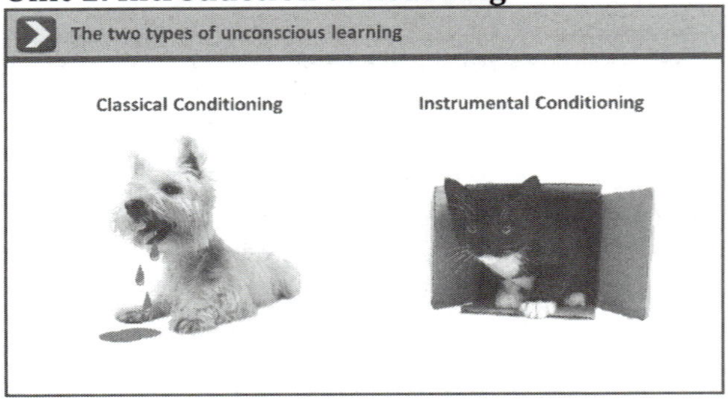

Classical Conditioning and Instrumental Conditioning describe two methods of learning.

Classical conditioning - allows us to associate two related events
instrumental conditioning - allows us to associate actions and their consequences

Unit 2: Classical Conditioning

Ivan Pavlov: was a Russian physiologist in the 1890s and 1900s, classical conditioning is also called pavlovian conditioning, he looked at stages of digestion and saw dogs would salivate even before any food reached their mouth
• tested sound of metronome signal to a dog that food was coming
• the behaviour of the dog is called a conditional reflex

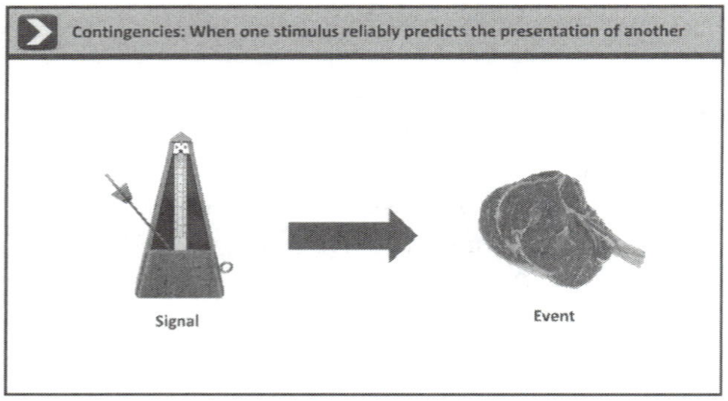

Define contingencies: the presentation of 1 stimulus reliably leads to the presentation of another
• When an organism learns the association between a signal and an event we say that a contingent relationship has been formed

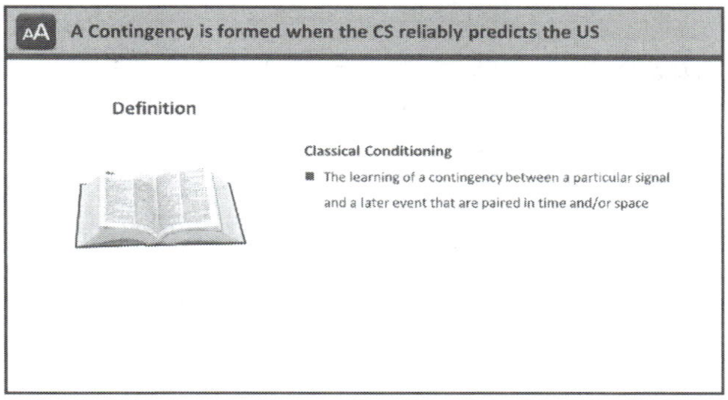

Classical Conditioning can be found in many organisms and involves learning the relationship between two events.

• learning the contingencies is the essence of classical conditioning

classical conditioning - the learning of contingency between a particular signal and a later event that are paired in time and/or space

Unit 3: Components of Classical Conditioning

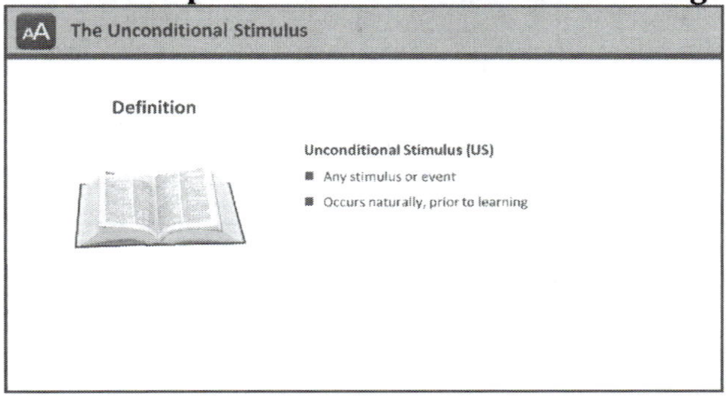

Unconditional stimulus: (US) is one that unconditionally and automatically triggers a response in the absence of learning

• no training needed for response

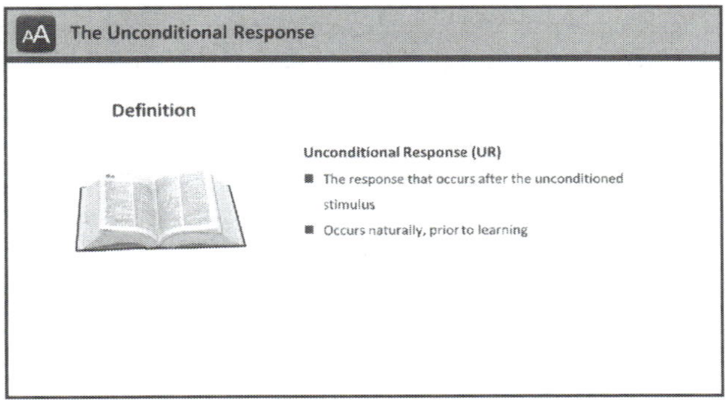

Unconditional response: (UR) when US occurs the UR follows with no training necessary

• response is a biologically programmed reflex

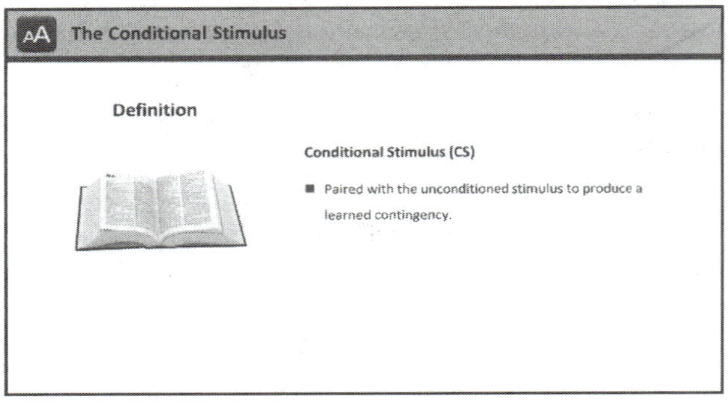

Conditional Stimulus: (CS) a previously neutral stimulus that becomes associated with an unconditional stimulus to eventually trigger a response on it's own

- conditional stimulus typically appears before the unconditional stimulus
- it may take several training trials in which the stimuli are paired before the CS alone elicits a response
- when this happens the organism has learned a contingent relationship

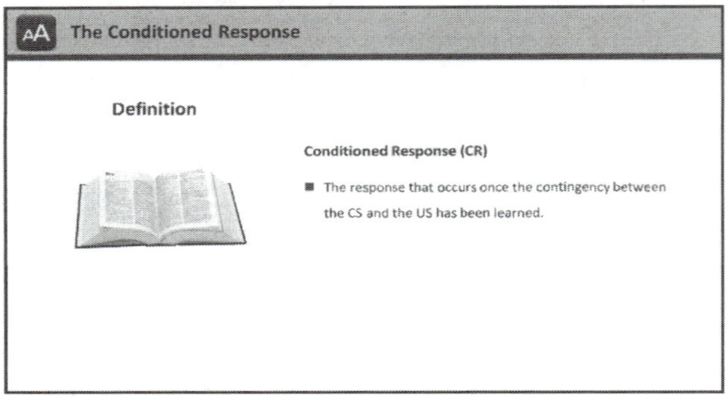

Conditioned Response: (CR) following pairing with the conditional stimulus, the CS begin to elicit a conditional response

- often this response is very similar to the unconditional response

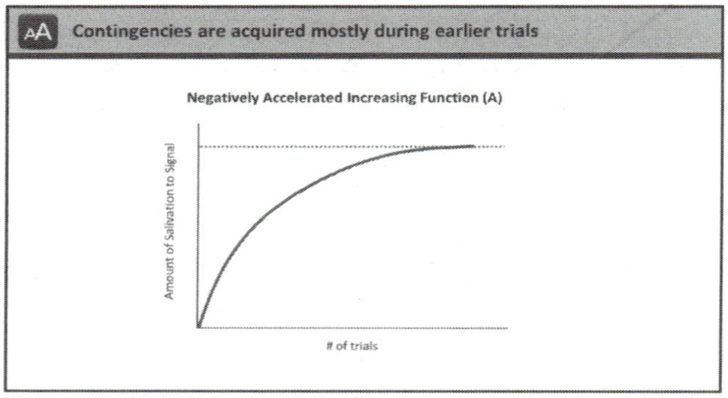

dietary neophobia - generally avoid unfamiliar foods

- rats try new foods in smaller quantities to tell what foods make them sick, they then can tell the contingency in a single trial

The acquisition of a contingency typically requires many trials, but can occur quickly in certain situations.

acquisition - the process by which a contingency between a CS and US is learned

- acquisition follows a negatively accelerating curve
- most learning happens during the early training trials
- acquisition typically takes several trials, special cases may only take one trial

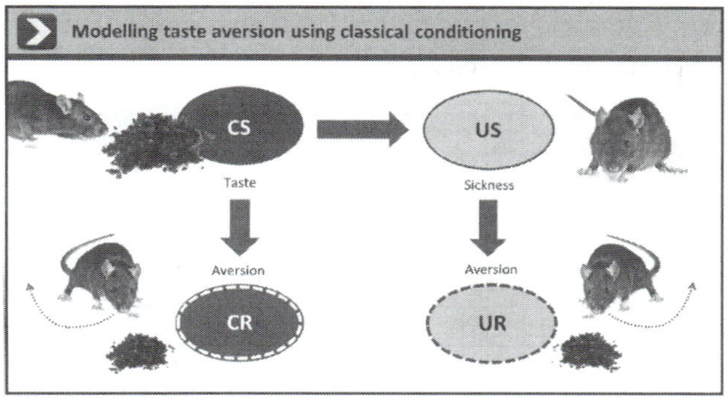

• the consumed poison makes a rat feel sick which elicits a strong aversion response
• the sickness the rat feels is paired with the novel taste of the food, a contingency the rat can learn in just one trial
• with this pairing, the novel food elicits a strong aversion response even before sickness occurs

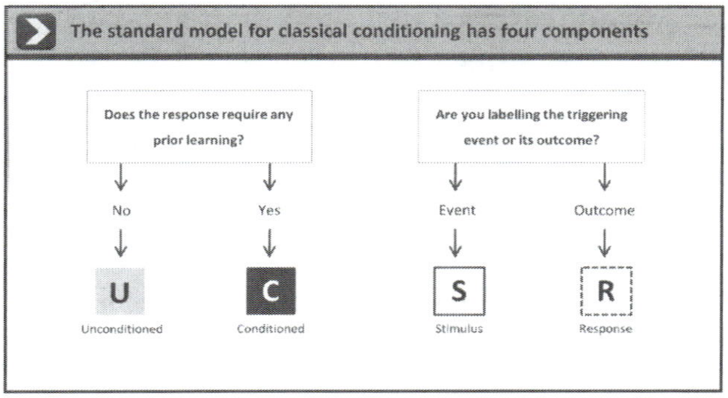

Figuring out each of the four components of classical conditioning.

* use chart when assigning the classical conditioning terms to a novel situation

Unit 4: Extinction

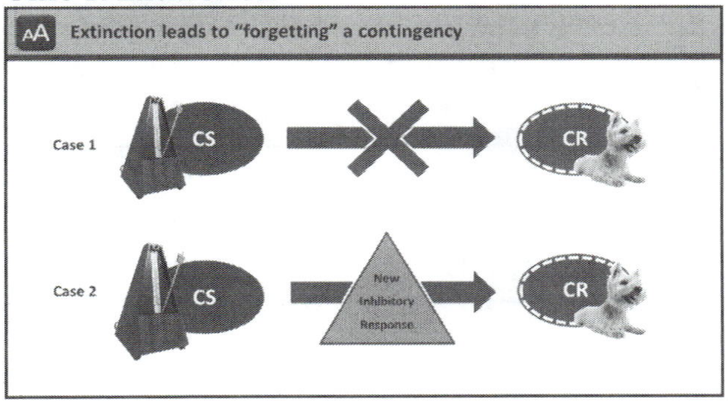

Extinction occurs when the CS can no longer elicit a CR.

case 1 - the previously learned contingency is unlearned or erased
case 2 - the old learned contingency remains, which now competes with a new inhibitory response that's learned to the same conditional stimulus

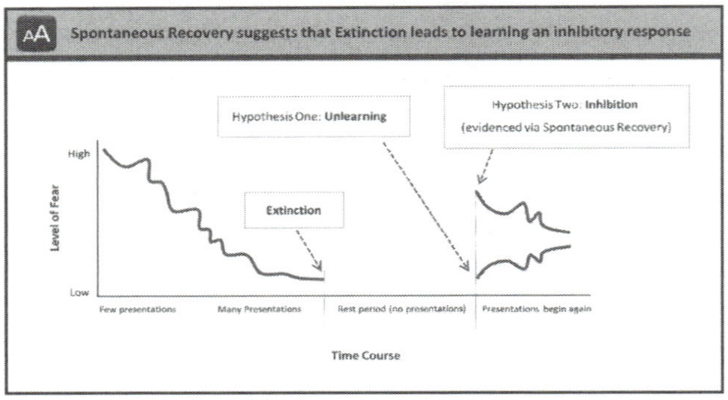

Spontaneous recovery demonstrates that the original contingency is not unlearned during extinction.

Spontaneous recovery - the sudden recovery of a conditional response following a rest period after extinction

- following an extinction procedure where a conditional stimulus is presented in the absence of the unconditioned stimulus, the conditional response gradually fades
- following a rest period, if the CS is presented once more it elicits a conditional response

Unit 5: Generalization and Discrimination

Generalization occurs when the organism produces a CR to stimuli that appear similar to the original CS.

Stimulus generalization - the process by which stimuli similar to the CS will also elicit a CR

- the strongest fear response is elicited by an image that has caused trauma in the past
- Some fear responses are still elicited by other images
- Stimulus generalization adds flexibility and efficiency to classical conditioning

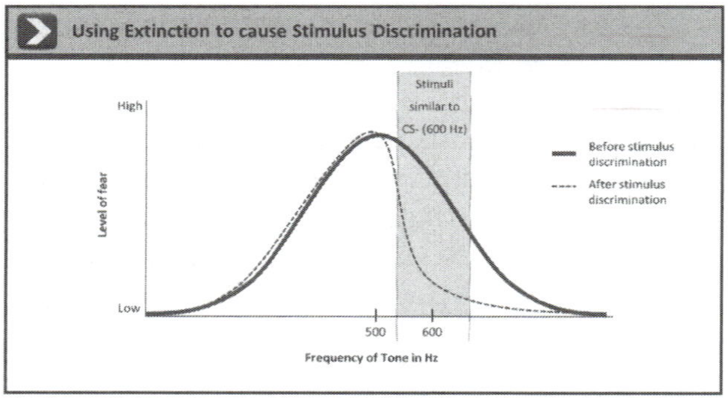

Stimulus discrimination allows the organism to produce a CR to only a restricted range of stimuli.

- Stimulus discrimination does the opposite of stimulus generalization
- it restricts the range of conditional stimuli that can elicit a response

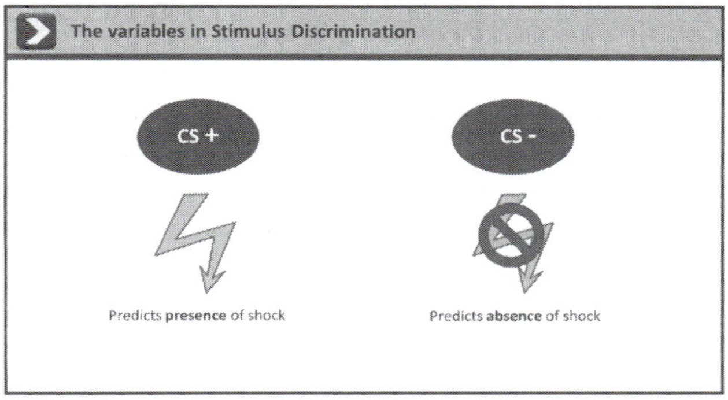

CS+: 500 hertz tone predicts the presence of an unconditional stimulus

CS-: 600 hertz tone predicts the absence of the unconditional stimulus

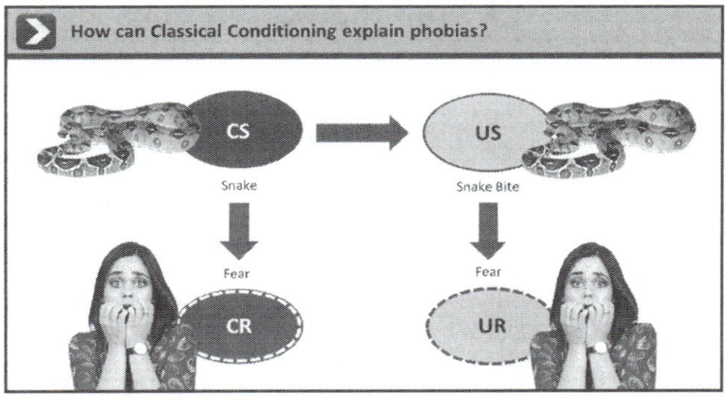

Phobias and their treatment can be understood in the context of classical conditioning.

Phobia- exaggerated intense and persistent fear of certain situations, activities, things, or people

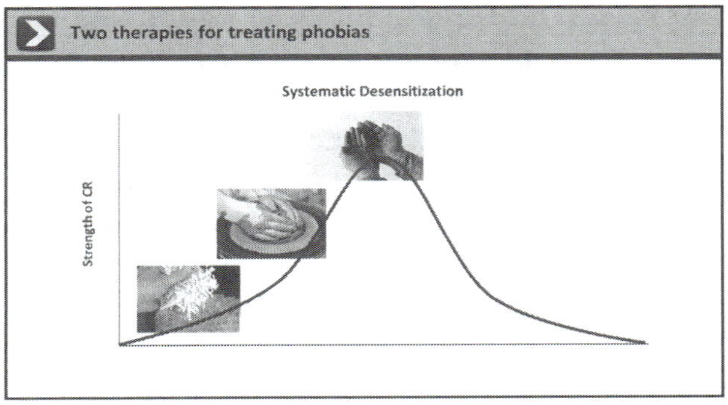

Implosive therapy: an individual with a particular phobia is encouraged to confront the CS that invokes their anxiety

- the CS is presented in the absence of the associated US

Systematic desensitization: start extinguishing stimuli at the far end of the curve, gradually working towards the middle

- gradually work through stages of increasingly fearful stimuli

Unit 6: Homeostasis and Compensatory Responses

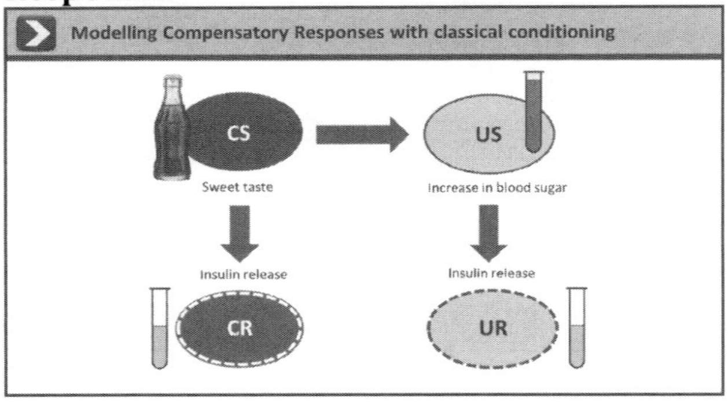

Homeostasis benefits greatly from classical conditioning mechanisms.

Compensatory responses: to allow our bodies to compensate for the effects of stimuli that we cannot consciously control

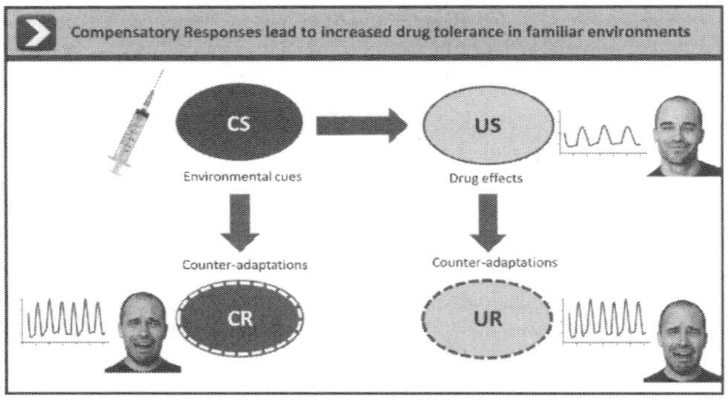

Addictions and withdrawal symptoms can be understood in the context of classical conditioning.

- US is the various naturally occuring effects of the drug
- UR is the counter-adaptations of the drug effects
- CS is the environmental cues paired with the drug effects
- CR is the counter-adaptations
- compensatory responses which prepare the body for the drug effects

Unit 7: Conclusion

Classical conditioning plays an important role in many aspects of our daily lives.

- classical conditioning is an adaptive process that many living things used to maintain homeostasis and avoid dangers in their environment

Classical Conditioning – Courseware Exercise

Imagine that you are in charge of advertising for a company that makes carbonated beverages. You have just performed a market survey and have found that you and your main competitor have approximately equal share of the market (you are both selling essentially the same amount of product). Use the principles of classical conditioning to:

1) Explain how you can mount a television ad campaign that will encourage consumers to have more positive thoughts associated with your product.

____

____

2) Explain how you can modify your campaign to associate negative thoughts with your competitor's product.

____

____

3) Identify the CS, US, CR, and UR and their relationship to one another in your ad campaign using the following figure from the module.

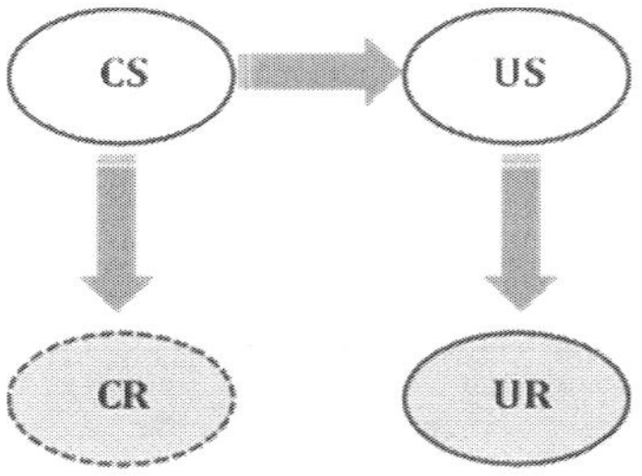

Classical conditioning can also be applied to clinical populations, particularly to those with anxiety disorders, such as phobias and to other maladaptive behaviours.

Imagine that you teach a 7th grade class and are helping students prepare for an oral history presentation. You notice, however, that one student is especially nervous about their upcoming presentation because they have been doing poorly in your class thus far. You fear that they may become flustered during their presentation and do poorly, which may consequently lead to them developing a fear of all future presentations, even those for courses outside of history.

4) What classical conditioning principle is at play in this hypothetical situation and how can you use stimulus discrimination to counter it? Describe how you would do so in a classroom setting.

____

____

____

5) Using the techniques described in the module, give three strategies that you could use to assure that none of your students develop a sudden fear of public speaking after this presentation.

a) ____

____

b) ____

____

c) ____

____

Classical Conditioning – Review Questions

1) In a classical conditioning framework, define:

   a) The US: ______________________________

   b) The UR: ______________________________

   c) The CS: ______________________________

   d) The CR: ______________________________

2) Describe the process of acquisition and explain what the negatively accelerating function suggests about classical conditioning.

____

____

____

3) Identify the US, UR, CS, CR for the following scenarios:

   a) You eat a new food and then get sick because of the flu. However, you develop a dislike for the food and feel nauseated whenever you smell it.

   US: __________ UR: __________ CS: __________ CR: __________

   b) Tyler's new girlfriend was wearing an alluring perfume on their recent date, which turned out to be very enjoyable. The following day, when Tyler gets into his car, he smells the lingering scent of his girlfriend's cologne and becomes overcome with joy.

   US: __________ UR: __________ CS: __________ CR: __________

   c) Deanna had a panic attack during a plane ride and became very afraid at the mere thought of an airplane. Twenty years later, Deanna is still afraid of airplanes even though she has never taken another flight.

   US: __________ UR: __________ CS: __________ CR: __________

4) Describe the process of generalization and discrimination that leads an individual to show a fear response to a 500Hz tone, but not to a 600Hz tone.

____

____

____

5) Describe the concept of extinction and spontaneous recovery and what they suggest about classical conditioning.

____

____

____

6) Use the example of drinking a cola to describe the process of homeostasis and why it is important.

____

____

____

7) Explain how drug addictions and withdrawal symptoms can be seen as a process of classical conditioning.

____

____

____

Classical Conditioning – Quiz Question

Which of the following correctly pairs a learning phenomenon with its example? Please reference the textbook if unfamiliar with any terms.

a. Discrimination: Xavier recalls particularly fond childhood memories whenever he smells his grandmother's pea soup, even though she cooked many other types of soup. (57.18%)
b. Habituation: Hillary is particularly afraid of her neighbour's dog after the dog bit her when they were playing once, but Hillary has no trouble interacting with any other dogs. (8.86%)
c. Generalization: Eli becomes increasingly responsive to the spontaneously scorching hot water in his shower when his roommate flushes the toilet. (9.36%)
d. Sensitization: Tanya taught her pet cockroaches to ignore a 500 Hz tone but respond to a 600 Hz tone. (24.59%)

This is an actual question from a previous Classical Conditioning Avenue Quiz that many students struggled with. We are going to go through this question together to identify what types of errors students made and how to avoid these mistakes in the future. To do so, we will look at each answer option individually and identify why it is correct or incorrect.

Often, exam developers will use correct information in an inaccurate way to describe or define certain concepts. In this example, various situations are described that encompass different concepts presented in the web module. It is your job to identify the correct match. Similar to questions we have walked through in the past, this question requires you to be able to understand and explain the various concepts from the web module in your own words. This will enable you to pick out the important information from each hypothetical scenario and compare it to what you've learned in the web module. Let's begin by examining the options:

a. Before reading the entire answer option we should already be defining discrimination in our own words. Once we've defined the concept we can now examine the answer option further. This option seems to be a correct example of discrimination because one type of soup elicits positive memories, while the others do not. We will hold onto it. (**Correct!**)
b. Again, we first define habituation in our own words. Is this scenario an example of habituation? It may seem like it at first, but it is not. Habituation is the decrease in responsiveness to a specific stimuli due to repeated exposure to that stimuli with no consequences. Is this exactly what is occurring in this example? No, because it doesn't say she is repeatedly being exposed to that dog or other dogs and therefore this option is incorrect. Let's move on.
c. First we define generalization in our own words. Is this scenario an example of generalization? Generalization is the process of applying a learned contingency to a set of similar stimuli. This does not seem to be what is occurring in this scenario. Let's move on.
d. After defining sensitization as a heightened responsiveness due to increased presentation of a stimulus, we understand that this is not what is occurring in this scenario.

We are left with only **option A**. Remember, it is important to be able to understand a concept to the point where you can explain and define it in your own words. This ability will be particularly useful when applying these concepts to new situations.

Key Terms

Acquisition	Discrimination	Phobia
Addiction	Drug Tolerance	Spontaneous Recovery
Classical Conditioning	Extinction	Systematic Desensitization
Compensatory Responses	Generalization	Taste Aversion
Conditioned Response (CR)	Generalization Gradient	Unconditional Response (UR)
Conditioned Stimulus (CS)	Homeostasis	Unconditional Stimulus (US)
Contingency	Implosive Therapy	Withdrawal
CS+	Inhibition	
CS-	Overdose	

Classical Conditioning – Bottleneck Concepts

Drug Overdose vs. Withdrawal
CS+ vs. CS-
Homeostasis
Spontaneous Recovery

Drug Overdose vs. Withdrawal

To understand drug overdose and withdrawal from a classical conditioning perspective, you must first understand homeostasis. Briefly, homeostasis is the process of keeping the internal environment of the body constant. When someone takes a drug, it changes their body in some way. For example, the drug might increase their heart rate. The body, wanting to maintain a constant internal environment, will in turn decrease the individual's heart rate to counteract the effects of the drug.

Often, people take drugs in a similar environment (e.g. for smokers: outside of their office building, using a certain brand of cigarettes, during their break at work, etc.). Over time, the environment becomes associated with consuming the drug and experiencing its effects. This means that being placed in the drug environment alone can elicit a conditioned response of counter-adaptations (processes that counteract the drug effects). This is the basis of both drug overdose and drug withdrawal.

When taking a drug in the same environment as usual, counter-adaptations occur before the drug is ingested. These measures prepare the body for the effects of the drug, leading a given dose of drug to elicit a smaller effect over time. However, if the person takes the drug in an unfamiliar environment, counter-adaptations will not occur. With a lack of countermeasures preparing the body, taking the same dose of drugs as usual may lead to an overdose when taken in an unfamiliar environment. In terms of drug withdrawal, being in the drug environment or seeing the apparatus needed to ingest a drug (e.g. a syringe) will elicit counter-adaptations. If no drug is taken, these counter-adaptations will cause the body to be abnormal (e.g. if a drug makes you ecstatic, the counter-adaptation might make you depressed). These counter-adaptations often make a person feel uncomfortable and may explain some of the withdrawal symptoms people experience.

Students often get confused about how these concepts work. A good way to think through these problems is to draw the CS, CR, US, and UR diagram (see following exercises). Then, you can ask yourself: What happens during withdrawal when you are in an environment associated with drugs, but did not take the drug? You would still experience the CR, but without drugs to counteract the effects, you would experience withdrawal. On the other hand, what do you suppose happens during a drug overdose where you have the drug effects but not the CS? There would be a UR, but no CR to help the body compensate for the drug effects!

Test your Understanding

1) Draw the US, UR, CS, CR diagram for the contingency between the environment and drug effects. Use this diagram to explain why drug withdrawal and drug overdose occur.

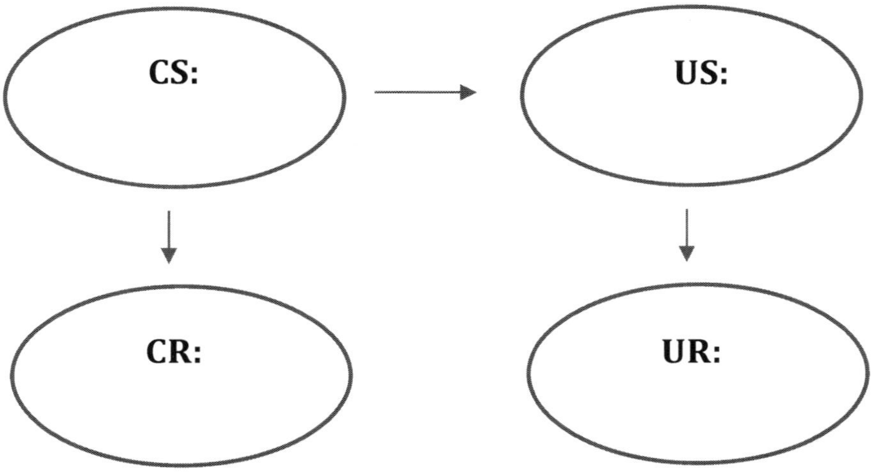

2) Gordon works out daily at the No Pain No Gain Gym. After a while at the gym, he starts being able to lift 200lbs without even having to warm-up. According to classical conditioning, which of the following statements is **incorrect**?

a) When going to a different gym, Gordon will likely not be able to bench-press as much weight without first warming up.
b) The No Pain No Gain Gym has become the CS and is associated with engaging in exercise. Therefore, being present at the gym leads Gordon's body to unconsciously prepare for oncoming exercise.
c) The No Pain No Gain Gym environment has become the CS for counter-adaptations, which act as the US.
d) If the No Pain No Gain Gym undergoes a complete renovation, Gordon may not be able to lift as much weight without warming up.

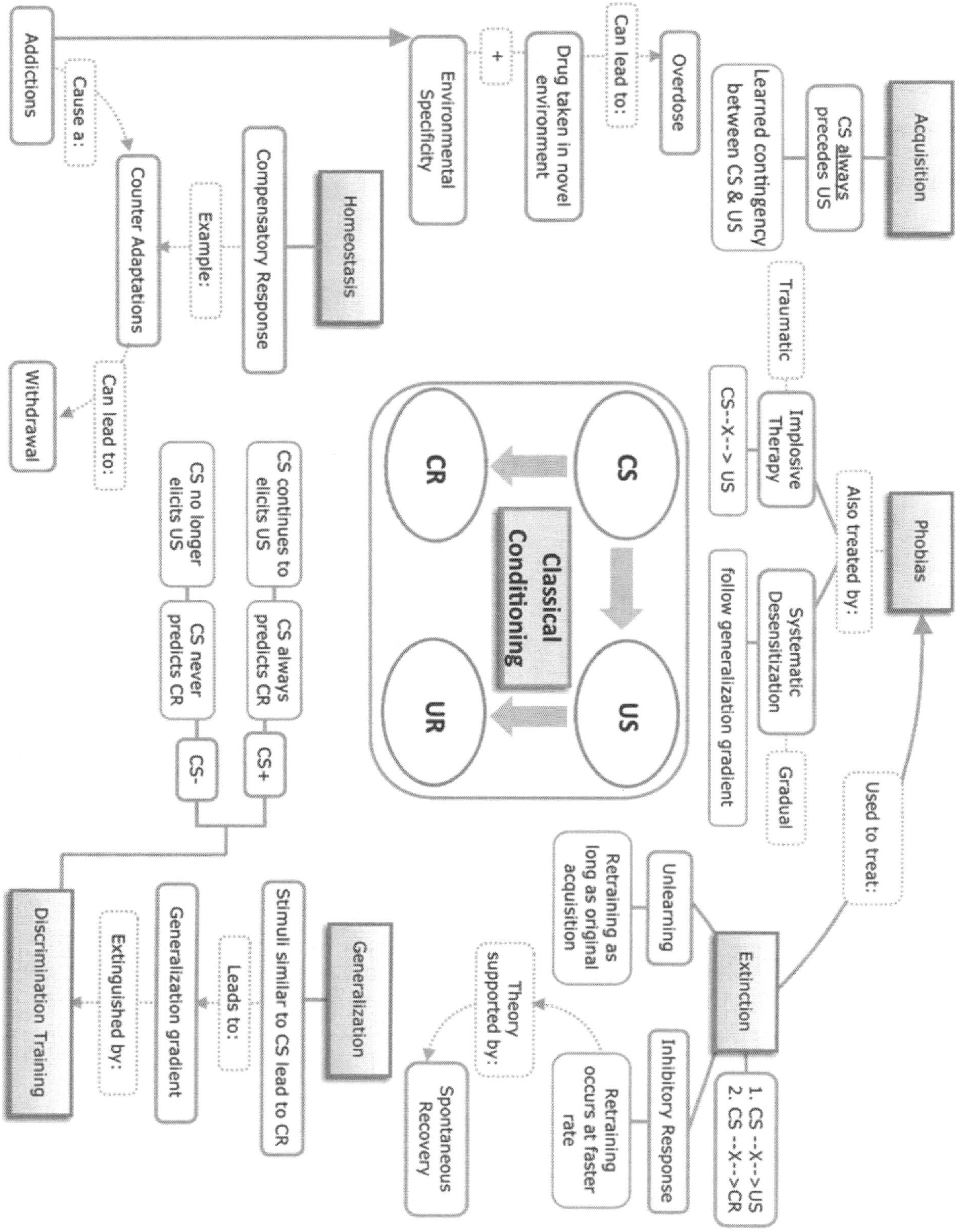

Acquisition
CS always precedes US
Learned contingency between CS & US
Overdose
Can lead to:
Drug taken in novel environment
+
Environmental Specificity
Addictions
Cause a:
Homeostasis
Compensatory Response
Example:
Counter Adaptations
Can lead to:
Withdrawal
Classical Conditioning
CS
US
CR
UR
Phobias
Also treated by:
Implosive Therapy
Traumatic
CS--X--> US
Systematic Desensitization
Gradual
follow generalization gradient
Used to treat:
Extinction
Unlearning
Retraining as long as original acquisition
Inhibitory Response
1. CS --X-->US
2. CS --X-->CR
Retraining occurs at faster rate
Theory supported by:
Spontaneous Recovery
CS continues to elicits US
CS always predicts CR
CS+
CS no longer elicits US
CS never predicts CR
CS-
Generalization
Stimuli similar to CS lead to CR
Leads to:
Generalization gradient
Extinguished by:
Discrimination Training

Acquisition
Classical Conditioning

MAC IntroPsych

Addiction
Classical Conditioning

MAC IntroPsych

Classical Conditioning
Classical Conditioning

MAC IntroPsych

Compensatory Response
Classical Conditioning

MAC IntroPsych

Conditioned Response (CR)
Classical Conditioning

MAC IntroPsych

Conditioned Stimulus (CS)
Classical Conditioning

MAC IntroPsych

Contingency
Classical Conditioning

MAC IntroPsych

CS+
Classical Conditioning

MAC IntroPsych

A stimulus, often a drug (US), elicits a compensatory response (UR). After continued use, the environment in which the drug is taken (CS) will be able to trigger compensatory responses (CR), preparing the body for the drug effect and attempting to maintain homeostasis. This can cause cravings for the drug.
Personal Example:

In classical conditioning, it is when a contingency between a CS (conditioned stimulus) and US (unconditioned stimulus) is learned.
Example: A researcher repeatedly rings a bell before presenting food to a dog. Now, when the dog hears the bell, he salivates in anticipation of food.
Personal Example:

A natural bodily response to maintain homeostasis by compensating for an oncoming or ongoing change.
Example: If an individual's body temperature increases, they will begin to sweat. In doing so, they cool their skin through the evaporation of water and maintain homeostatic levels.
Personal Example:

Learning a contingency or association between a particular stimulus and a later event that are paired together in time and/or space.
Example: Ivan Pavlov's dog learned a contingency between the ringing of a bell and the arrival of food. When the dog heard the bell, it would begin to salivate.
Personal Example:

The stimulus that, when paired with the US, creates a learned contingency where the CS reliably predicts some event.
Example: Every winter, James works at a restaurant with a bell on the door that rings (CS) every time the door opens. When the door opens, the restaurant becomes very cold (US) and James shivers (UR). The next day, James is at a warm spa where he hears a bell ring (CS) and begins to shiver (CR).
Personal Example:

The response that occurs when presented with the CS once a contingency between the CS and US has been learned.
Example: James gets regular allergy shots (US) that cause him fear (UR). If the doctor he sees each time wears a distinct lemon perfume (CS), he may form a contingency between the smell of lemons (CS) and his allergy shot (US). If so, the next time he smells lemons (CS), he will begin to feel fear (CR), even if he isn't at the doctor's clinic.
Personal Example:

A signal that reliably predicts an event (US).
Example: At a railway crossing, the signal of flashing red lights and train bells reliably predicts an oncoming train.
Personal Example:

An association formed between two stimuli after acquisition has occurred. If the presentation of one stimulus reliably leads to the presentation of another stimulus, a contingency can be formed.
Example: In Pavlov's dog example, a contingency is formed between the sound of the bell and the presentation of food.
Personal Example:

CS-
Classical Conditioning

MAC IntroPsych

Discrimination
Classical Conditioning

MAC IntroPsych

Drug Tolerance
Classical Conditioning

MAC IntroPsych

Extinction
Classical Conditioning

MAC IntroPsych

Generalization
Classical Conditioning

MAC IntroPsych

Generalization Gradient
Classical Conditioning

MAC IntroPsych

Homeostasis
Classical Conditioning

MAC IntroPsych

Implosive Therapy
Classical Conditioning

MAC IntroPsych

Restricting the range of CSs that can elicit a CR. **Example:** A certain sound (CS) signals that a phone has received a text message (US) which leads to the individual checking their phone (UR and CR). If a similar sound is repeatedly presented without a text message, then the individual would stop expecting a text message in response to the similar sound. **Personal Example:**	A signal that reliably predicts the absence of an event (US). **Example:** A green light at a traffic intersection indicates that there will be no traffic from perpendicular lanes, signalling that it is safe to drive ahead. **Personal Example:**
In classical conditioning, it is the loss of the CR when the CS no longer predicts the presentation of the US. This occurs after repeated trials of presenting the CS without the US. **Example:** James associates the smell of lemons with getting his allergy shot. If James was repeatedly exposed to the smell of lemons (CS) without receiving his allergy shot (US) and experiencing fear (UR), he would no longer experience fear (CR) when smelling lemons (CS). **Personal Example:**	With each successive drug trial, the drug's effectiveness decreases, especially when the drug is always taken in the same environment. This is because the environment reliably triggers compensatory responses before the drug is taken, thus requiring more of the drug to be administered to achieve the same effects. **Personal Example:**
A graph demonstrating the extent to which similar stimuli elicit the same CR as the CS. It often appears like a bell shaped curved, in which the original CS elicits the strongest response and less similar stimuli elicit weaker responses. **Example:** If a certain sound (CS) signals that a phone has received a text message (US), this sound will lead to the user checking their phone in. A similar sound may also lead to the user checking their phones frequently. Sounds less similar to the CS will illicit less frequent responses. **Personal Example:**	When a stimulus similar to the CS also produces a CR. **Example:** If a certain sound (CS) signals that a phone has a received a text message (US), which leads to the user checking their phone (UR and CR), then another similar sound may also elicit the same response. **Personal Example:**
A mechanism used to treat phobias, encouraging the individual to directly confront the CS that causes them anxiety by repeatedly presenting it in the absence of the anxiety-causing US. **Example:** Someone who fell from a ladder as a child and now has a phobia of heights may be asked to ride to the top of the CN tower (which results in exposure to heights without falling), thereby treating the phobia **Personal Example:**	The process of keeping the internal state of the body constant, including but not limited to temperature, glucose, and ion levels. **Example:** Sweating is a compensatory response that occurs when the body becomes too warm and must cool down to maintain a constant body temperature. **Personal Example:**

Inhibition
Classical Conditioning

MAC IntroPsych

Overdose
Classical Conditioning

MAC IntroPsych

Phobia
Classical Conditioning

MAC IntroPsych

Spontaneous Recovery
Classical Conditioning

MAC IntroPsych

Systematic Desensitization
Classical Conditioning

MAC IntroPsych

Taste Aversion
Classical Conditioning

MAC IntroPsych

Unconditioned Response (UR)
Classical Conditioning

MAC IntroPsych

Unconditioned Stimulus (US)
Classical Conditioning

MAC IntroPsych

When an individual administers too much of a drug, which the body cannot compensate for. It often occurs when an individual takes a drug they have previously taken in a new environment.
Example: If they usually do drugs in their room, they may have increased their dosage over time as the drug became less effective due to compensatory responses triggered from their environment. If they move to a new environment, their body no longer experiences the same compensatory responses, leading to a much stronger effect from the drug.
Personal Example:

When extinction leads to the learning of a new, inhibitory response to the CS. This suggests there are two learned processes: the original learned response to the CS and the inhibitory learned response to the CS.
Example: After extinguishing a fear of bees by repeatedly presenting bees (CS) in the absence of being stung (US), a new learned inhibitory response to bees is learned rather than the contingency between bees and being stung being unlearned.
Personal Example:

When a CS again elicits a CR after a rest period takes place following extinction in which the CS is repeatedly presented without the US.
Example: Sarah is afraid (CR) of bees (CS) after being stung (US) which caused fear (UR). This fear (CR) is gradually extinguished by repeatedly presenting Sarah with bees (CS) without being stung (US), but the following spring, she suddenly experiences fear (CR) again when she sees a bee (CS).
Personal Example:

An anxiety disorder, in which a person exhibits an exaggerated, intense, and persistent fear of certain situations, activities, things, or people, which is often disproportional to the danger that is posed. They are often the result of a specific traumatic experience involving the feared stimulus.
Example: A common phobia is apiphobia (fear of bees).
Personal Example:

A rapid form of acquisition in classical conditioning specifically related to taste.
Example: Often, it only takes one trial of eating spoiled food and experiencing sickness to learn to avoid the food. The CS is taste, the US is sickness, and the UR and CR are aversion.
Personal Example:

A mechanism used to treat phobias, in which the individual is presented with gradual exposure to the feared CS without exposure to the US.
Example: An individual with a fear of dogs may initially be presented with four-legged animals that do not quite resemble dogs, with each successive step involving conditional stimuli that are more similar to dogs.
Personal Example:

A stimulus, which automatically triggers a response in the absence of learning.
Example: If James receives an allergy shot (US), he will automatically experience pain (UR).
Personal Example:

A response, which is automatically triggered by a stimulus in the absence of learning.
Example: If James is exposed to a cold environment (US), he will automatically shiver (UR).
Personal Example:

Withdrawal
Classical Conditioning

MAC IntroPsych

MAC IntroPsych

MAC IntroPsych

MAC IntroPsych

MAC IntroPsych

MAC IntroPsych

MAC IntroPsych

MAC IntroPsych

	A group of symptoms occurring after a discontinuation of a medication or drug. Symptoms occur most often when an individual is in the environment in which they previously took drugs. These symptoms are internal compensatory responses that would normally oppose the drug effect. But without the presence of a drug, these symptoms would bring the body to levels away from homeostasis (and lead to discomfort). **Personal Example:**

INSTRUMENTAL CONDITIONING

"Give me a dozen healthy infants, well-formed, and my own specified world to bring them up in and I'll guarantee to take any one at random and train him to become any type of specialist I might select— doctor, lawyer, artist, merchant-chief and, yes, even beggar-man and thief, regardless of his talents, penchants, tendencies, abilities, vocations, and race of his ancestors. "
-John B. Watson, author of "Psychology as the Behaviourist Views It."

For a number of years, there was an unusual display in the lobby of the psychology building at Harvard University. Remarkably, two pigeons would hit a ping-pong ball back and forth to each other in a spirited match. Visitors were amazed at how such a complex skill could be taught to birds. Although impressive, training was actually straightforward and less complex than people realized. B.F. Skinner first trained each pigeon individually. The desired behaviour of hitting a moving ping-pong ball was broken down into particular bits of behaviour and reinforced (rewarded) with food. The bird might first be reinforced for just approaching the ball, then only for touching the ball, later only for pushing it, and finally only for hitting a moving ball. All that was left was to place the two trained pigeons at opposite ends of a table and start keeping score. By a similar process, Skinner taught pigeons to walk in figure-eights, dance with each other, and even operate a prototype missile guidance system (Skinner lamented that "no one would take us seriously.") The core principles that actions are determined by the environment and that behaviour is shaped and maintained by its consequences are used in many applied settings including cognitive behaviour therapy, game design, and educational psychology. However, Skinner went a step further and believed that these foundational principles could introduce positive change to our society as a whole. As summarized by one interviewer, "In the Skinnerian world, man will refrain from polluting, from overpopulating, from rioting, and from making war, not because he knows that the results will be dangerous, but because he has been conditioned to want what serves group interests."

Watson, J.B. (1913). Psychology as a behaviourist views it. Psychological Review, 20, 158-177. Skinner, B.F. (1950). Are theories of learning necessary? Psychological Review, 57, 193-216.

Weekly Checklist:

- ☐ **Web Module to watch: Instrumental Conditioning**
- ☐ **Readings: Chapter 4**
- ☐ **Avenue Quiz 3**

Upper Year Courses:

If you enjoyed the content in this week's module, consider taking the following upper year course:

- PSYCH 2H03 Human Learning and Cognition

Instrumental Conditioning – Outline

Unit 1: Introduction

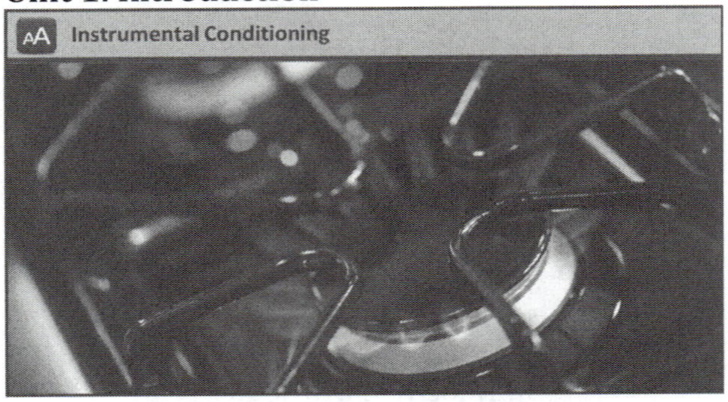

Instrumental conditioning: involves explicit training between voluntary behaviours and their consequences

* • the learning of a contingency between behaviour and a consequence

Unit 2: Instrumental Conditioning

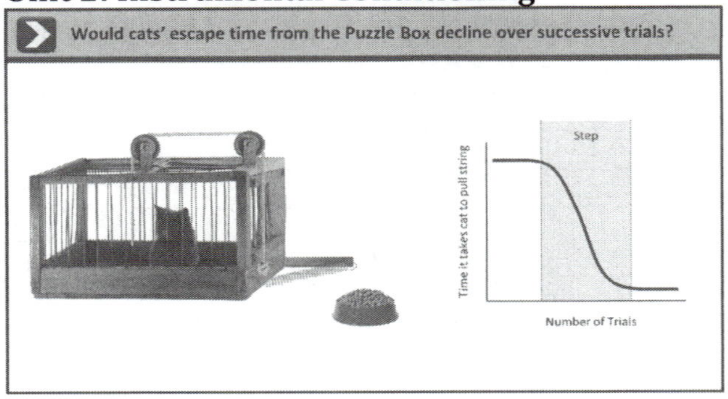

Early research on instrumental conditioning was often performed on non-human animals.

Thorndike: doing studies on non-human animals put focus on overt behaviour rather than on mental elements or conscious experiences

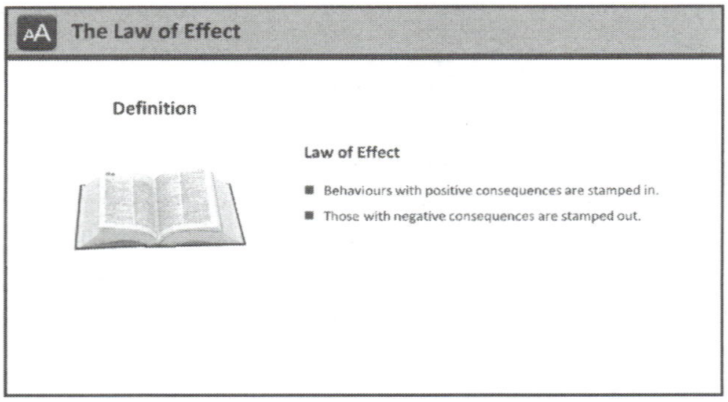

Stamping in: rope pulling because they were followed by the favourable consequences of access to food

* •behaviours with positive consequences

Stamping out: random behaviours like turning in a circle

* • those with negative consequences

Unit 3: Types of Instrumental Conditioning

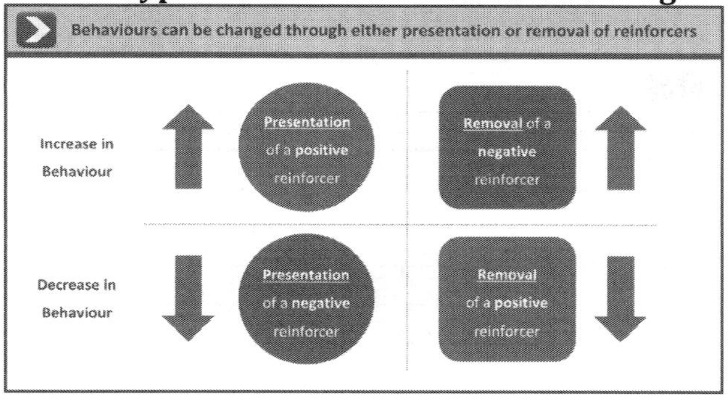

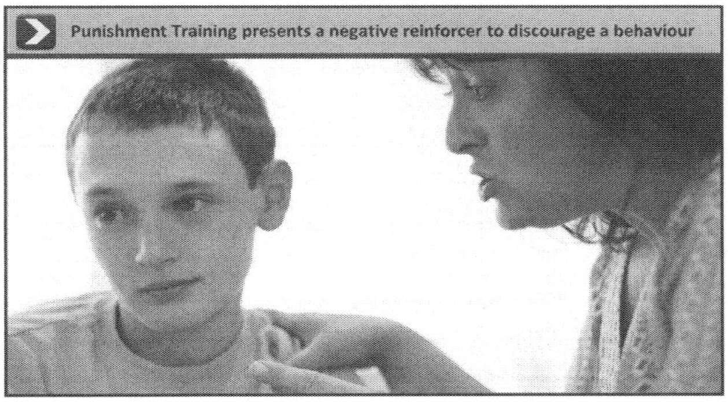

Behaviour can be influenced by four types of consequences.

behavioural responses are changed by positive and negative reinforcers, which can be either presented or removed

- 4 types of instrumental training: presenting or removing positive reinforcement and presenting or removing negative reinforcement

Reward training: presentation of a positive reinforce are following a response, which increases frequency behaviour

Punishment: a response followed by the presentation of a negative reinforcement, which leads to decrease in behaviour being reinforced

Omission training: reinforcement is omitted (removed) and this leads to decrease in behavior being reinforced
• time out procedure

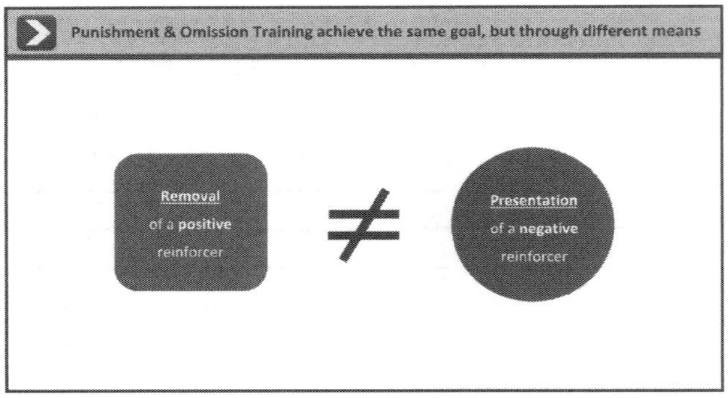

• omission training and punishment lead to the same decrease in responding, they use different means

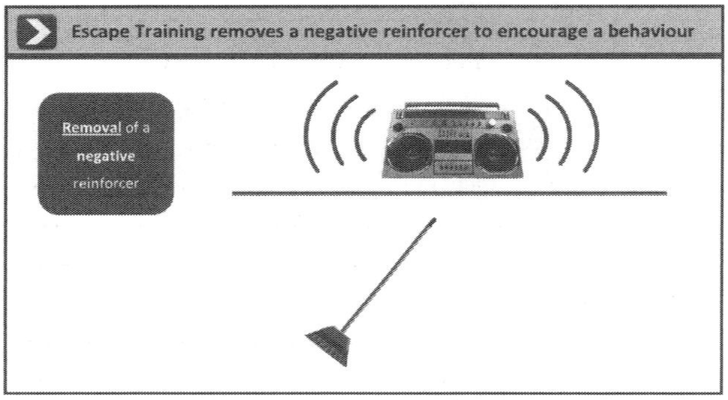

Escape training: a response is followed by removal of a negative reinforcer, almost like escaping a bad situation
• constant negative reinforcer being presented that the learner is motivated to have removed
• a specific response removes negative reinforcement which leads to an increase in that response behaviour

Unit 4: Acquisition and Shaping

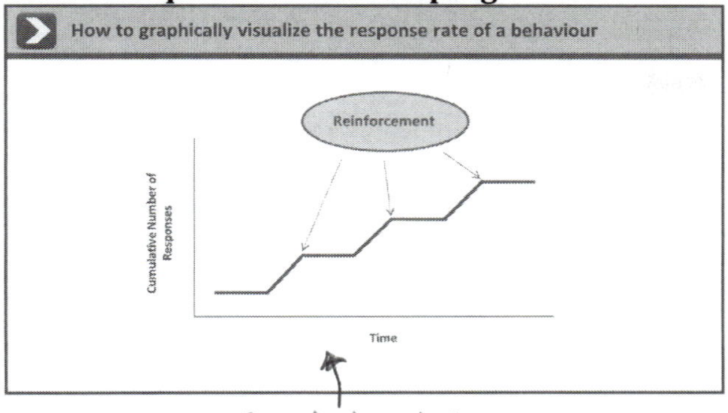

reward training

Responses to each type of training can be graphed to visualize the acquisition of a contingency.

cumulative recorder

- long piece of paper flows through machine drawing a straight line, with each response made the pen moves up a notch leading to a characteristic pattern of acquisition

straight line = no response

upward slope = response

- can change depending on the subject, the complexity of the behaviour, and type of reinforcement

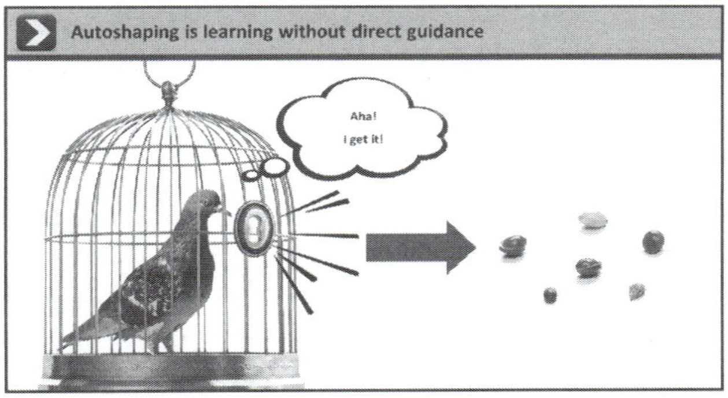

Organisms can learn the contingency between a behaviour and its consequence without explicit training.

Autoshaping: behaviours are learned without the careful guidance of the researcher, it will learn the contingency on it's own

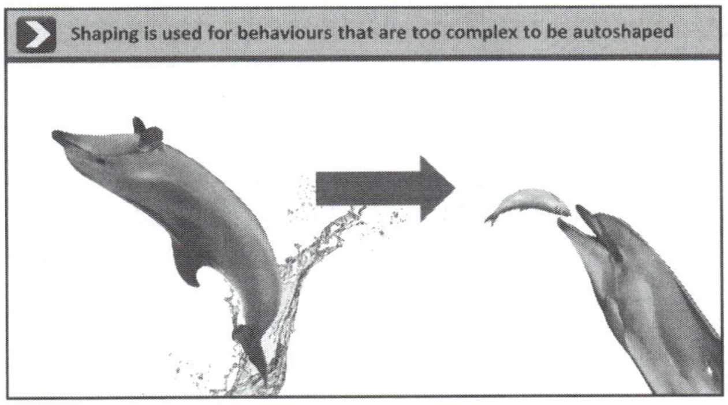

Some behaviours require a more systematic form of training to enable the acquisition of a contingency.

Shaping by successive approximation: complex behaviour is organized into smaller steps which gradually build to the full response

- each step can be reinforced through reward training

Unit 5: Generalization and Discrimination

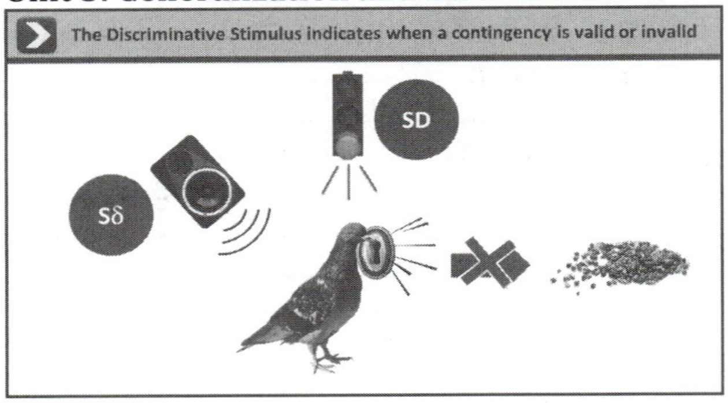

The discriminative stimulus indicates the validity of a contingency.

S+ SD: (discriminative stimulus) signals when a contingency between the particular reinforcement is on

S- S-delta: a cue when the contingent relationship is not valid

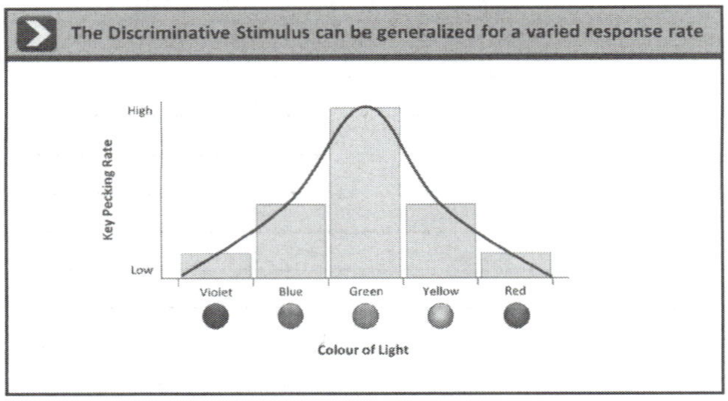

Stimuli similar to the SD can indicate the validity of a contingency to a certain degree.

- range of responding could be graphed on a generalization gradient
- similar thing happens with discriminative stimulus in instrumental conditioning

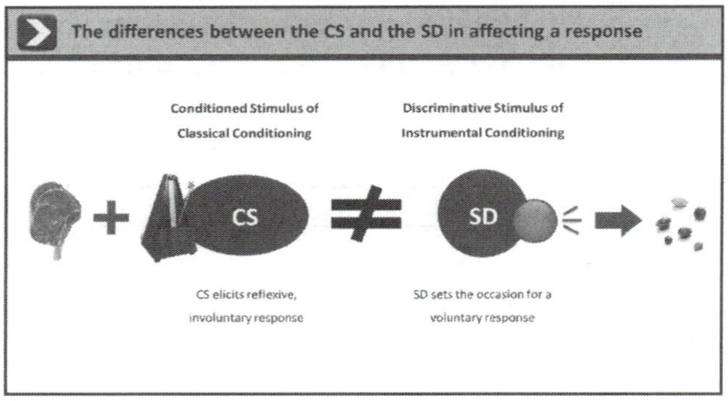

The ability to elicit a response involuntarily marks an important distinction between the CS and the SD.

classical conditioning →
- CS is paired with US and elicits response reflexively, response is automatic

instrumental conditioning →
- SD is paired with response reinforce or outcome, SD doesn't reflexively elicit the response, SD sets the occasion for a response by signaling when the respone reinforcer outcome is valid
- in instrumental conditioning the response is voluntary

Unit 6: Schedules of Reinforcement

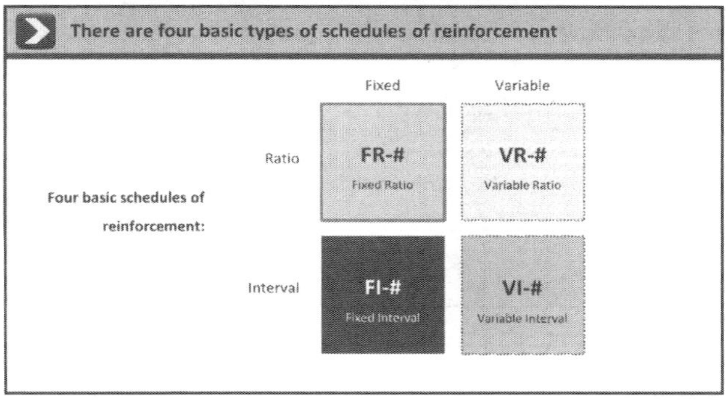

Four basic schedules guide the delivery of reinforcement.

FR • schedule of reinforcement is based on number of responses which determines when reinforcement is given

FI • interval schedule of reinforcement is based on the time since the last response was reinforced

VR + VI • variable ratio and interval scales are provided following a variable amount of work or length of time

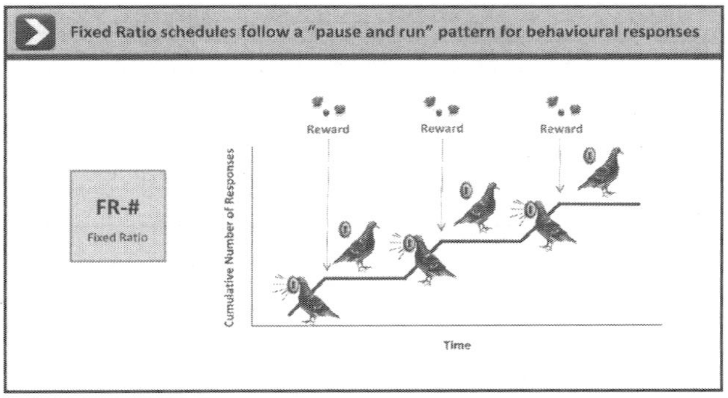

Fixed ratio: pigeon must peck multiple times to recieve food reward, if to much is required it can lead to ratio strain and the subject will stop responding

• display a characteristic type of cumulative record called pause, and run pattern

• following reinforcement participant will pause within activity before beginning the next run of responding

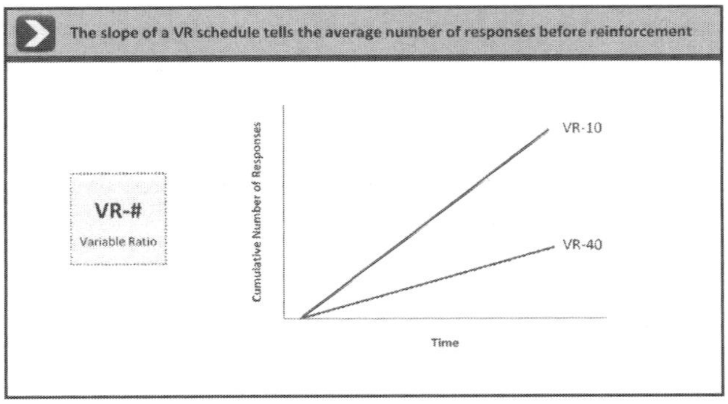

Variable ratio: reinforcement is delivered after some random number of responses around the characteristic mean

• supporting very constant and high response rates

• cumulative record of response is reinforced on a variable ratio schedule may almost look like a diagonal line with no pauses in between

• slope of a variable ratio schedules cumulative record reflects the average number of responses required before reinforcement is delivered

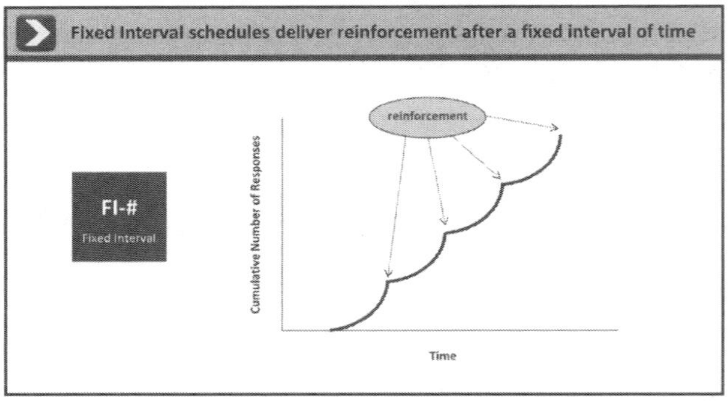

Fixed interval: reinforcement is delivered following the first response after a set interval of time

- following reinforcement there is a lull period where responding drops then slowly starts picking up again and peaking just before the next reinforcement is scheduled to be delivered following a response

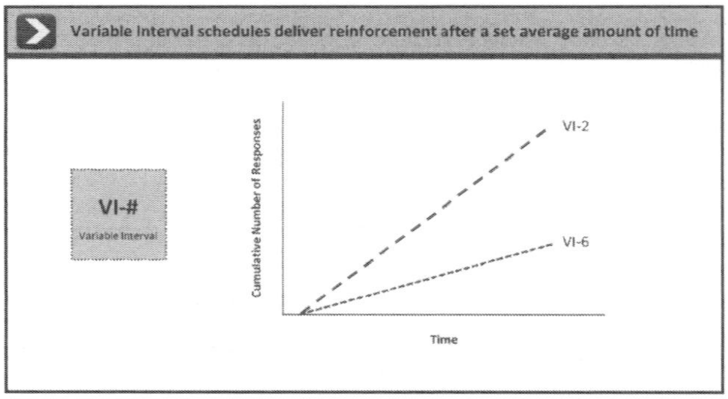

Variable interval: could recieve reinforcement at anytime, but you do have an idea of how often reinforcement is likely to come up

- subject tends to respond at a very steady rate that ensures it will not miss an opportunity for reinforcement

Instrumental Conditioning – Courseware Exercise

1) Name and describe each of the four types of instrumental conditioning and provide an example of how a parent can use each technique to train her child, Billy, to pick his jacket off the floor.

a) Name: ______________________
   Description: ______________________
   Example: ______________________

b) Name: ______________________
   Description: ______________________
   Example: ______________________

c) Name: ______________________
   Description: ______________________
   Example: ______________________

d) Name: ______________________
   Description: ______________________
   Example: ______________________

e) Despite using these techniques, the parent is having no luck with the child at all! Based on the information provided in lecture, what might the child's parent be doing wrong? How could the parent fix this problem?

____

____

____

____

2) Carrie, a first year psychology student, is backpacking across Europe during the summer. She is running low on funds and decides to work at an organic strawberry farm as a fruit picker. She is paid 15 Euros for every 3 buckets of strawberries that she picks. Based on this information, respond to the following questions:

a) What is her schedule of reinforcement?

____

b) If Carrie begins working for another farm that pays her 15 Euros for every 2 buckets of strawberries, what is her new schedule of reinforcement?

____

c) How will Carrie's rate of work change with this new schedule of reinforcement?

____

d) Carrie's employers are considering the possibility of paying their workers hourly. If they decide to pay their employees 15 Euros per hour, what would her new schedule of reinforcement be?

____

Instrumental Conditioning – Review Questions

1) Compare and contrast classical and instrumental conditioning.

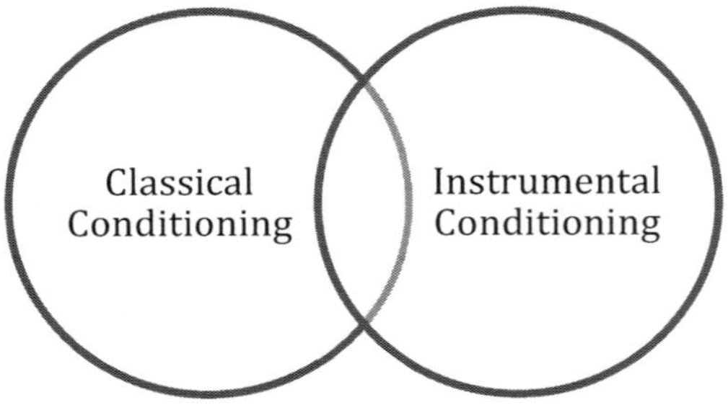

2) Which of the following definitions best describes the law of effect in instrumental conditioning?

a) When contingencies are fully established between behaviours that lead to positive or negative outcomes, these behaviours are stamped in.

b) Behaviours that do not lead to any outcomes are stamped in and behaviours that lead to negative outcomes are stamped out.

c) Behaviours that lead to positive outcomes are stamped in and behaviours that lead to negative outcomes are stamped out.

d) Behaviours that lead to rewards are stamped in and behaviours that that lead to punishment are stamped out.

3) Your friend Sally always tries to talk to you about her weekend while your IntroPsych TA is reviewing the course concepts. This is really distracting and you want her to stop. Being the expert in instrumental conditioning that you now are, you offer her a piece of candy when she stops talking. What kinds of instrumental conditioning are now associated with candies and talking in IntroPsych tutorials?

a) For **Sally**, this is a form of **punishment**; for **you**, this is a form of **escape training**.

b) For **Sally**, this is a form of **reward training**; for **you**, this is a form of **escape training**.

c) For **Sally**, this is a form of **omission training**; for **you**, this is a form of **reward training**.

d) For **Sally**, this is a form of **escape training**; for **you**, this is a form of **punishment**.

4) How does SD differ from S-delta?

a) SD is a stimulus that will lead to positive reinforcement; S-delta is a stimulus that will lead to negative reinforcement.

b) SD is a stimulus that signals that a behaviour will be followed by reinforcement; S-delta is a stimulus that signals that a behaviour will not be followed by reinforcement.

c) SD automatically elicits a response; S-delta sets the occasion for a response.

d) SD is a stimulus that is associated with generalization; S-delta is a stimulus that is associated with discrimination.

5) Graph the typical response patterns of each of the schedules. Always make note of a graph's axes!

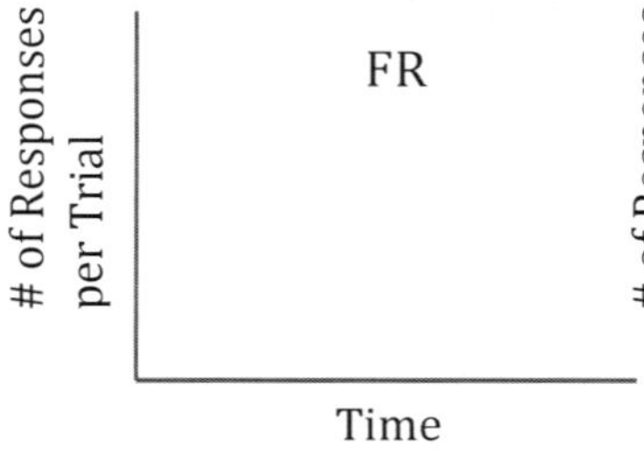

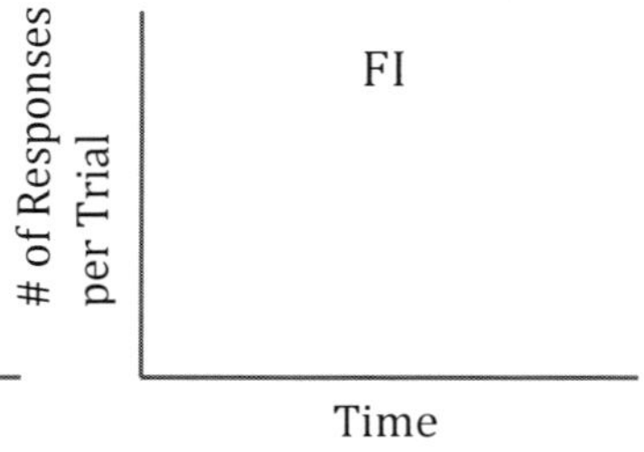

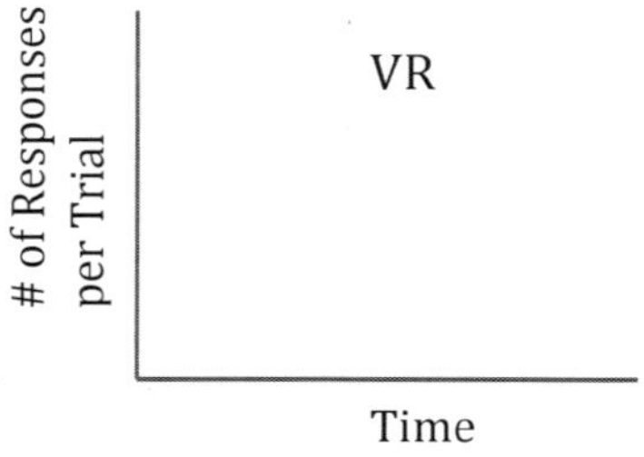

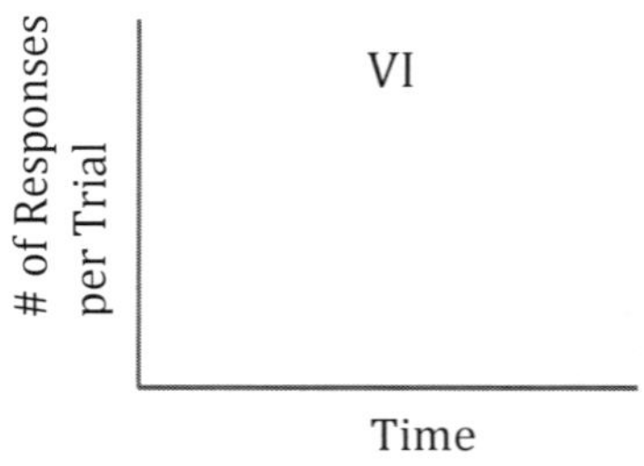

Instrumental Conditioning – Quiz Question

Which of the following is a **correct** comparison of classical and instrumental conditioning?

a. The S-Delta cues a response to negative reinforcement, while the CS- signals the absence of a stimulus. (14.25%)
b. The S-Delta cues the absence of a response, while the CS- signals a negative response. (7.06%)
c. The SD indicates a valid contingency, while the CS+ elicits a conditioned response. (62.04%)
d. The SD indicates a positive response, while the CS+ cues a conditioned response. (16.65%)

This is an actual question from a previous Instrumental Conditioning Avenue Quiz that many students struggled with. We are going to go through this question together to identify what sort of errors students were making and how to avoid them in the future. To do so, we will look at each answer option individually and identify why it is correct or incorrect.

Similar to what we have done in the past, it is important that we are able to explain and describe the concepts from the web module in our own words. In addition, be sure to read every answer option carefully. Reading an answer option with a critical and sceptical eye will allow you to better identify the inconsistencies in an option. Keeping this in mind, let's examine the answer options:

a. In this case, we should be able to describe a CS+, CS, discriminative stimulus and S-Delta. Furthermore, we are told the S-Delta cues (initiates) a response. Have we ever talked about cueing a response in either type of conditioning? No. In fact, the S-Delta is a signal that a particular contingency is not valid. This option is incorrect. Let's move on.
b. Again, does the description of the S-Delta match the description we have given in our words? No. What about the CS-? Well, the CS- signals the absence of a stimulus (US). Is this how the CS- is described in this question? No. It is described as a predictor of a negative response. It may sound right but we can identify it as being incorrect when we compare it to our description of the CS-. Let's move onto option C.
c. Does the description of the S-Delta match ours? Yes! What about the CS+? Well, sort of. While not explicitly mentioning that the CS+ predicts the presence of the US, it mentions that it will elicit a UR. We know that if a CS predicts the presence of a US, then once a CS-US contingency is learned, the CS will elicit a CR. It is important to keep a flexible mind when reading questions, the answer may not be directly from the definition. This option seems to be correct so we will hold onto it. (**Correct!**)
d. This option states that the SD indicates a positive response. What does that even mean? The SD makes you feel good? Makes you perform a good deed? This is a nonsense statement designed to sound like a good option. Remember, it is important to be critical of each answer option. The correct option can always be supported by information from the web module without having to "stretch" the information to fit the option. Therefore, this is an incorrect alternative.

This leaves us with **option C,** the correct answer in this question. Often, answer options are designed to sound like good answers. If we take the time to think critically and apply the information we have learned from the web module, it is easy to pick out these answer options as incorrect.

Key Terms

Acquisition	Four Consequences	Puzzle Box
Autoshaping	Interval Schedule of Reinforcement	Ratio Schedule of Reinforcement
Continuous Reinforcement	Instrumental Conditioning	Reward Training
Discriminative Stimulus (SD)	Law of Effect	S-delta
Escape Training	Omission Training	Shaping
Fixed Interval	Partial Reinforcement	Variable Interval
Fixed Ratio	Punishment	Variable Ratio

Instrumental Conditioning – Bottleneck Concepts

Classical Conditioning vs. Instrumental Conditioning
Omission vs. Escape Training
Schedules of Reinforcement
SD vs. S-delta

Classical Conditioning vs. Instrumental Conditioning

Both classical and instrumental conditioning are based on learning a contingency—an association or relationship between two things. Classical conditioning involves learning a contingency between two events or stimuli. Instrumental conditioning involves learning a contingency between a behaviour and its consequence. For classical conditioning, the two stimuli can be unrelated events; however, they must occur close to each other in both time and space. For instrumental conditioning, the behaviour leads to a certain consequence, meaning that the two stimuli are related in some way.

Students often have trouble identifying whether a situation is an example of classical or instrumental conditioning. The easiest way to differentiate between them is to ask whether the conditioning results in a voluntary or an involuntary response. In classical conditioning, the response (CR) is always involuntary. If you get bitten by a dog and, as a result, associate pain with dogs, you will experience fear every time you see a dog whether you want to or not. In instrumental conditioning, however, the subject's response is always voluntary. You might know that not studying will lead to poor marks on a test, but that does not automatically mean you will study hard—you have to make a choice to study.

Test your Understanding

1) Read the following scenarios and determine if they are examples of classical or instrumental conditioning. If you classify a scenario as classical conditioning, determine the US, CS, UR, and CR. If the situation fits the description of instrumental conditioning, determine the behaviour and its consequence.

a) Tom is a curious boy who likes to explore his surroundings. One day he notices an electrical socket and wonders what it does. He decides to stick a paperclip into the hole and receives a painful shock. Ever since that day, Tom has never stuck anything into an electrical socket again.

b) Francine's favourite fruit is watermelon and she eats it throughout the day. One day, she became very ill from food poisoning and felt terribly nauseous and sick. Once she felt better, Francine wanted to eat watermelons again. However, this time she felt nauseous as soon as she saw the fruit.

2) Come up with an example of instrumental and classical conditioning based on your everyday life. If you are unsure about their accuracy, feel free to ask your TA for their opinion!

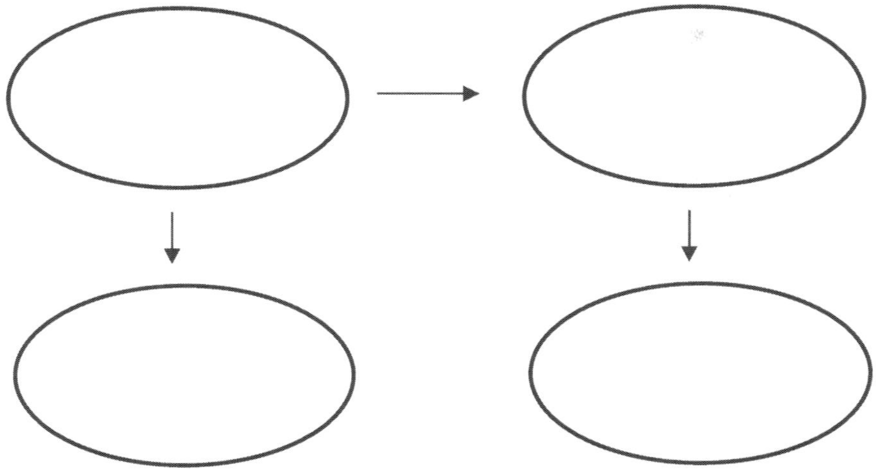

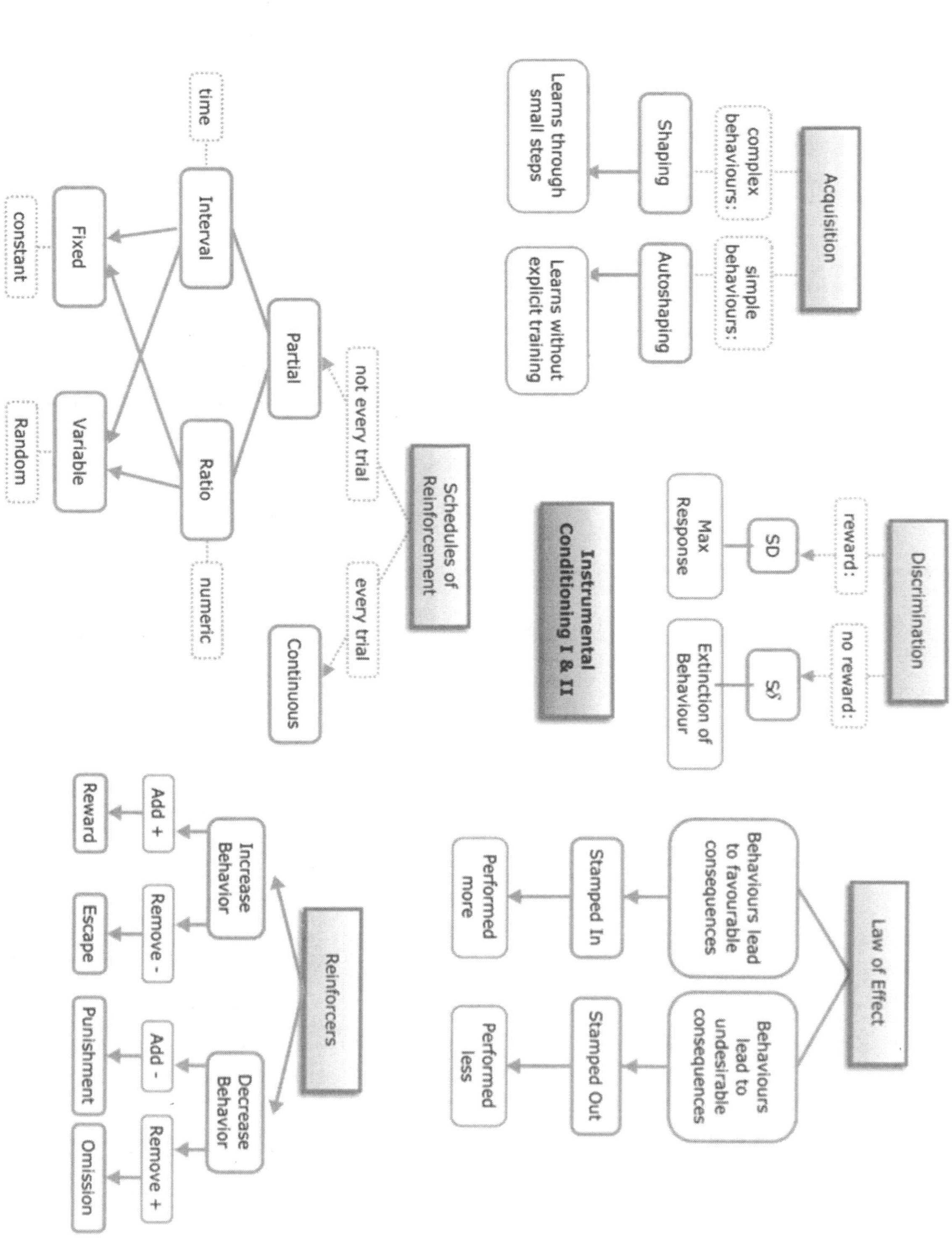

Instrumental Conditioning I & II
Acquisition
complex behaviours:
simple behaviours:
Shaping
Autoshaping
Learns through small steps
Learns without explicit training
Discrimination
reward:
no reward:
SD
S∆
Max Response
Extinction of Behaviour
Law of Effect
Behaviours lead to favourable consequences
Behaviours lead to undesirable consequences
Stamped In
Stamped Out
Performed more
Performed less
Schedules of Reinforcement
not every trial
every trial
Partial
Continuous
Interval
Ratio
time
numeric
Fixed
Variable
constant
Random
Reinforcers
Increase Behavior
Decrease Behavior
Add +
Remove -
Add -
Remove +
Reward
Escape
Punishment
Omission

Acquisition
Instrumental Conditioning

MAC IntroPsych

Autoshaping
Instrumental Conditioning

MAC IntroPsych

Continuous Reinforcement
Instrumental Conditioning

MAC IntroPsych

Discriminative Stimulus (SD)
Instrumental Conditioning

MAC IntroPsych

Escape Training
Instrumental Conditioning

MAC IntroPsych

Fixed Interval
Instrumental Conditioning

MAC IntroPsych

Fixed Ratio
Instrumental Conditioning

MAC IntroPsych

Four Consequences
Instrumental Conditioning

MAC IntroPsych

When a behaviour can be learned without explicit training by an experimenter. **Example:** When a cat tries to escape a puzzle box, its random behaviour will eventually lead it to pull the rope without any explicit instructions to do so. Over time, it is able to consistently do this on its own. **Personal Example:**	In instrumental conditioning, it is when a contingency between a behaviour and its consequence is learned. **Example:** As a child, you learned that being polite lead to positive consequences and now, as an adult, you are still polite in hopes of positive consequences. **Personal Example:**
A cue in instrumental conditioning, signalling when a contingency between a particular response and reinforcement is available. **Example:** When a dog is asked to roll over by its owners, it may be rewarded with a treat. However, a vet may not necessarily reward a dog for rolling over. The contingency between the behaviour (rolling over) and the reinforcement (a treat) is only valid in the presence of the owners (discriminative stimulus). **Personal Example:**	A schedule of reinforcement in which reinforcement always follows a particular behaviour. These are infrequent in the real world. **Example:** A dog trained to sit is given a treat every time she obeys. **Personal Example:**
An instrumental conditioning schedule of reinforcement in which reinforcement is delivered after a constant period of time. **Example:** Employees of many companies are paid for every two weeks of work, a fixed interval schedule of reinforcement. **Personal Example:**	The removal of a negative reinforcer following a behaviour in order to increase the frequency of that behaviour. **Example:** If you are consistently getting sunburned while tanning at the beach, you may learn to wear sunscreen to prevent yourself from getting burned further. **Personal Example:**
Four mechanisms of describing how reinforcement can be used to influence behaviour. The four consequences are the presentation of positive reinforcement, presentation of negative reinforcement, removal of positive reinforcement, and removal of negative reinforcement. **Personal Example:**	An instrumental conditioning schedule of reinforcement in which reinforcement is delivered after a constant number of responses. **Example:** An agent for an actress may only receive payment for every 5 auditions he books. **Personal Example:**

Interval Schedule
Instrumental Conditioning

MAC IntroPsych

Instrumental Conditioning
Instrumental Conditioning

MAC IntroPsych

Law of Effect
Instrumental Conditioning

MAC IntroPsych

Omission Training
Instrumental Conditioning

MAC IntroPsych

Partial Reinforcement
Instrumental Conditioning

MAC IntroPsych

Punishment
Instrumental Conditioning

MAC IntroPsych

Puzzle Box
Instrumental Conditioning

MAC IntroPsych

Ratio Schedule
Instrumental Conditioning

MAC IntroPsych

The overall training paradigm that allows for the learning of a contingency between a behavior and a consequence
Example: A cat may no longer chew wires if it finds itself getting shocked when doing so.
Personal Example:

A schedule of reinforcement in which reinforcement is provided once some amount of time has passed since the last response was reinforced.
Example: If a shoemaker is paid for his work every week, then he will receive a pay cheque regardless of how many shoes he has made.
Personal Example:

The removal of a positive reinforcement following a behaviour to decrease the frequency of that behaviour.
Example: Billy steals his sister's laptop, which causes their mom to take away his bike for a week.
Personal Example:

Behaviours with positive consequences become stamped in (Example: being rewarded with a cookie after reaching for the cookie jar at the top of the fridge). Behaviours with negative consequences are stamped out (Example: being blamed and punished for stealing the cookies from the cookie jar would be categorized as a negative behaviour, and you probably won't repeat it).
Personal Example:

The presentation of a negative reinforcer following a behaviour to decrease the frequency of that behaviour.
Example: If Sally cheats on a test and is sent to detention (the presentation of a negative reinforcer), this is meant to decrease the frequency of cheating.
Personal Example:

A schedule of reinforcement in which a form of reinforcement does not follow every single time a particular behaviour is performed.
Example: If a young child has a bad habit of sucking his thumb, his mother may reward him with a chocolate for every five days that he does not suck his thumb.
Personal Example:

A schedule of reinforcement in which reinforcement is provided once a predetermined number of responses has been provided.
Example: If a salesperson sells 4 cars, he receives his paycheck.
Personal Example:

A cat trapped in a box with a rope exhibits random behaviours. Its random behaviour would eventually lead it to find that when it pulls the rope, it can escape from the box. Over time, the number of behaviours before the cat finds the rope would decrease, suggesting the animal followed a stimulus-response process, or instrumental conditioning.
Personal Example:

Reward Training
Instrumental Conditioning

MAC IntroPsych

S-Delta
Instrumental Conditioning

MAC IntroPsych

Shaping
Instrumental Conditioning

MAC IntroPsych

Variable Interval
Instrumental Conditioning

MAC IntroPsych

Variable Ratio
Instrumental Conditioning

MAC IntroPsych

MAC IntroPsych

MAC IntroPsych

MAC IntroPsych

A stimulus that cues when a contingency between a particular response and reinforcement is no longer valid.
Example: When a dog is asked to roll over by its owners' guests, it will not be rewarded with a treat and therefore, over time will learn not to do so because the guests (S-delta) indicate an invalid contingency.
Personal Example:

The presentation of a positive reinforcer following behaviour to increase the frequency of that behaviour.
Example: If a dog is rewarded with a treat for rolling over, he is most likely to repeat that behaviour to obtain the reward.
Personal Example:

An instrumental conditioning schedule of reinforcement in which reinforcement is delivered after some variable period of time around a characteristic mean.
Example: In the case of an employee's bonus, they will receive it at random times during some point of the year regardless of how much work they have done.
Personal Example:

Ordering a complex behaviour into a series of smaller, more feasible steps, which when put together, lead to the final complex behaviour.
Example: An animal trainer may train a dog to carry a toy across the room. First, the dog would be rewarded when they make any movement toward the toy. Once this is reinforced, the dog must pick up the toy to be rewarded. Once this behaviour is reinforced, the dog is then rewarded when it crosses the room with the toy.
Personal Example:

An instrumental conditioning schedule of reinforcement where reinforcement is delivered after some variable number of responses around a characteristic mean.
Example: For slot machines, payout occurs after a random number of plays around a pre-set mean. Behaviour is reinforced randomly, causing people to play for hours.
Personal Example:

PROBLEM SOLVING & INTELLIGENCE

"If I had an hour to solve a problem and my life depended on the solution, I would spend the first 55 minutes determining the proper question to ask. For once I know the proper question, I could solve the problem in less than five minutes."
- Albert Einstein

In the TV game show, *Are You Smarter than a 5th Grader?,* adult contestants competed to win a million dollar prize. In order to win, players were required to answer ten questions correctly. The questions were taken from elementary school textbooks and ranged in difficulty from grade one to grade five. Although the premise of this game seems simple, there were only two winners in the history of the show. These surprising results lead us to ask, "are adults *not* smarter than 5th graders?".

A dramatic and potentially controversial finding in intelligence research could suggest that no, adults are not smarter than current fifth graders. This finding, termed the Flynn Effect, states that the mean score for intelligence testing in the population has been steadily increasing since it was first measured in 1932. It proposes that IQ test scores are steadily on the rise, with each generation becoming more intelligent than the previous one. Despite the many ideas set forth to explain the Flynn effect, no one is actually sure why it occurs. Is it the result of better nutrition and better quality schooling? Or perhaps is it due to our ever-increasing access to information? Although its cause has yet to be determined, the Flynn effect is significant as it raises important questions in our minds. Specifically, it makes us wonder what contributes to this abstract and often confusing concept we call "intelligence".

Flynn, J. R. (2006). O efeito Flynn: Repensando a inteligencia e seus efeitos [The Flynn Effect: Rethinking intelligence and what affects it]. In C. Flores-Mendoza & R. Colom (Eds.), Introducao a Psicologia das Diferencas Individuais [*Introduction to the psychology of individual differences*] (pp. 387–411). Porto Alegre, Brazil: ArtMed.

Weekly Checklist:

- ☐ **Web Module to watch: Problem Solving & Intelligence**
- ☐ **Readings: Journal Article**
- ☐ **Avenue Quiz 4**

Upper Year Courses:

If you enjoyed the content in this week's module, consider taking the following upper year courses:

- PSYCH 2H03 Human Learning and Cognition

Problem Solving & Intelligence – Outline

Unit 1: Introduction

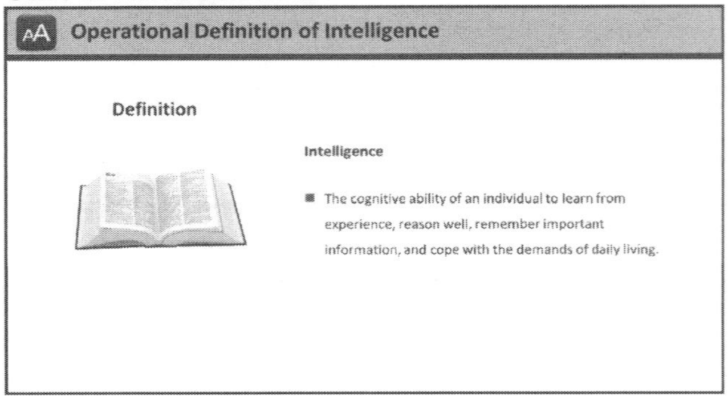

Intelligence: the cognitive ability of an individual to learn from experience, reason well, remember important information, and cope with the demands of daily living

Unit 2: Problem Solving

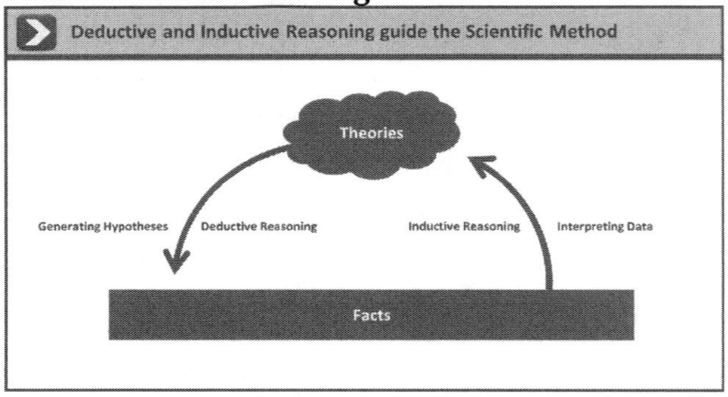

We use two main types of reasoning to explain the world around us.

Deductive: when a person works from ideas and general information to arrive at specific conclusions

Inductive: moves from specific facts and observations to broader generalizations and theories

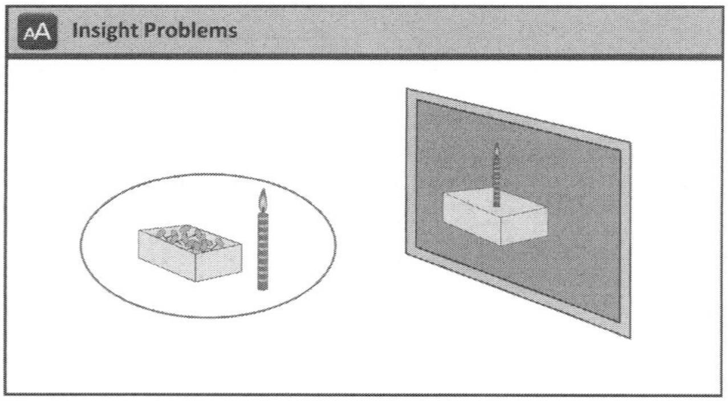

Insight problems are a special type of puzzles that engage our problem-solving skills.

Functional fixedness: difficulty seeing alternative use for common objects and only thinking about a specific use

Unit 3: A History of Intelligence Testing

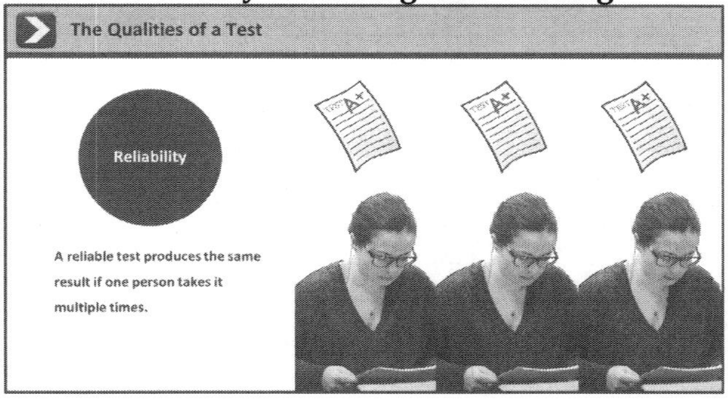

An effective test of intelligence must be both reliable and valid.

Reliability: measures the extent to which repeated testing produces consistent results
• especially important for intelligence because psychologists assume intelligence is a static internal quality

Validity: measures the extent to which a test is actually measuring what the researcher claims to be measuring

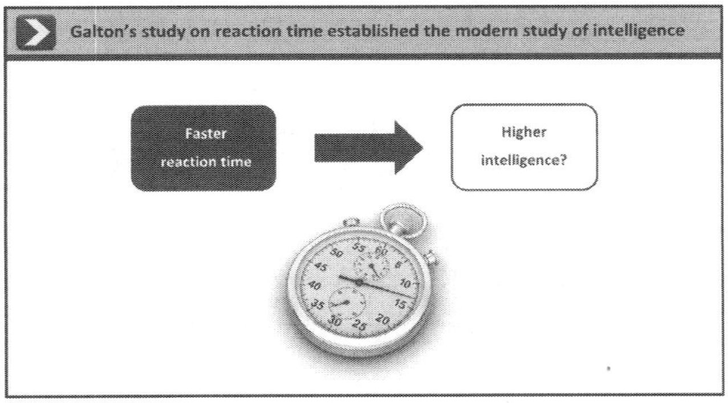

Historically, intelligence has been tested in several different ways and each method has employed a variety of assumptions.

Francis Galton: goal was to formally quantify intelligence in an unbiased manner
• recorded how quickly participants could respond to sensory motor tasks by reaction time
• faster reaction time = higher intelligence

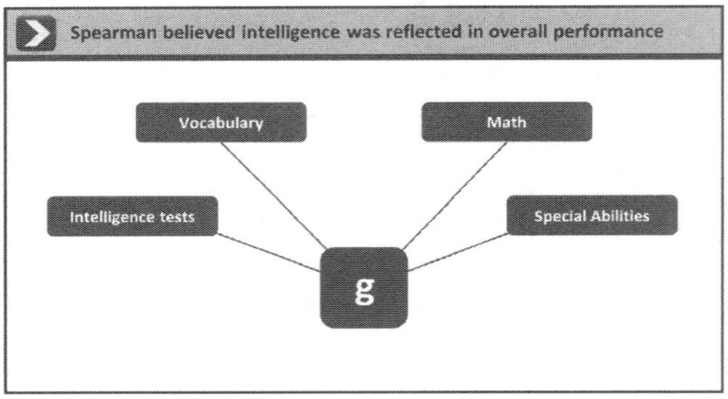

Charles Spearman: believed in a single type of intelligence

• observed that most people who performed well on classical intelligence tasks performed well on all kinds of tasks

• believed there was one general intelligence named G

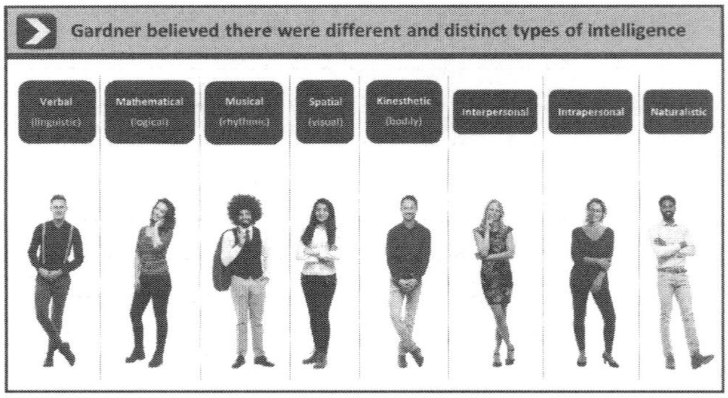

Howard Gardner: proposed multiple intelligence theory and test

• argued 8 types of intelligence; verbal, mathamatical, musical, spatial, kinesthetic, interpersonal, intrapersonal and naturalistic

• each type of intelligence was seen as independent from the others

• open possibility that everyone may excel in some form of intelligence

Unit 4: Human Intelligence

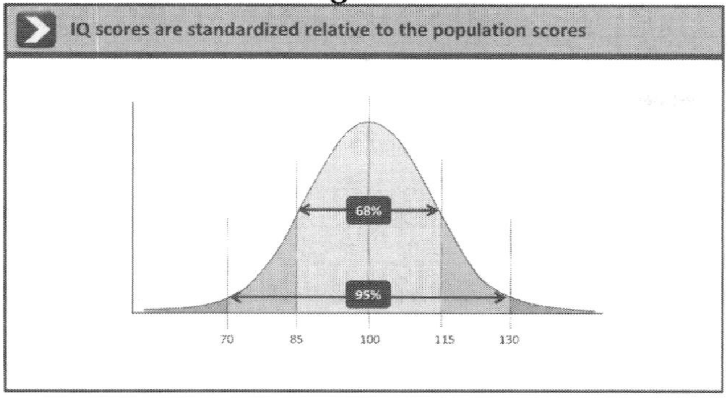

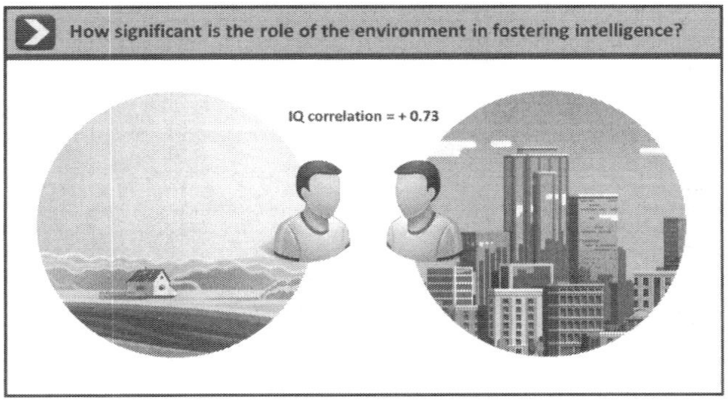

IQ tests remain popular today and allow scientists to research intelligence.

Characteristics of modern-day IQ tests:

- IQ scoring is based on results of large samples of individuals who have taken the test
- the tests are standardized so that someone who achieves the mean score has an IQ of 100
- IQ scores surrounding the mean are assigned around the perfect normal distribution with a standard deviation of 15
- your IQ is relative to the performance of the rest of the population

Methods used to determine the influence of genes and environment on intelligence: correlation studies

Findings from twin studies: researchers found IQ between identical twins as a strong + correlation of plus 0.8

- fraternal twins had a positive correlation of plus 0.6

Implications of findings: researchers can explore environmental impact by correlating IQs of identical twins raised in different environments

- correlation is still high + 0.73
- researcher cannot consider all environmental similarities and differences between the twins homes
- both genetics and environment play a role in intelligence development

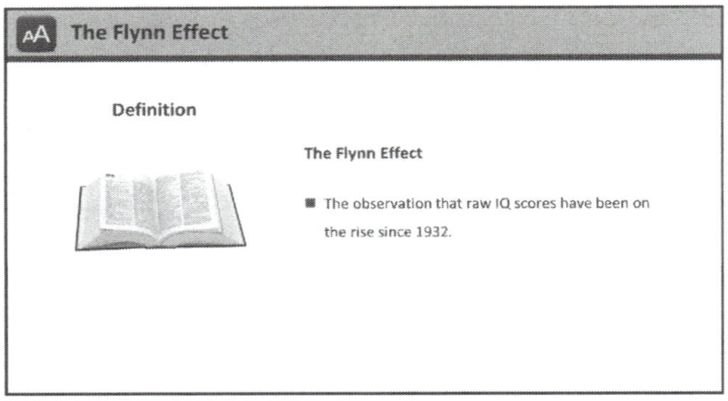

The Flynn Effect: the mean score for intelligence testing in the population has been steadily increasing since it was first measured in 1932

Potential reasons for the Flynn Effect:
- increase quality of schooling !
- increased access to information and ideas through books, TV and internet
- may be increased nutrition and health

Unit 5: Piaget and Intelligence Development

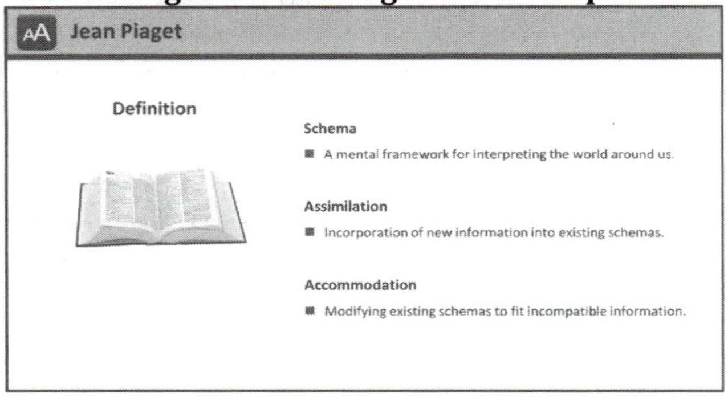

Jean Piaget suggested theories of intelligence development that remain influential to this day.

Schema: a mental framework for interpreting the world around us

Assimilation: incorporation of new information into existing schemas

Accommodation: modifying existing schemas to fit incompatible information

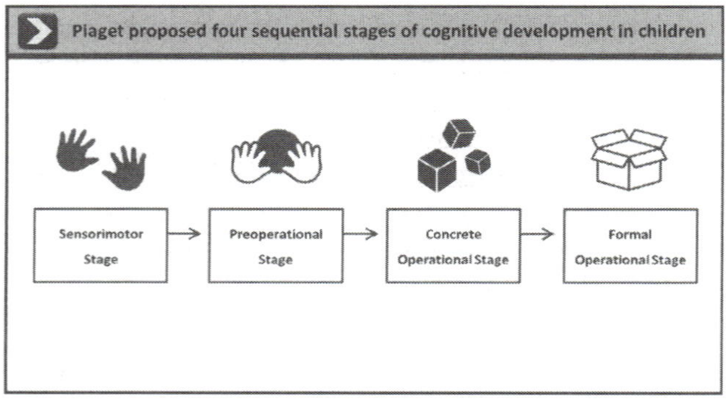

Characteristics of the four stages of development: must be in order and no stages can be skipped
- sensory motor – lasts until 2nd birthday, a child begins to recognize that he can affect change on his environment, object permanence: objects can continue to exist even when he can't see them anymore
- pre-operational – ages 2-7, mastered object permanence, still have to master egocentrism, seriation, reversible relationships, and conservation, only sees world from his view, cannot logically order objects
- concrete operational – 7-12, can perform all tasks that couldn't in pre-operational, cannot think in abstract terms or reason based on hypothesis,
- formal operational stage – 12+ years able to think in abstract terms, work with hypothesis and do everything else that makes up the range of adult cognitive abilities

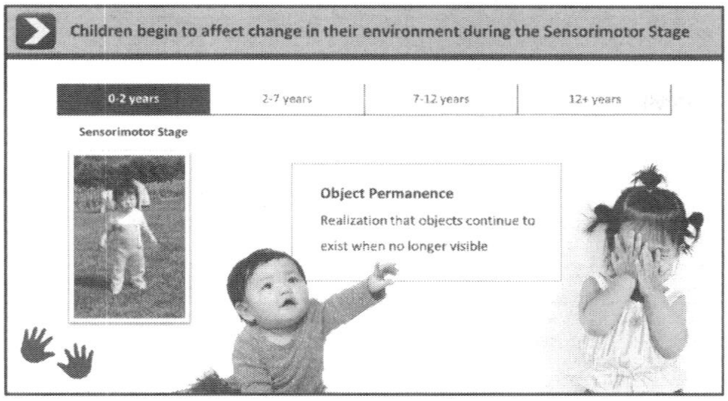

The Sensorimotor Stage

Age: ____________________

Milestones: ____________________

Additional information: ____________________

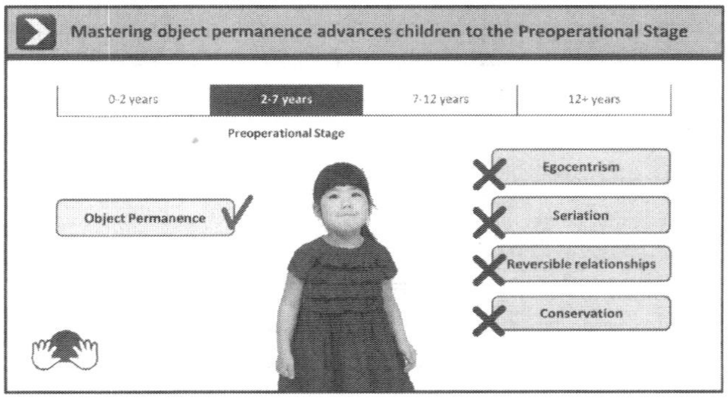

The Preoperational Stage

Age: ____________________

Egocentrism: ____________________

Reversible relationships: ____________________

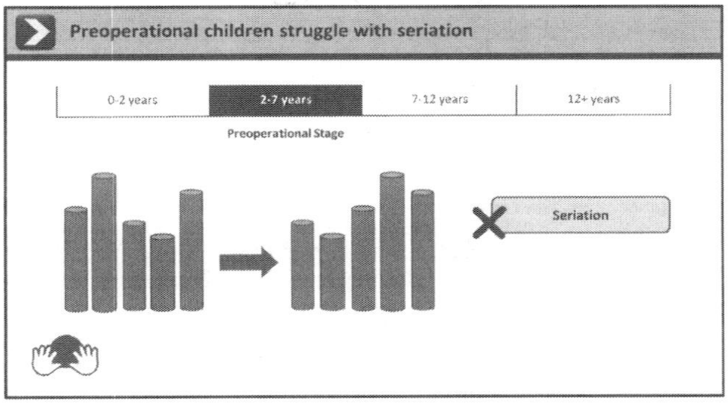

Seriation: ____________________

Conservation: ____________________

The Concrete Operational Stage

Age:

Characteristics:

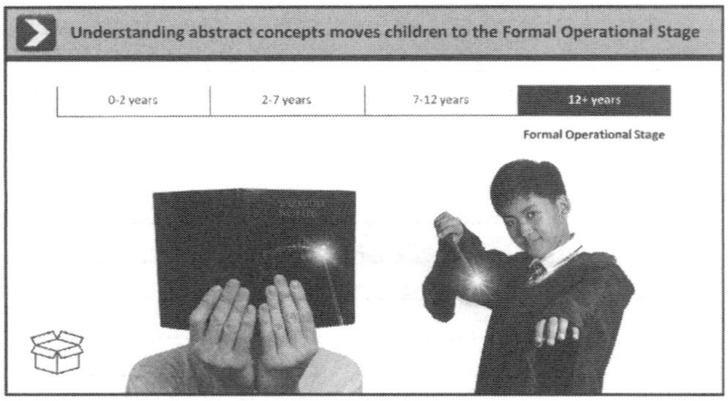

The Formal Operational Stage

Age:

Characteristics:

Criticisms of Piaget's Theories

Decalage: the finding that children sometimes develop some skills out of order in the strictest sense of Piaget's theories

Children's language abilities: the very tasks of Piaget used to formulate this hypothesis rely heavily on this

Unit 6: Biases and Heuristics

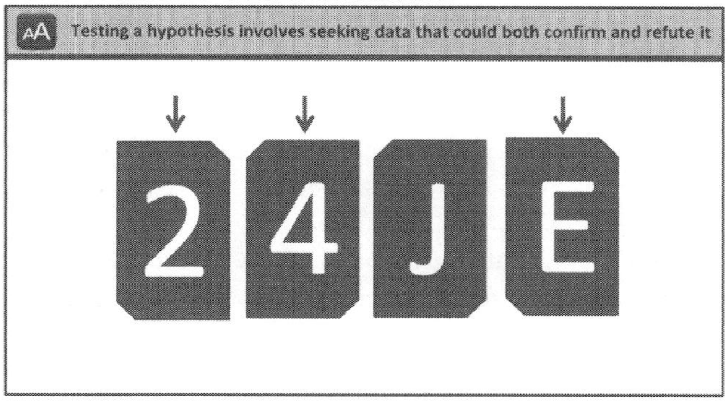

Biases and heuristics are often used to make quick decisions; however, they may make humans prone to errors.

Confirmation bias: a tendency to seek out information that directly supports the hypothesis

Confirmation bias in everyday life: physician making a diagnosis, makes initial diagnosis, then hears symptoms to further support initial diagnostic hypothesis, by

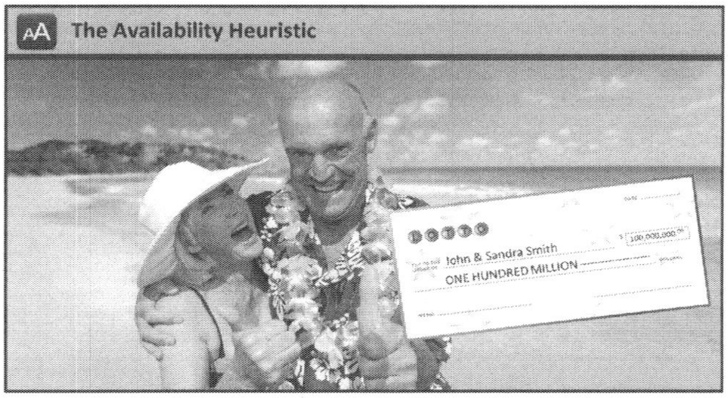

Heuristics: mental shortcut used to solve a problem quickly and often correctly, reduce effort and simplify decision making

Availability heuristic: more available to your memory

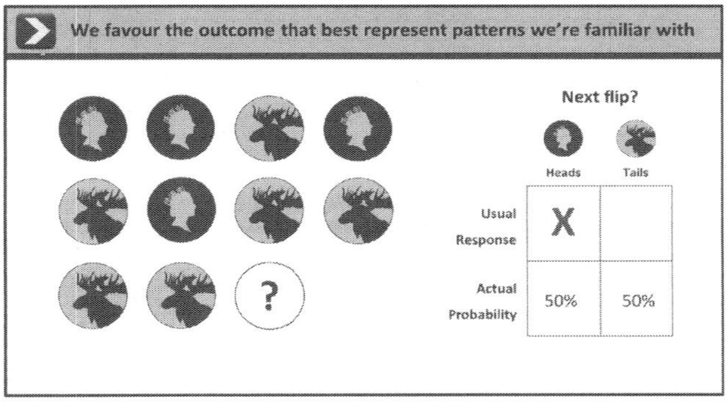

• think it should be heads to better match a pattern of randomness
• casinos use this

Representativeness heuristic: tendency to estimate the likelihood of a current example by comparing it to an existing prototype in our mind of what we consider to be the most relevant or typical example of a particular category

Representativeness heuristic in everyday life: flip a coin and get this sequence
• each coin flip is independent of the others
• there is equal chance of landing heads or tails on any flip

Problem Solving & Intelligence – Courseware Exercise

Now that you've learned about problem solving, you can do a couple of actual tasks to demonstrate insight learning. Try your best at the following problems (and try not to look at the answers on the next page).

Wine problem

You have a glass of red wine and a glass of white wine, both with equal volume. You take exactly one teaspoon of red wine, put it into the white wine glass, and stir. Then, you take exactly one teaspoon of this new mixture and put it back into the red wine glass. In the end, both glasses have the same volume.

Question: Which glass is more pure (contains more of its original liquid)?

This is a tough problem and it may help if you give yourself simple values and to map it out on paper. If you manage to solve it in this way, you can see that giving yourself tangible values or a diagram really help in problem solving.

Now, try your hand at a second problem.

Tumour Problem

You are a doctor with a patient that has a malignant tumour in his stomach. To operate on the patient is impossible, but unless the tumour is destroyed, the patient will die. A kind of ray, at a sufficiently high intensity, can destroy the tumour. Unfortunately, at this intensity the healthy tissue on the way to the tumour will also be destroyed. At lower intensities, the rays are harmless to healthy tissue, but will not affect the tumour.

Question: Can the rays be used to destroy the tumour without injuring the healthy tissue?

This question may be a bit difficult and have you thinking that the solution lies in some obscure medical textbook. However, if we reframe the question with something practical, it becomes easier.

Tumour Problem Rephrased

You are raiding a castle and need 100 men attacking at once to win. Your men know how to construct a bridge that carries 10 men to the castle.

Question: How can you storm this castle?

The interesting thing is that if we present this question using a practical example like a castle with bridges, most people get it right. Problem solving is best with tangible things!

Solution to the Wine Problem

They are actually equally pure. To try to simplify it: suppose you have 100ml in each class, and you take 10ml out of the red and put it in the white. The white now was 100ml white, and 10ml red. If you take 10ml out again, 100/110 of that teaspoon will be White, and 10/110 will be Red. Those are just the proportions in the glass. Basically, you take lots of red out of the red and put it in the white, then you take lots of white out of the white and put it in the red, putting some red back with it. In the end, both glasses will have lost the same amount; the white lost it all at once, but the red lost more, then got a bit back. Tricky, tricky.

Solution to the Tumour Problem

When you rephrase the problem in terms of a castle under attack, the answer is obviously to build 10 bridges! That way 10 men per bridge can get across for a grand total of 100 men charging the castle.
The easiest solution for the tumour problem is to use many of the low power rays from many directions such that they all meet and sum at the point of the tumour.

After solving these problems, do you think that problem solving ability is related to intelligence? How so?

____

____

____

Obviously, these types of problems would be incredibly difficult to administer to animals. Is problem solving a uniquely human trait?

____

____

____

How is problem solving different in animals? Can you think of a way to administer an insight-like problem to an animal?

____

____

____

Problem Solving & Intelligence – Review Questions

1) Describe the difference between deductive and inductive reasoning.
   a. How are these types of reasoning relevant when using the scientific method?

2) What is the confirmation bias? Provide an example.

3) What is the availability heuristic? Provide an example.

4) What is the representativeness heuristic? Provide an example.

5) James' friends never read their textbooks, but consistently get A+ grades. James thinks this must be the best way to study, tries it, and gets an F on his first biology midterm. Which cognitive short-cut did James use to make this decision? Explain.

6) What is the difference between reliability and validity?

7) Which of the following statements is the primary explanation of the Flynn Effect?
   a. Humans are becoming increasingly more educated, thus getting smarter.
   b. Due to the increased supply of nutritious foods, children today enjoy more rapid growth in their intellectual abilities.
   c. Humans are provided with more opportunities to be intellectually simulated, thus becoming more intelligent.
   d. None of the above.

8) Is IQ genetic, environmental, or both? Explain.

9) Suppose you ask Sam (6 years old) and Ella (9 years old) to tell you whether the following statement is correct. "If all squares are rectangles, and all rectangles are red, are all squares red?" Which of these children might Piaget expect to answer this question correctly?
   a. Sam
   b. Ella
   c. Neither of them
   d. Both of them

Problem Solving & Intelligence – Quiz Question

Using the Wechsler scale of intelligence tests, which of the following is correct?

a. Identical twins Sam and Simon showed very different IQ scores, suggesting genetic factors play an insignificant role on intelligence. (9%)
b. Marge scores an IQ of 113, while her mother Sandra scored the same IQ when she was Marge's age. Marge thinks this supports her claim that she is more intelligent than her mother. (26%)
c. The consistent mean IQ of 100 reflects how the overall raw scores from intelligence tests of the population have remained stable. (27%)
d. Research on fraternal twins suggests a smaller role of the environment in determining one's intelligence. (38%)

This is a question from a previous Problem Solving and Intelligence Avenue Quiz that the majority of students struggled with. Together, we are going to identify the correct answer option and the reasons why each distractor is incorrect. In this example, only 26% of students selected the correct answer option, B. Let's look at the options:

a. This option provides us with a hypothetical situation in an attempt to prove a point, that genetic factors are insignificant when it comes to their influence on intelligence. If we think back to the web module for a second, a significant portion of time was devoted to explaining that both environment and genetics play important roles in one's intelligence, so this option must be incorrect. In fact, most students recognized this as an incorrect option.

b. Once again, this option presents us with a hypothetical situation in which an IQ score is being compared to an IQ score received many years prior. It is always important to pull out the crucial information (comparing raw IQ scores from two different time periods) from a hypothetical answer option or question stem as this makes it much easier to identify whether the information contained within is correct or not. In this case, we know that for some strange reason (Flynn Effect), **raw** scores on the IQ test have been on a steady rise since the 1950's. Remember, an IQ score of 115 is standardized, which means the original raw score is compared to the raw scores of everyone else at the time of examination and then given a standardized score with a mean of 100. It is possible, therefore, that a standardized score of 115 today corresponds to a higher raw score (Flynn Effect) than one associated with 115 many years ago. Let's hold onto this option for now. (**Correct!**)

c. This is a tricky option. Many times, question developers will use factual information in an inappropriate manner to prove a point. In this case, that a consistent, **standardized** mean IQ of 100 is evidence that the overall **raw** scores of the population have remained stable. It is true that the standardized mean of 100 always remains the same, but is this really evidence to suggest that the raw scores also remain the same? For starters, we know that in order to receive a standardized score, a raw score must first be compared to everyone else taking the test at the same time. This fact alone suggests to us that it is possible that mean raw scores can change while the standardized mean score of 100 remains the same. On top of that, we know that there is an observation called the Flynn Effect in which raw scores have been on the rise since the early 1950s while the mean standardized score always remains 100. After considering all of this, this option does not seem correct.

d. Let us go back to the question once again. It reads as follows: "**Using the Wechsler scale of intelligence tests**, which of the following is correct?". Any answer option we consider must have to do with the Wechsler scales of intelligence. When first examining this option, there is no direct mention of an IQ test, only intelligence. This is our first red flag that this option may be incorrect, so we should continue cautiously. This option is trying to convince us that there is evidence to suggest a smaller role of the environment in determining intelligence. Smaller than what? This is another red flag. Let's assume the question writer is implying genetics. Was there ever information in the web module definitively stating that genes or the environment were more important in determining intelligence? No. There was evidence to suggest that each was important, but in no way was there evidence put forth to suggest that one was more important than the other. It is for this reason that we can eliminate this option.

This leaves us with **option B**, which is the correct response.

Key Terms

Arch of Knowledge	Functional Fixedness	Representativeness Heuristic
Availability Heuristic	Inductive Reasoning	Reversible Relationships
Concrete Operational Stage	Intelligence	Sensorimotor Stage
Confirmation Bias	Multiple Intelligences	Seriation
Conservation	Object Permanence	Stanford-Binet Intelligence Test
Deductive Reasoning	Piaget's Stages of Development	Validity
Flynn Effect	Preoperational Stage	Weschler Scales
Formal Operational Stage	Reliability	

Problem Solving & Intelligence – Bottleneck Concepts

Piaget's Stages of Development
IQ Scores vs. the Flynn Effect
Inductive vs. Deductive Reasoning
Confirmation Bias

Inductive vs. Deductive Reasoning

Inductive reasoning takes place when you know a specific fact and create a generalization from that fact. For example, concluding that all dogs are vicious when you get attacked by one involves inductive reasoning. This type of thinking is what often leads to stereotypes. Deductive reasoning, on the other hand, occurs when you know a general idea and you use it to predict specific facts that must be true if the general idea is true. For example, if you believe that studying diligently results in good marks, you may predict that your classmate, Fred, must have exceptional grades since you always see him studying at the library. These two concepts are often confused. The easiest way to differentiate them is to first identify the information you have (is it a general idea or a specific fact?) and then identify what you can hypothesize based on the information (is it a concrete/more specific conclusion or a general idea?). Let's try an example:

Marcus knows that when people don't get enough sleep, their mind does not function optimally. He notices one day that his friend Kathy did uncharacteristically poorly on a midterm and concludes it must be because she didn't get enough sleep.

In this case, Mark starts off with the assumption that when people don't get enough sleep, their brains do not function as well. This is just a general idea about how the world works. He applies this fact to Kathy's situation. She didn't do as well as she normally does on a midterm and he concludes that it must be because she didn't get enough sleep and so her brain did not function as well during the midterm (a specific case). Since Mark goes from a general idea to a prediction, this is an example of deductive reasoning.

Test your Understanding

1) In the following scenarios, identify if inductive or deductive reasoning is being used and explain why.

a) Karen was surprised to find out that her friends Brian and Patricia started a relationship with each other. They are not alike whatsoever! This leads her to guess that maybe, in romantic relationships, opposites attract.

b) One day, Matthew notices that Wendy has come to class with a completely new outfit. He knows that Wendy only buys clothes when they are on sale. He concludes that there must be a big sale happening at the mall.

2) Come up with your own examples of inductive or deductive reasoning. Ask your TA or post it on the discussion boards to receive feedback on whether or not your example is correct.

CONCEPT MAP: PROBLEM SOLVING & INTELLIGENCE

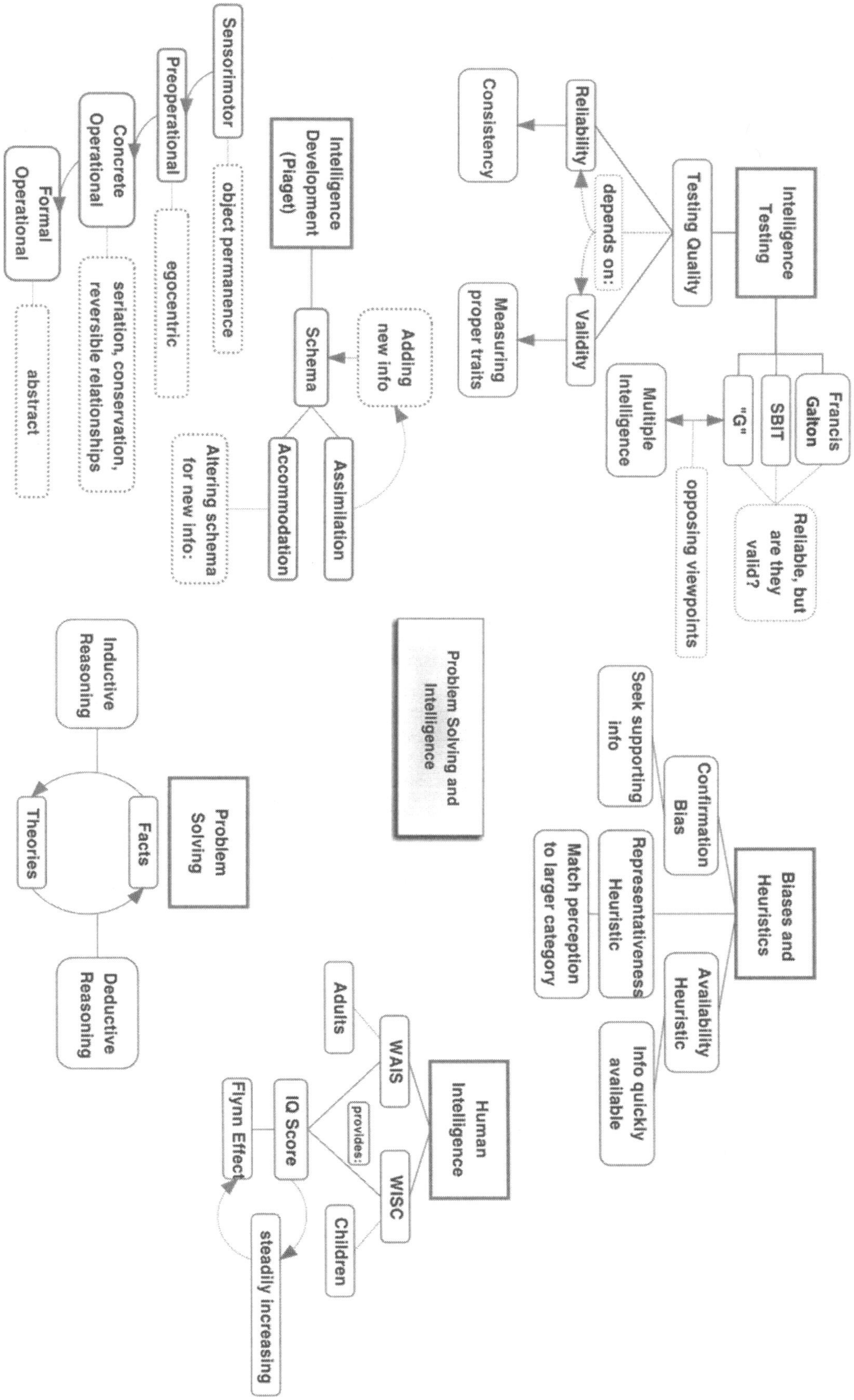

Arch of Knowledge
Problem Solving and Intelligence

MAC IntroPsych

Availability Heuristic
Problem Solving and Intelligence

MAC IntroPsych

Concrete Operational Stage
Problem Solving and Intelligence

MAC IntroPsych

Confirmation Bias
Problem Solving and Intelligence

MAC IntroPsych

Conservation
Problem Solving and Intelligence

MAC IntroPsych

Deductive Reasoning
Problem Solving and Intelligence

MAC IntroPsych

Flynn Effect
Problem Solving and Intelligence

MAC IntroPsych

Formal Operational Stage
Problem Solving and Intelligence

MAC IntroPsych

The tendency to make decisions based on the information that is most quickly available to us. **Example:** You may believe that typical lottery winnings are in the millions of dollars because these are most often publicized and readily available in the news; however, most winnings are actually a few dollars. **Personal Example:**	A diagram used to illustrate the different mechanisms of reasoning in problem solving. Scientists use deductive reasoning to generate specific, testable hypotheses from general theories. The data collected through experimentation can be interpreted and related back to general theories through inductive reasoning. **Personal Example:**
Our tendency to seek information that supports our hypothesis. One way to overcome the confirmation bias is to actively seek and collect information that may disprove our hypothesis. **Example:** If an individual is opposed to oil drilling in the Arctic, they may naturally tend to collect information about the negative impacts of offshore oil drilling rather than considering the benefits. **Personal Example:**	The third of Piaget's stages of development, from ages 7 – 12, at which the child has mastered all tasks from the preoperational stage. However, they have difficulty thinking in abstract terms, which means that they have difficulty reasoning using hypotheses. **Example:** A child in this stage might understand the conservation of mass but couldn't understand something more abstract, such as algebra **Personal Example:**
Arriving at a specific fact based on a general theory. **Example:** If you know that dogs are generally friendly, you will be able to deduce that because your neighbour's new pet is a dog, he is likely friendly. **Personal Example:**	The ability to understand the constant mass or volume of an object using multiple representations. **Example:** A child in the concrete operational would understand that regardless of whether you break a cookie into two or three pieces, you still have the same amount of cookie. **Personal Example:**
The fourth and last of Piaget's stages of development, occurring at 11+ years of age. It is the stage at which a child has mastered the tasks from the concrete operational stage and is able to think in abstract terms. **Example:** A child in this stage would be able to learn algebra and enjoy fantasy games. **Personal Example:**	The observation that raw IQ scores have continued to increase every year since 1932. It is argued that this effect may be due to a number of factors, such as increased quality of schooling, accessibility to information, an increased nutrition and health. **Personal Example:**

Functional Fixedness
Problem Solving and Intelligence

MAC IntroPsych

Inductive Reasoning
Problem Solving and Intelligence

MAC IntroPsych

Intelligence
Problem Solving and Intelligence

MAC IntroPsych

Multiple Intelligences
Problem Solving and Intelligence

MAC IntroPsych

Object Permanence
Problem Solving and Intelligence

MAC IntroPsych

Piaget's Stages of Development
Problem Solving and Intelligence

MAC IntroPsych

Preoperational Stage
Problem Solving and Intelligence

MAC IntroPsych

Reliability
Problem Solving and Intelligence

MAC IntroPsych

Coming to a general theory based on a specific fact. **Example:** If you see your neighbour's dog is friendly, you may use inductive reasoning to determine that all dogs or furry four-legged creatures are also friendly. **Personal Example:**	The difficulty of seeing alternative uses for common objects. **Example:** It is obvious that a flashlight is used to illuminate dark areas. However, it is less obvious that you would be able to use it as a paperweight on a windy day. **Personal Example:**
A theory arguing that there are separate and independent intelligences for different purposes. Therefore, one could be brilliant in one area while lacking in another. The eight intelligences specified were verbal, mathematical, musical, spatial, kinaesthetic, interpersonal, intrapersonal, and naturalistic. **Personal Example:**	The cognitive ability of an individual to learn from experience, reason well, remember important information, and cope with the demands of daily living. **Personal Example:**
A set of four basic stages that children actively partake in during cognitive development. The stages are called sensorimotor, preoperational, concrete operational, and formal operational. Each stage is characterized by different abilities and limitations. While different children progress through them at different rates, children must pass through them in the same sequential order. **Personal Example:**	The understanding of infants that objects continue to exist even when no longer visible. **Example:** In a game of peek-a-boo with their father, an infant has achieved object permanence if they are not continuously surprised every time they see their dad's face again. **Personal Example:**
A measure of the extent to which repeated testing produces consistent results. **Example:** If an individual performs a certain fitness test multiple times and achieves similar results each time, then the test can be considered reliable. **Personal Example:**	The second of Piaget's stages of development, from 2-7 years of age, where the child has mastered the tasks from the sensorymotor stage but is very egocentric and has difficulty seeing the world from the perspective of others. **Example:** An egocentric child would think if they were hungry and wanted to eat, everybody around them must feel the same. **Personal Example:**

Representativeness Heuristic
Problem Solving and Intelligence

MAC IntroPsych

Reversible Relationships
Problem Solving and Intelligence

MAC IntroPsych

Sensorimotor Stage
Problem Solving and Intelligence

MAC IntroPsych

Seriation
Problem Solving and Intelligence

MAC IntroPsych

Stanford-Binet Intelligence Test
Problem Solving and Intelligence

MAC IntroPsych

Validity
Problem Solving and Intelligence

MAC IntroPsych

Weschler Scales
Problem Solving and Intelligence

MAC IntroPsych

MAC IntroPsych

The ability to understand relationships from multiple perspectives.
Example: If a preoperational child is asked if he has a mother, he may say, "Yes, I do! That's my mommy!" If he is asked if mommy has a son, he might say, "Mommy has no son!"
Personal Example:

The tendency to assume that what we see is representative of a larger category we have in our minds, and to classify based on this.
Example: In the gambler's fallacy, individuals believe that previous results influence later games, not considering that each game is completely independent of one another. Therefore, they may assume that a win on one game may represent a larger "winning streak".
Personal Example:

The ability to logically order a series of increasing size in objects.
Example: If a preoperational child is asked to place a series of cones of increasing size order, they may have difficulty ordering them from smallest to largest.
Personal Example:

The first of Piaget's stages of development, from birth until 2 years of age. It is the stage at which a child realizes they can affect change on their environment. Object permanence is achieved at the end of this stage.
Example: A child at this stage may realize that if they push a ball, it will roll across the floor.
Personal Example:

Measures whether a test is actually measuring what it is supposed to.
Example: Conventional eye charts that test vision at different distances may not always produce valid results. A person may struggle reading aloud the letters on these charts, despite seeing the letters perfectly fine, perhaps because they have dyslexia.
Personal Example:

An intelligence test, developed in the early 1900s, involving 30 short tasks related to everyday life using all types of reasoning. The test is still used in some forms today.
Personal Example:

Scales standardized to produce an intelligence quotient for every individual. They consist of the Weschler Adult Intelligence Scale (WAIS) and Weschler Intelligence Scale for Children (WISC). An individual who achieves the mean score will be assigned an IQ of 100. Scores around the mean fall along a perfect normal distribution with a standard deviation of 15.
Personal Example:

LANGUAGE

"It depends on what the meaning of the word 'is' is."
- Bill Clinton, during his 1998 grand jury testimony on the Monica Lewinsky affair

Ellie and Janet are sitting in an art class working on their self-portrait painting project. Ellie, who is just beginning to explore her artistic side, turns to Janet looking for approval. Janet takes a look at Ellie's painting and casually says, "Actually, that's pretty." Ellie goes back to her work unsure what to make of the comment. Was this a compliment or an underhanded dig? The problem is the word "actually". Remove it from the sentence and it is clearly a compliment and social norms are upheld. But add that single word and an innocent comment can take on a negative connotation. The word "actually" implies a sense of surprise that what follows is not expected. Ellie can translate the comment to mean, "Wow, usually what you do is not good, but this time, it's good." Although we are often casual in the language we use, you can probably think about a misinterpreted conversation or email that created a problem. Whether you are applying for a grant, filling out an application, or meeting with a potential client, language does matter. It's something that speechwriters, editors and advertisers think about very carefully. A single word or turn of a phrase can profoundly alter the meaning, impact, and even the legality of a sentence. Consider the sensational case of the Clinton-Lewinsky affair in which the question of whether Bill Clinton perjured himself before the grand jury depended on the definition of the word "is". Clinton rationalized that he wasn't lying when he said to his top aides that with respect to Monica Lewinsky, "there is nothing going on between us." According to Clinton: "It depends on what the meaning of the word 'is' is. If 'is' means is and never has been, that is not—that is one thing. If it means there is none, that was a completely true statement...Now, if someone had asked me on that day, are you having any kind of sexual relations with Ms. Lewinsky, that is, asked me a question in the present tense, I would have said no. And it would have been completely true." In returning to our example on the impact of the word "actually," add or delete it from a few other sentences and see how you feel about receiving the following comments:

- Those jeans actually look good on you.
- You actually don't look fat.
- That dinner was actually really good.

It's not just being nit-picky. Word choice actually is a matter of importance. Think about this the next time you are writing an important email.

Weekly Checklist:

- ☐ **Web Modules to watch: Language**
- ☐ **Readings: Chapter 5**
- ☐ **Avenue Quiz 5**
- ☐ **QuizTerm NEXT WEEK!**

Upper Year Courses:

If you enjoyed the content in this week's module, consider taking the following upper year courses:

- PSYCH 3C03 Child Language Acquisition
- PSYCH 3UU3 Psychology of Language
- PSYCH 3NL3: Cognitive Neuroscience of Language

Language – Outline

Unit 1: Introduction to Language

Language is regulated by the rules of grammar

The quick brown fox jumps over the lazy dog

The lazy dog was jumped over by the quick brown fox

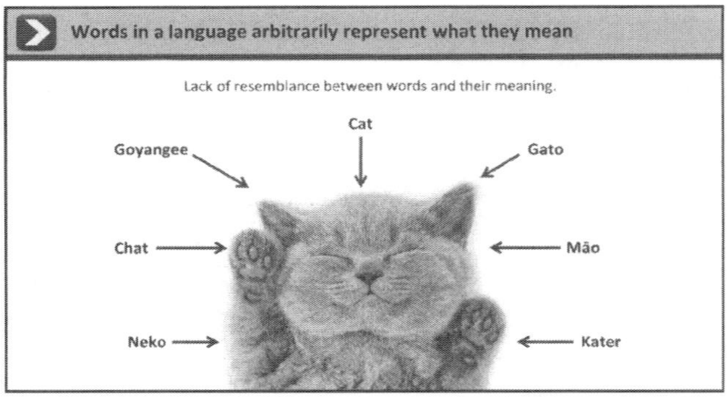

To classify a form of communication as language, several important criteria must be met.

Regular: it's governed by rules and grammar, a scentence can be reorganized and still retain its meaning because a system of rules details how each word fits with the ones around it

Arbitrary: the specific sound that is assigned to represent a concept

Productive: there are almost limitless ways to combine words to describe objects, situations, and actions

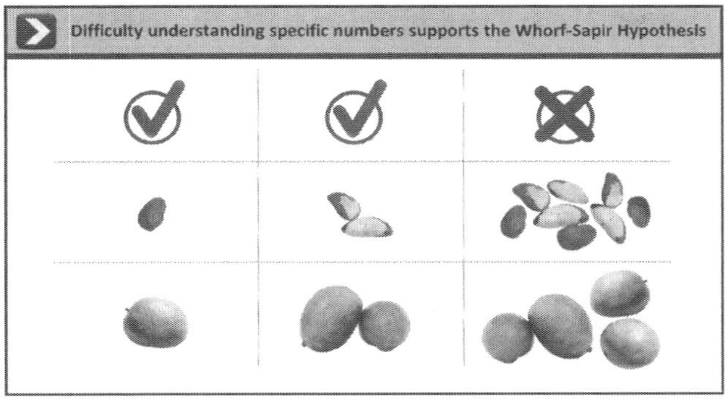

The Whorf-Sapir Hypothesis suggests that language has the power to influence our thoughts and perceptions.

Evidence supporting the Whorf-Sapir Hypothesis:

tribe that counted 1, 2, many was tested with different numbers
- performance worsened with test sets greater than three objects

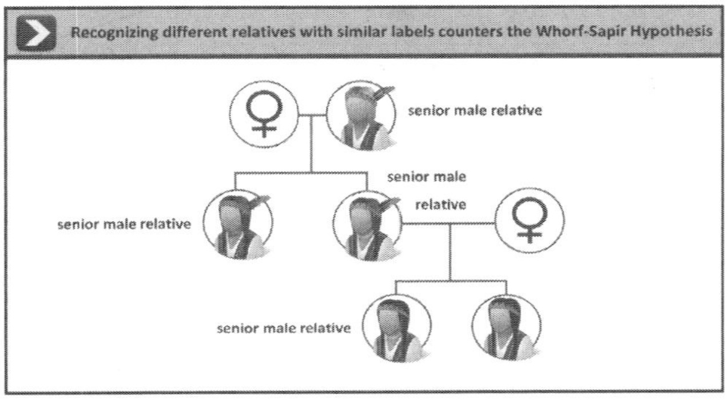

Evidence against the Whorf-Sapir Hypothesis:

- use a single word to describe any male relative

Unit 2: The Structure of Language

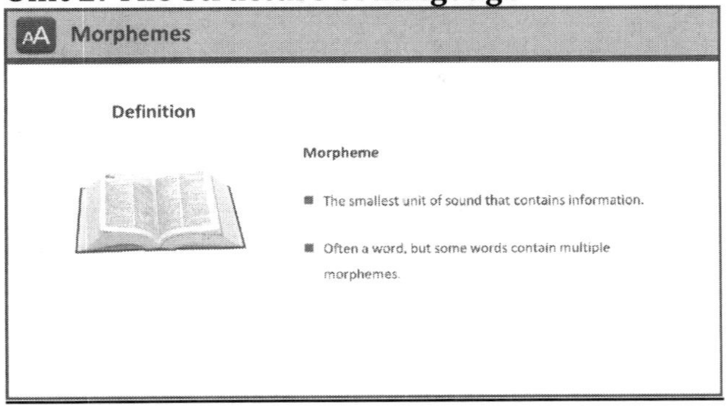

Languages often contain multiple layers of structure to allow for effective communication.

Morphemes:

- smallest unit of sound that contain information
- often a word, but some words contain multiple morphemes
- not all morphemes can be used as an individual word, some must be added to another morpheme to make sense

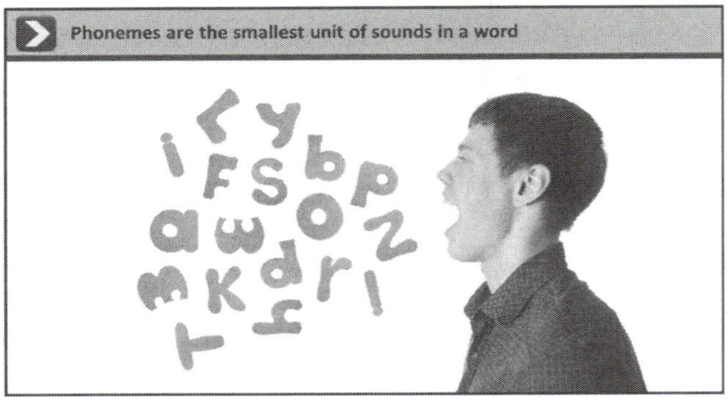

Phonemes: the breakdown of a morpheme into its constituent sound

Variation between languages: each language has its own distinct rules about the order in which sounds and words can be combined

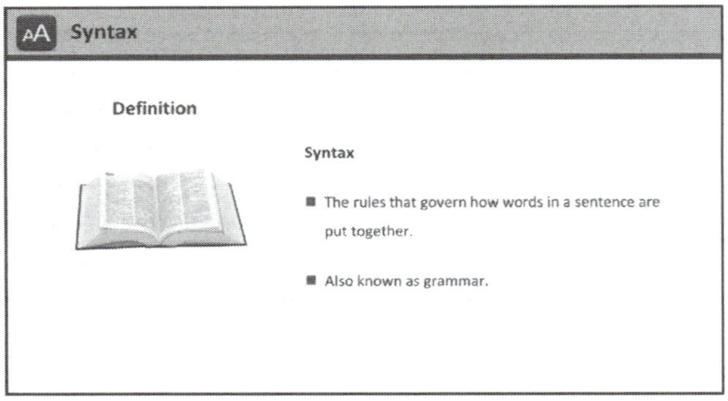

Syntax and semantics: Syntax - rules that govern how words in a sentence are put together
• also known as grammar
• Semantics - meaning of each individual word

Variation between languages: syntax rules among languages are as varied as the cultures they originate from

Unit 3: Development and the Segmentation Problem

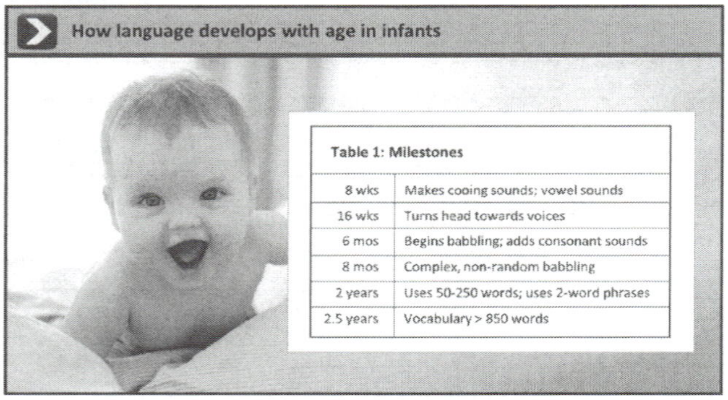

8 wks	Makes cooing sounds; vowel sounds
16 wks	Turns head towards voices
6 mos	Begins babbling; adds consonant sounds
8 mos	Complex, non-random babbling
2 years	Uses 50-250 words; uses 2-word phrases
2.5 years	Vocabulary > 850 words

The acquisition of language is a challenging process that occurs at different rates over many years.

The general course of language development: young infants show language related skills such as responding to the presence of another and smiling socially

Babbling: wide range of drawn out sounds that combine consonants and vowels
• includes rythm and inflection so they seem as part of conversation

Language Explosion: 1 ½ - 6 years, vocabulary increases rapidly
• mastered the major concepts of language

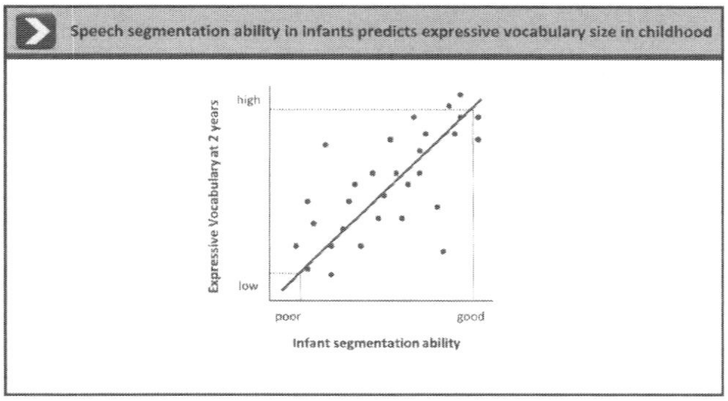

The segmentation problem: the illusion is called by the difficulty you have segmenting the speech stream into word units

The relation of infant's segmentation ability to their later vocabulary: found that early speech segmentation skills showed a strong positive correlation with expressive vocabulary at 2 yrs of age

Unit 4: Universal Phoneme Sensitivity

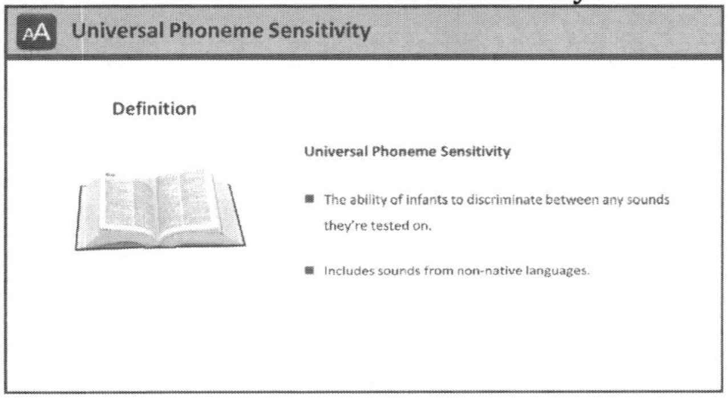

Universal phonemic sensitivity: infants can discriminate between virtually all sounds that they've been tested on
•adults cannot do this so there may be some developmental basis for phoneme discrimination that is influenced early in life

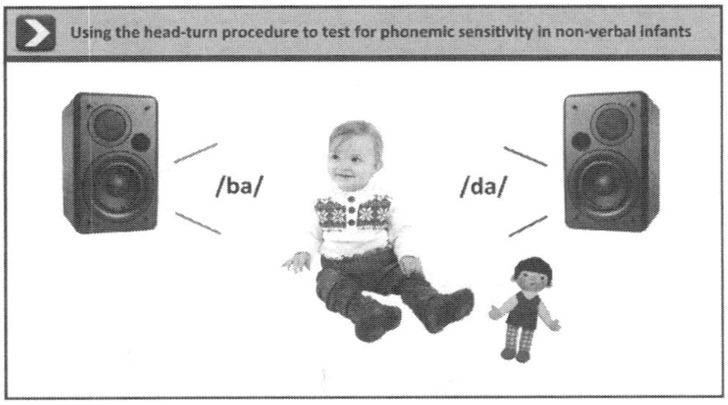

Methods of testing phoneme sensitivity in infants: head turn procedure

Compare infants' phonemic sensitivity with that of adults:

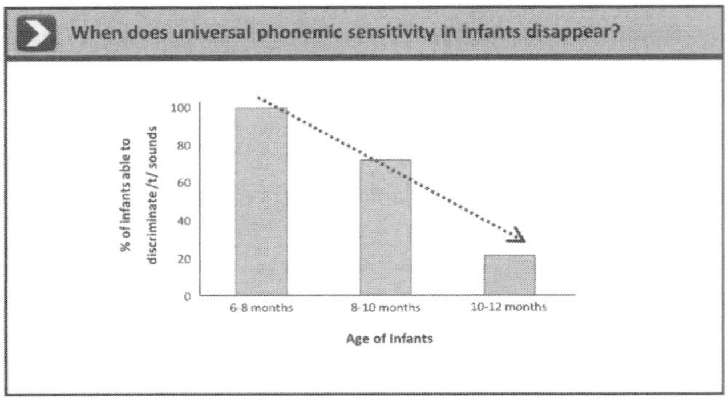

The disappearance of universal phoneme sensitivity in infants: by the end of the first year of life, infants had already lost most of their ability to discriminate the non-native phonemes

Implications of varying degrees of phonemic sensitivity when learning a novel language: adults will need much more time and a very intensive practice program before being able to discriminate the phonemic contrast

Unit 5: Theories of Langage Development

Two major theories of language development guide how researchers understand the acquisition of language.

Social Learning Theory: children learn language through a combination of imitation and operant conditioning

Evidence supporting Social Learning Theory: Genie*, growing up with no language skills or exposure to it, children fail to develop these skills

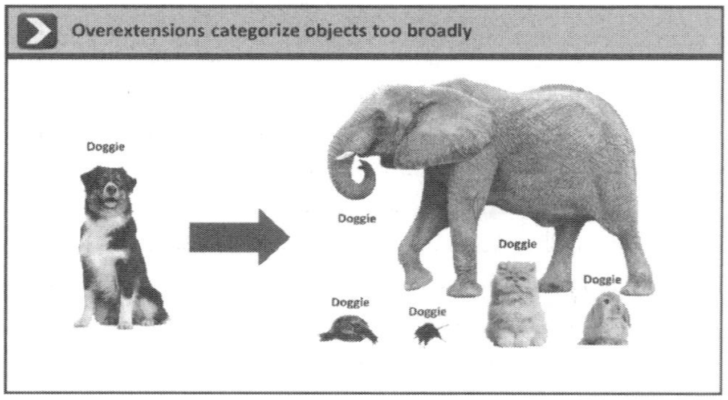

Evidence against Social Learning Theory: children's langage development is too rapid and complex to be driven by imitation and reinforcement alone

1) Overextensions: when children apply a rule to broadly and can occur at the level of meaning or syntax (runned instead of ran)

2) Underextensions: When children apply a rule to a specific object only

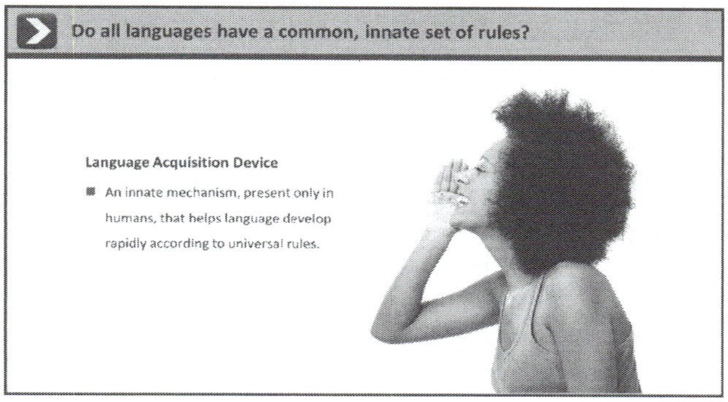

Innate Mechanism Theory: humans have innate mechanisms that allow them to understand and use these universal grammar rules, which allow language skills to develop rapidly

Noam Chomsky:

Evidence for the Innate Mechanism Theory:

1) Sign language: they haven't been taught sign language but the signs they make follow grammar rules
- signing didn't follow parents native language, so was using the innate mechanism

2) Neural activation: young infants show neuro physiological responses to the first language they are exposed to
- infants brains are prewired to adapt to sounds and their associated meanings

Unit 6: Animal Communication

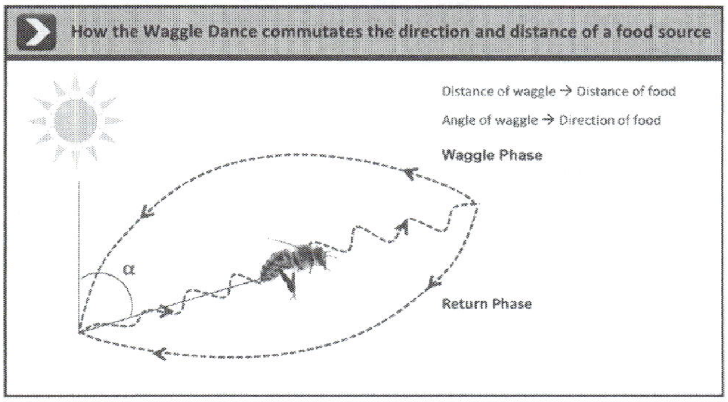

Human language can be compared to various methods of communication used by non-human animals.

Waggle dance: honey bees, when they find a food source, they return to the hive and do the waggle dance to communicate location

Two phases: waggle phase - bee moves forward in direction of food source

Duration: duration of waggle is the distance of food source from the hive

- as many as 100 repetitions

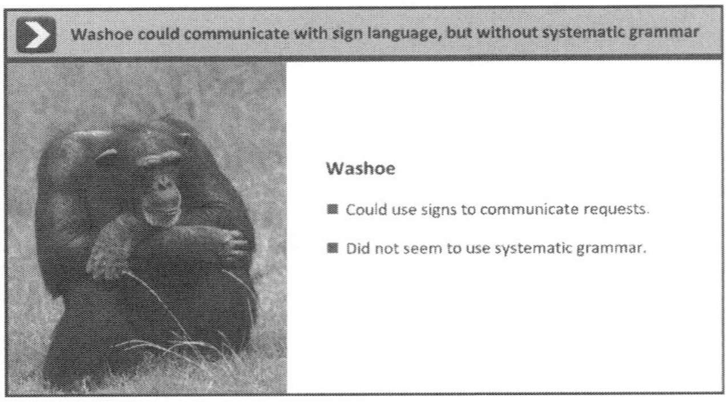

Washoe: chimps raised by scientists ad learned how to communicate using American Sign Language

Washoe's strengths: learn science to communicate simple requests and combie them to communicate more complex requests

Washoe's limitations: did not communicate using any systemic grammar

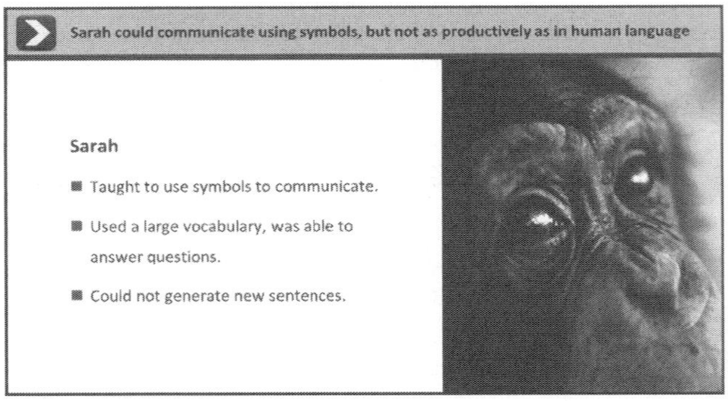

Sarah: raised in lab, taught to use plastic symbols to communicate demands

Sarah's strengths: large vocabulary and was able to answer simple questions, she developed the ability to use complex symbols to communicate

Sarah's limitations: did not learn to combie them in novel combinations

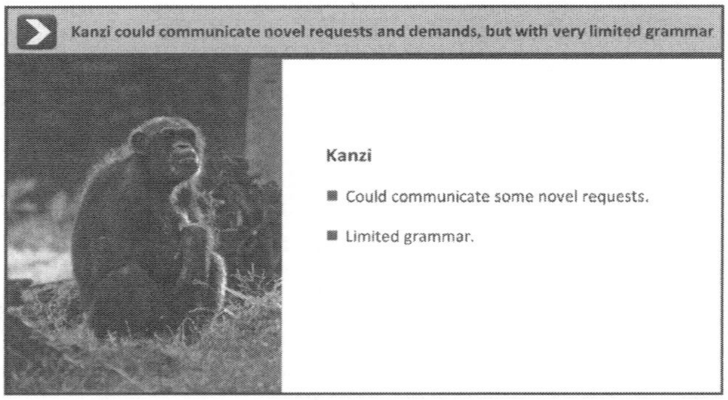

Kanzi: taught to communicate using geometric figures (lexigrams) arranged on a keyboard

Kanzi's strengths: communicate requests and respond to demands as well as understand some requests that had never been previously seen

Kanzi's limitations: grammar was limited, limited ability to create novel combinations of words

Language – Courseware Exercise

Now that you have a rough idea of how cognitive researchers define language, it's important to apply these criteria to the animal communication examples that were covered in lecture and determine whether they exemplify true language.

Remember that language is *regular* in that it is governed by rules and grammar. Additionally, language is *arbitrary* because there is a lack of resemblance between a word and its meaning. Finally, language is *productive* because it can be recombined infinitely to describe countless new situations or ideas.

Use these criteria to evaluate each of the methods of communication in the following table. You may need to do a bit of online research to evaluate all three criteria for each example. If an example fulfills all three criteria, it can be considered language!

Animal example	**Regular?**	**Arbitrary?**	**Productive?**	**Is it language?**
Waggle Dance				
Bird Song				
Washoe				
Sarah				
Kanzi				
Human Speech				

Language – Review Questions

1) Which of the following exemplifies the smallest unit of sound in the English language that contains information, i.e., a morpheme?
   a) The word "drivers".
   b) The letter "s" in the word "sock".
   c) The word "watch".
   d) The letter "y" in the word "party".

2) Which of the following situations best demonstrates the Whorf-Sapir Hypothesis?
   a) Infants born in an English-speaking family can discriminate phonemes presented in Vietnamese.
   b) Adults who fluently speak the Inuit language have many words for "snow" and are better able to distinguish between different types of snow.
   c) Children who are not exposed to language from an early age still have the ability to spontaneously develop grammatical rules .
   d) Animal communications are limited in their motor abilities, thus they can only convey messages relevant to their natural lifestyle.

3) What are the milestones of infant language development? Make a chart!
   a. What is the language explosion, and when does it occur?

4) What is the segmentation problem?
   a. How is an infant's ability to solve the segmentation problem related to their later language abilities?

5) What is universal phoneme sensitivity?
   a. Provide some evidence for the existence of this phenomenon.

6) Compare and contrast the two theories of language development

	Social Learning Theory	Innate Mechanism Theory
Supporting Evidence		
Opposing Evidence		

Language – Quiz Question

What does the **language explosion** refer to?

a. The peak of language development. (53%)
b. Mastery of most linguistic components. (22%)
c. Receptive vocabulary catches up with expressive vocabulary. (18%)
d. Syntax is explicitly understood and used appropriately. (7%)

This is an actual question from a previous Language Avenue Quiz that many students struggled with. We are going to go through this question together to identify what sort of errors students were making and how to avoid them in the future. To do so, we will look at each answer option individually and identify why it is correct or incorrect.

To answer this question correctly, you must be reading each answer option carefully when comparing it to information from the web module. This question utilizes a number of answer options that, at first glance, seem correct but are, in fact, not. Let's have a look at the options.

a. This is a very attractive option but, upon careful examination, is actually incorrect. Is the language explosion the peak of language development? The peak of language development suggests that language will develop no more as your language skills have been maxed out. When you reach the peak of a mountain there is no place to go but down. Does language development stop after the language explosion? No. In fact, mastery of syntax occurs long after the language explosion. Thus, this option is incorrect.
b. This seems like something we have seen in the web module and textbook verbatim. Let's keep this option. (**Correct!**)
c. If this option seems unfamiliar, consider checking your textbook. The textbook explains that receptive vocabulary develops before expressive vocabulary. Additionally, the language explosion refers to expressive vocabulary. Considering this fact alone, this answer option appears incorrect.
d. Is syntax explicitly understood? Do we cease to develop our understanding of syntax past the age of 6? No. We continue to master the syntax of language past the language explosion. Therefore, this answer option is also incorrect.

We are left with **option B**. It is often helpful to look for familiar wording. If a concept is worded in a bizarre way, this is often a clue that it is a nonsense answer option and should be eliminated.

Key Terms

Accent	Morpheme	Social Learning Theory
Foreign Accent Syndrome	Overextensions	Syntax
Infant-Directed Speech	Phoneme	Underextensions
Innate Mechanism Theory	Segmentation	Universal Phoneme Sensitivity
Language	Segmentation Problem	Waggle Dance
Language Acquisition Device (LAD)	Semantics	Whorf-Sapir Hypothesis
Language Explosion		

Language – Bottleneck Concepts

Whorf-Sapir Hypothesis
Innate Mechanism Theory vs. Social Learning Theory
Universal Phoneme Sensitivity
Segmentation Problem

Whorf-Sapir Hypothesis

The Whorf-Sapir Hypothesis states that language influences our thoughts and the way we perceive and experience the world. If some words aren't present in a particular language, it may affect how people perceive the world if that is the only language they know. For example, in lecture, we discussed the Piraha, a group of Brazilians, and their language. They only have three counting words: one, two, and many. The Whorf-Sapir hypothesis would predict that these people should have difficulty counting objects that are three or more. Consistent with this hypothesis, the Piraha had great difficulty making groups of objects as the groups became greater or equal to three. However, this hypothesis does not gain consistent support. For example, in Chinese, a separate word is used to describe an aunt and an uncle from your mother's side of the family versus your father's side of the family. Even though these words are not in the English language, people who only know English are still able to distinguish which side of the family their aunts and uncles belong to. Questions surrounding the Whorf-Sapir hypothesis will usually involve whether or not statements or scenarios agree with it. Always ask yourself if people's understanding of a concept is limited because their vocabulary lacks a word or enhanced due to the presence of a word; if either scenario is true, the Whorf-Sapir hypothesis is supported. Below are a few examples related to this concept. Determine which ones lend support to or go against the Whorf-Sapir hypothesis.

Test your Understanding

1) Which of the following statements <u>do not</u> support the Whorf-Sapir hypothesis?

a) In English, there are separate words for the colours, green and blue. The Tarahumara people on the other hand, have a single word that describes green/blue. English speakers are better at distinguishing green and blue than the Tarahumara people.
b) The Inuit language has more words describing snow compared to English. People who only know English have a harder time distinguishing between different types of snow.
c) In Greek, there are many words for love including: Agápe (unconditional love), Éros (romantic love), Philia (friendship love), and Storge (family love). Even though Fred only knows English, he has no trouble recognizing that when his best friend Kyle says, "I love you man," he means it as a friend, and not in a romantic way.
d) In spoken Chinese, there is no distinction between he, she, or it. When people learn English as a second language, they have a hard time differentiating deciding whether to use he, she, or it in sentences.

2) Can you name other examples where words are present in one language but not another? In those cases, do you think having that extra word influences how people perceive or experience the world? Does this example support or go against the Whorf-Sapir Hypothesis?

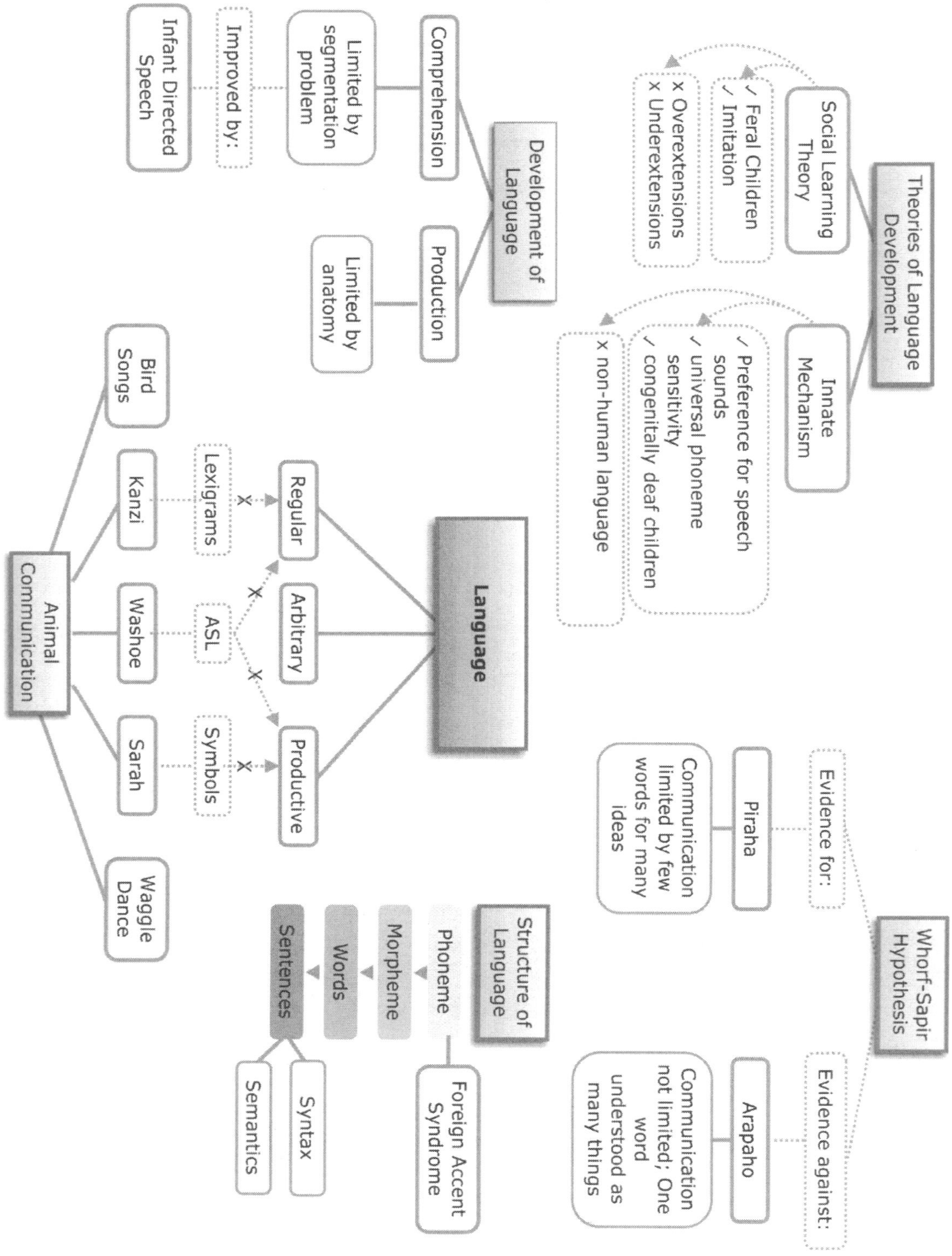

Theories of Language Development
Social Learning Theory
✓ Feral Children
✓ Imitation
x Overextensions
x Underextensions
Innate Mechanism
✓ Preference for speech sounds
✓ universal phoneme sensitivity
✓ congenitally deaf children
x non-human language
Whorf-Sapir Hypothesis
Evidence for:
Piraha
Communication limited by few words for many ideas
Evidence against:
Arapaho
Communication not limited; One word understood as many things
Development of Language
Comprehension
Limited by segmentation problem
Improved by:
Infant Directed Speech
Production
Limited by anatomy
Language
Regular
Arbitrary
Productive
Lexigrams
ASL
Symbols
x
Animal Communication
Bird Songs
Kanzi
Washoe
Sarah
Waggle Dance
Structure of Language
Phoneme
Morpheme
Words
Sentences
Foreign Accent Syndrome
Syntax
Semantics

Accent
Language

MAC IntroPsych

Foreign Accent Syndrome
Language

MAC IntroPsych

Infant-Directed Speech
Language

MAC IntroPsych

Innate Mechanism Theory
Language

MAC IntroPsych

Language
Language

MAC IntroPsych

Language Acquisition Device
Language

MAC IntroPsych

Language Explosion
Language

MAC IntroPsych

Morpheme
Language

MAC IntroPsych

In very rare cases following serious brain injury or stroke, some individuals sound as though they are speaking their native language with a novel, acquired foreign accent.
Example: A person with a British accent may sound like they are speaking English with a Russian accent.
Personal Example:

A manner of pronunciation unique to an individual, geographical location, or nation. It occurs both between and within languages. It may be influenced by location and dominant speech patterns in the environment in which an individual is raised.
Personal Example:

The theory that humans are born with instinctual mechanisms to help them understand universal grammar rules, allowing them to develop language skills rapidly.
Personal Example:

The natural tendency for people to use higher pitched and exaggerated tones when speaking to infants, which may help infants learn to segment speech.
Personal Example:

An innate mechanism, which Noam Chomsky argues is present in humans of all languages, that helps language develop rapidly according to universal grammar rules.
Personal Example:

The human capacity for acquiring and using complex systems of communication. Language is governed by rules and grammar, the symbols used in language are completely arbitrary and language is productive, meaning there are limitless ways to combine words.
Personal Example:

The smallest unit of sound that contains information. A word can contain one or multiple morphemes.
Example: In the word horseshoes, there are three morphemes. The word is divided as (horse)(shoe)(s), where one morpheme refers to the animal, the next to what goes on its feet, and the last to the fact that there are more than one.
Personal Example:

The point in children's language development, between 1.5-6 years of age, where vocabulary increases very rapidly and most children have mastered the major aspects of language.
Personal Example:

Overextensions
Language

MAC IntroPsych

Phoneme
Language

MAC IntroPsych

Segmentation
Language

MAC IntroPsych

Segmentation Problem
Language

MAC IntroPsych

Semantics
Language

MAC IntroPsych

Social Learning Theory
Language

MAC IntroPsych

Syntax
Language

MAC IntroPsych

Underextensions
Language

MAC IntroPsych

The smallest unit of sound in language, regardless of meaning. **Example:** The word happy can be broken down into four phonemes: /h/, /a/, /pp/, /y/, each of which has a sound but not necessarily meaning. **Personal Example:**	When children apply language rules too broadly, leading to semantic and grammatical errors. **Example:** When a child learns a TV has a screen that shows images, they may then address a computer, a smartphone, and any other device with a screen as a TV. **Personal Example:**
The difficulty in segmenting words when hearing an unfamiliar language. **Example:** If you do not speak Polish, it will be very difficult to segment a Polish sentence if listening to someone speaking the language. **Personal Example:**	In spoken language, the process of determining when one word ends and the next begins. Segmentation is the process of naturally spacing the sentence into individual words to improve comprehension. **Example:** In this sentence, "Itisdifficulttoreadthisifeverythingisbunchedtogether." **Personal Example:**
Suggests that children learn language through imitation and operant conditioning by adults. **Example:** if a baby babbles and stumbles upon the phonemes to say "mama", they will receive positive reinforcement, encouraging the child to repeat it again. Parents may also then start repeating this word so that the child will imitate them. **Personal Example:**	The meaning of each individual word used in a sentence. While a sentence may follow syntactic rules, it can potentially carry no semantic meaning. **Example:** The sentence "Amazing colourless pink flowers jump inside banks" contains no semantic meaning. **Personal Example:**
When children only apply a language rule to a specific context, and do not generalize it to other situations in which they should generalize it. **Example:** A child may use the word car to refer only to his or her family's car, and to no other cars. **Personal Example:**	Refers to the rules that govern how sentences are put together; also known as grammar. Language influences syntactic rules. **Example:** In French, gender is assigned to all nouns while in English, gender is only assigned to those of biological gender. A table would be referred to as "it" in English, not "she". **Personal Example:**

Universal Phoneme Sensitivity
Language

MAC IntroPsych

Waggle Dance
Language

MAC IntroPsych

Whorf-Sapir Hypothesis
Language

MAC IntroPsych

MAC IntroPsych

MAC IntroPsych

MAC IntroPsych

MAC IntroPsych

MAC IntroPsych

A form of bee communication that uses physical movement to convey the distance and direction of food away from the hive.
Personal Example:

An infants' ability to discriminate between speech sounds in any language, including those from non-native languages.
Example: Infants in English-speaking families can discriminate Hindi speech sounds almost as well as Hindi-speaking adults while English-speaking adults are unable to accurately discriminate these speech sounds.
Personal Example:

The hypothesis that says language influences our thoughts and the way we perceive and experience the world.
Example: In a culture whose language does not have a word for war, they do not participate in war or understand the concept of war.
Personal Example:

CATEGORIES & CONCEPTS

"What's in a name? That which we call a rose by any other name would smell as sweet."
- Shakespeare, Romeo and Juliet

The label used to identify a disease—whether it is common language or medical terminology— can influence how serious people think the condition is. For example, impotence is now widely known as erectile dysfunction; excessive sweatiness is also known as hyperhidrosis. When people are presented with the medicalized term for these recently medicalized conditions, they are perceived to be more severe, more likely to be a disease, and more likely to be rare compared to the same disorder presented with its synonymous lay label. Participants in a study were given a survey that included 16 disorders, eight of which were chosen due to the increased popular use of a medical label within the last 10 years (e.g. erectile dysfunction versus impotence). The remaining eight were established medical disorders with both lay and medical terminology in popular use for more than 10 years (e.g. hypertension versus high blood pressure). "A simple switch in terminology can result in a real bias in perception," says Meredith Young, one of the study's lead authors and a graduate student in the Department of Psychology, Neuroscience & Behaviour at McMaster University. "These findings have implications for many areas, including medical communication with the public, corporate advertising, and public policy." The pattern of results also has direct implications for the patient. If a patient is informed that she has gastroesophageal reflux disease, for example, rather than chronic heartburn, she might think she is more ill. An important implication is that the patient's understanding of the condition heavily influences how she goes about taking care of her own health. Pharmaceutical companies may have an inherent interest in the medicalization of disease. The more serious a condition is perceived to be, the more convinced you may be that a drug treatment is appropriate. And so, while a red rose or rosaceae may smell just as sweet, they may be perceived very differently.

Young, M. E., Norman, G. R., & Humphreys, K. R. (2008). Medicine in the popular press: The influence of the media on perceptions of disease. *PLoS One*, *3*(10), e3552.

Weekly Checklist:

- ☐ **Web Module to watch: Categories & Concepts**
- ☐ **Readings: Journal Article**
- ☐ **Avenue Quiz 6**

Upper Year Courses:

If you enjoyed the content in this week's module, consider taking the following upper year course:

- PSYCH 2E03 Sensory Processes
- PSYCH 2H03 Human Learning and Cognition

Categories & Concepts – Outline

Unit 1: Categorization

Categorization allows us to deal with our surroundings quickly and effectively.

Unit 2: Functions of Categorization

Categorization serves three specific functions.

1) Treating non-identical objects in a similar manner:

Classification: the ability to treat objects that appear differently as belonging together
• different colour apples are different due to colour, but classifying them as apples means they are safe to eat

2) Understanding our surroundings: ability to evaluate a situation based on prior experience and act appropriately
• we see two people shouting, based on prior experiences, we understand that they probably don't need our opinion

AA Communication uses specific words to describe ideas efficiently

3) Communication: the ability to describe complex ideas or objects using a single label

- many words in our language refer to a category or concept (cat, sport, classroom), using the category name allows for efficient communication

AA The Illusion of the Expert

Definition

Illusion of the Expert

- The feeling that a task must be simple for everyone because it is simple for oneself.

Categorization seems to be a simple process because humans can perform it with great ease.

Illusion of the expert: feeling that something must be simple because you're really good at it

- Categorization is a complex field with a number of conflicting theories seeking to explain the ease with which humans are able to categorize

Unit 3: Rules

Simple, rather than complex categories, leave us susceptible to the Illusion of the Expert

% yes	Category	Include...	But not...
84%	table	coffee table, pedestal	bed, counter, iron board
88%	bottle	baby bottle, pill bottle	jar, glass, carton
64%	dog	chihuahua, greyhound	wolf, fox, coyote
84%	tree	sapling, pine, palm, bonsai	bush, vine, bamboo
40%	fruit	melon, coconut, grape	squash, almond
56%	furniture	rug, chair, desk	table, saw

Rules are often insufficient to describe all members of a category.

Research by Dr. Brooks: asked 1st + 2nd year students are there some sets of features you can use to identify a new member of a given category

- Chart is results

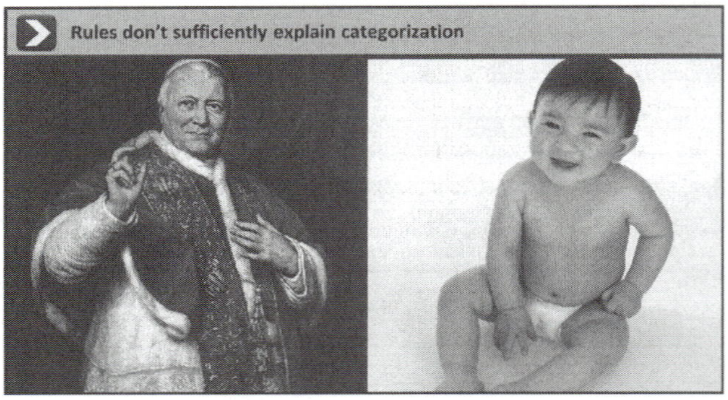

Implications of humans' inability to articulate rules for various categories:

bachelor = unmarried male
• pope and 6 month old fit the typical image of a bachelor
• when asked to define rules, you may find it difficult to properly include and exclude items for category membership

Unit 4: Prototype Theory

Prototype theory suggests that we categorize our current experience by comparing it to average representations of various categories.

prototype theory: we categorize objects by comparing them to an internal representation of the category called a prototype
• prototypes are thought to be the average or best member of a category

The role of experience: prototypes are formed through experience
• can be very personal because all the objects you've previously encountered are averaged together

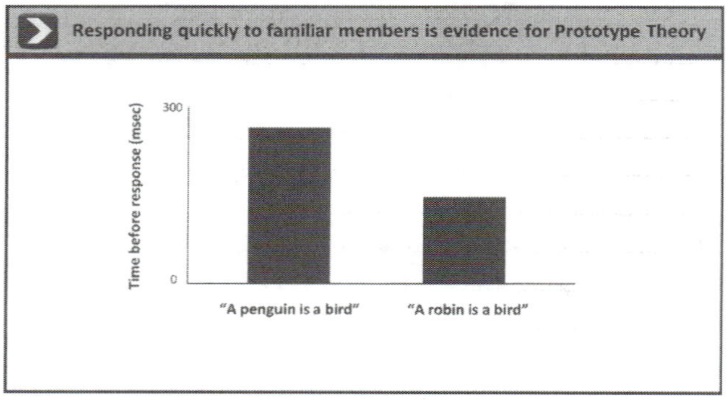

Evidence supporting prototype theory:
• more typical category members which are likely closer to the prototype, are categorized more quickly and easily than are a typical category member

Evidence against prototype theory:
• study asking to give prototype examples and then also a week later
• if we are comparing our experiences to an internal prototype, we should expect it to be stable over time

Unit 5: Exemplar Theory

Exemplar theory suggests that our entire lifetime of experiences is stored and used to categorize our current experiences.

exemplar theory- suggests that instead of storing only one average category prototype, you actually store your entire lifetime worth of experiences

Use the exemplar theory to explain how robins can be classified as birds more quickly than penguins: you have many more exemplars in memory for robins than you do for penguins, that is why you know a robin is a bird faster than a penguin being a bird

The dermatologist experiment: dermatologists were asked to diagnose patients, two weeks later were asked again but using different slides. In the second series, the experts were 20% more accurate if they were exposed to a single exemplar 2 weeks later

Prototype Theory can explain simple categorization better than Exemplar Theory

	Prototype Theory	Exemplar Theory
Categorizes by comparing the object to:	internal average	past, similar objects
Can explain why a single encounter changes categorization patterns?	no	yes
Can explain why we respond faster to more representative objects?	yes	yes
Other	explains simple categorization better	-

Prototype Theory vs. Examplar Theory

exemplar- seems to provide a more compelling account of human categorization abilities

prototype- still has its place with some evidence suggesting that prototypes explain categorization of relatively simple objects in situations better than exemplar theory

Unit 6: The Development of Categorization

Children begin developing their categorization skills during the first few years of life.

• children as young as 3 are able to understand general categories
• can generalize small facts from past experiences

Children's innate understanding of categories: understand you can change the nature of a machine but can't change the nature of an animal

Unit 7: Animal Categorization

Some animal species can become highly skilled at categorization.

Food versus non-food: baboons learned food vs non-food categorization very quickly and were eventually able to categorize new objects into these categories with 90% accuracy

Same versus different: with practice the baboons also reached 90% accuracy even using a variety of novel test objects

Categories & Concepts – Courseware Exercise

A researcher is measuring typicality and group membership ratings for a variety of objects. To determine typicality ratings, she asks participants to rate how typical objects are to their greater category (i.e. how well does "cow" *represent* the category "barnyard animals"?). She then asks participants for the membership ratings of the same objects (i.e. how well does "cow" *belong to* the category of "barnyard animals"?).

She found the following results for the objects "maple" and "palm" for the category "trees": palm trees were found to be non-typical, but were generally thought to belong in the category "trees". Maple trees were rated high on both typicality and membership.

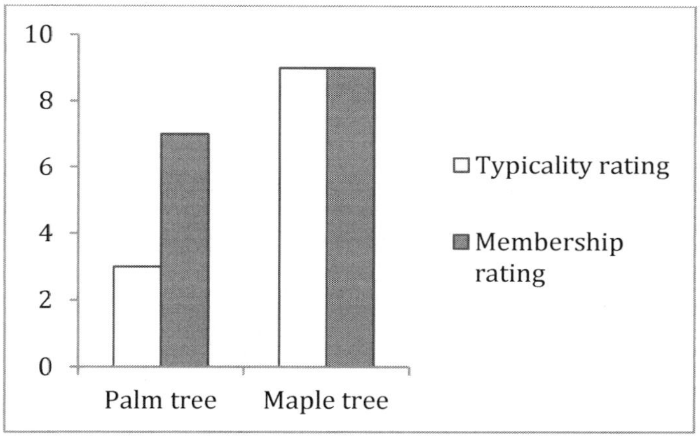

If you were told that the participants in this experiment had lived their entire lives in Canada, what theory would you use to explain the discrepancy between typicality and membership ratings for the object "palm tree"?

____

____

____

Which of these two trees would be regarded as the ideal member of the category "trees"? What piece of data from the study supports your answer?

____

____

____

Could the results of this study be explained using exemplar theory? Explain your answer.

____

____

Categories & Concepts – Review Questions

1) Provide your own example to explain each of the three advantages of categorization.

2) Is it possible to describe every category with a set of rules?
   a. What do experiments on the use of rules tell us about categorization?

3) Compare and contrast prototype theory with exemplar theory.

	Prototype Theory	Exemplar Theory
Similarities		
Differences		
How does the theory explain the categorization of an "orange" into the category "fruit"?		

4) Describe the development of categories and concepts in humans.
   a. List evidence that provides support for the idea that children can apply categories.

5) List evidence that provides support for the idea that animals can apply categories and concepts.

Categories & Concepts – Quiz Question

The results of the study conducted by Rips (1973) on the reaction time needed to categorize a penguin and a robin as birds can be explained by both prototype and exemplar theories. Which of the following statements is accurate?

a. According to **prototype** theory, it should take longer to classify a robin as a bird because the average representation of the category *bird* is likely closer to a robin than a penguin. (4%)
b. According to **exemplar** theory, *robin* should be matched to existing experiences of *bird* more quickly than *penguin* because there are likely many more robin exemplars. (75%)
c. According to **prototype** theory, *robin* should be matched to existing experiences of *bird* more quickly than *penguin* because there are likely many more *robin* exemplars. (19%)
d. According to **exemplar** theory, it should take longer to classify a robin as a bird because the average representation of the category *bird* is likely closer to a robin than a penguin. (2%)

This is a question from a previous Categories & Concepts Avenue Quiz. This question asks students to apply their knowledge about exemplar and prototype theories to the Rips (1973) study. When approaching this question, it is beneficial to consider what was presented in the web module about this study and about each theory of categorization. Let's look at our options:

a. This option uses a common question writing technique where a portion of the answer is correct but one aspect is incorrect. It is true that prototype theory considers the average representation of a bird and this average or best example is probably closer to a robin than a penguin for people in our society. However, because this is true, it should also take longer to classify a *penguin* as a bird, whereas this option says that it should take longer to classify a robin. Therefore, this option is incorrect.
b. This option correctly describes categorization by exemplar theory as comparing new experiences with a bird to existing experiences (exemplars) of birds. Because people in our society likely have many more experiences with robin-like birds than with penguins, they should be faster to categorize a robin as a bird. This answer seems to be correct. (**Correct!**)
c. This option correctly states that robins are likely to be categorized faster than penguins; however, it describes prototype theory as using previous experiences or exemplars to categorize. Therefore, we know option C is incorrect.
d. There is no correct portion to this option. We know from the study discussed in the web module that robins are categorized as birds faster than penguins. We also know that prototype theory uses comparison to an average or best example of a category member, while exemplar theory uses comparisons to all previous experiences with category members to categorize. Therefore, we can rule out option D when selecting the best choice.

This leaves us with **option B** as the correct choice!

Key Terms

Categorization	Exemplar Theory	Prototype Theory
Classification	Illusion of the Expert	Understanding
Communication		

Categories & Concepts – Bottleneck Concepts

Exemplar vs. Prototype theory
Rips' (1973) experiment
Brooks et al. (1991) experiment with skin experts
Animal Categorization

Brooks et al. (1991) experiment with dermatologists

Understanding the results of experiments and how they support or contradict certain theories is an excellent way to test your understanding of course content. Examining the experiment performed by Brooks et al. in 1991 will help you better differentiate between the exemplar and prototype theories. In this experiment, experienced dermatologists were asked to diagnose various skin diseases after viewing their pictures on slides. Diagnosing a disease requires an individual to categorize the patient's symptoms as belonging to, and characteristic of, that disease. After 2 weeks, the same dermatologists returned to perform the task again. This time around, the slides were different, but some of them depicted the same disorders presented during the previous session. The researchers wanted to determine if being exposed to certain skin disorders during the first week would help dermatologists better diagnose the same disorders two weeks later.

According to the prototype theory, examples from the previous week should not affect dermatologists' accuracy because recent examples would simply be averaged with the hundreds of previously seen cases of the disorders. Therefore, the first phase of the experiment would cause a minimal change in the doctors' prototype for certain disorders, resulting in virtually no improvement in their diagnostic accuracy.

On the other hand, the exemplar theory argues that recent examples would enable dermatologists to be more accurate in their diagnosis. To conceptualize exemplar theory, you can imagine accessing a big filing cabinet where each exemplar of a given category is stored. Everything you try to categorize is compared to each example until a similar match is found. Recent examples will be compared first so any recent examples of a certain disorder would help dermatologists better and more quickly diagnose skin disorders. Adding support to the exemplar theory, researchers found that skin experts were 20% more accurate in diagnosing the disorders they had been tested on two weeks earlier. This experiment also highlights the process of scientific research. Investigators can use evidence from this study to argue that certain categorization tasks are performed in the manner outlined by the exemplar theory. However, keep in mind that the prototype theory is still a valid theory for certain categorization tasks.

Test your Understanding

1) What would be the results of this experiment if they had supported the prototype theory instead of the exemplar theory?

2) Although people differ slightly in how they say certain words or phrases, we are able to understand their speech. Categorization may play a role in this phenomenon. This difference is more noticeable when visiting another country. When Frederick was 25, he travelled to Australia for 2 weeks. Their accent seemed strange to him at first, but he eventually became accustomed to it. When he returned home from his vacation, Frederick thought that people in his hometown also had a strange accent that he hadn't noticed before. Does Fredrick's case support the exemplar or the prototype theory? Explain.

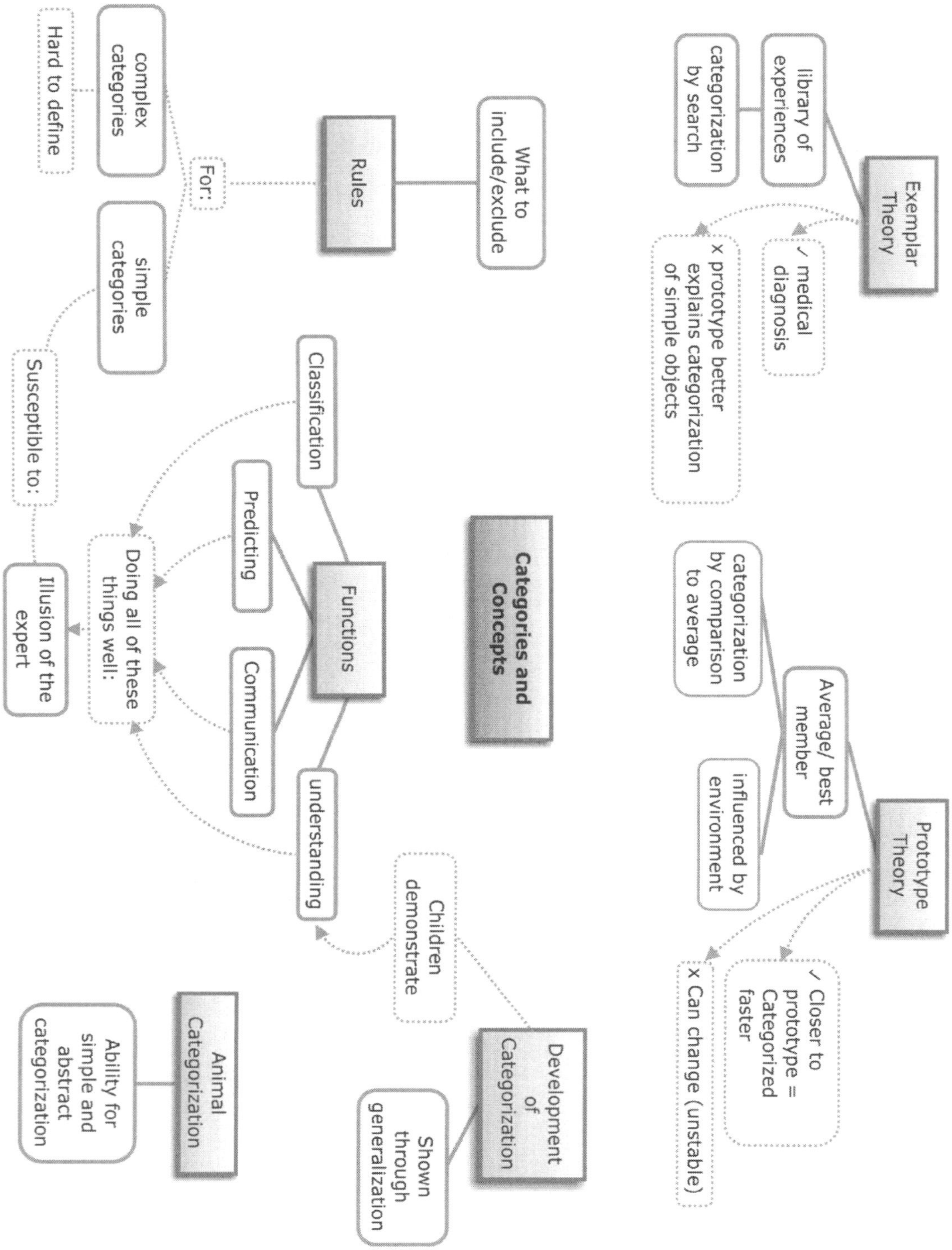
Categories and Concepts
Exemplar Theory
library of experiences
categorization by search
✓ medical diagnosis
x prototype better explains categorization of simple objects
Prototype Theory
Average/ best member
categorization by comparison to average
influenced by environment
✓ Closer to prototype = Categorized faster
x Can change (unstable)
Rules
What to include/exclude
For:
complex categories
Hard to define
simple categories
Susceptible to:
Functions
Classification
Predicting
Communication
understanding
Doing all of these things well:
Illusion of the expert
Children demonstrate
Development of Categorization
Shown through generalization
Animal Categorization
Ability for simple and abstract categorization

Categorization
Categories and Concepts

MAC IntroPsych

Classification
Categories and Concepts

MAC IntroPsych

Communication
Categories and Concepts

MAC IntroPsych

Exemplar Theory
Categories and Concepts

MAC IntroPsych

Illusion of the Expert
Categories and Concepts

MAC IntroPsych

Prototype Theory
Categories and Concepts

MAC IntroPsych

Understanding
Categories and Concepts

MAC IntroPsych

MAC IntroPsych

Allows you to treat objects that appear differently as belonging together **Example:** Green apples, red apples, and yellow apples can appear differently on a colour dimension, but by categorize them all as 'apples' you can treat them similarity and assume they are safe to eat. **Personal Example:**	The process by which objects or ideas are recognized, understood, and differentiated by grouping based on some underlying criteria. **Personal Example:**
The theory that suggests we categorize new objects by comparing them to all the objects we have encountered in our past experiences. **Example:** When seeing a breed of dog that you have never seen before, you recognize that it is a dog by comparing it to all other dogs you have seen in the past and identifying similar characteristics. **Personal Example:**	The ability to describe complex ideas or objects using a single label. **Example:** The label "furniture" easily describe a wide range of things.
This theory suggests we categorize new objects by comparing them to *one* internal representation of the category called a "prototype", which is the "average" or "best" member of the category. **Example:** When viewing a new dog for the first time, you may compare it to one typical representation of what you consider a "dog", which is the average of every other dog you have seen before. **Personal Example:**	The perception that something is simple because we are good at it. **Example:** A math professor may assume that because they can do the math easily, it must be simple enough for first year students to also understand challenging concepts. **Personal Example:**
The ability to evaluate a situation and act appropriately based on prior experiences. **Example:** If we see two people shooting in a private conflict, we immediately understand that they probably don't need our opinion **Personal Example:**	

ATTENTION

"Productivity in 11 words – one thing at a time. Most important thing first. Start now."
- Anonymous

Chances are that you are attending to many other things while reading this article. You may also be listening to music, surfing the web, or messaging friends via phone or email. Although attending to multiple tasks at the same time may make one feel both efficient and productive, there is much psychological research that indicates that our ability to engage in simultaneous tasks is, at best, limited and at worst, virtually impossible. The implications of these findings are significant, especially when we consider the use of technology in the classroom setting. With the ever increasing speed of information technology and the increasing use of laptops in the classroom, it is quite possible to be listening to one of the world's brightest minds, while also checking your email and reading the news at the same time. Given that the controlled processes involved in conscious attention are limited, are you really absorbing any information presented in a lecture while engaging in simultaneous tasks that require your attention? Hembrooke and Gay (2003) investigated the effects of multitasking in the classroom. In their experiment, two groups of students heard the exact same lecture and were tested immediately following it. One group of students was allowed to use their laptops to engage in browsing, search, and social computing behaviours during the lecture. In the other condition, students were asked to keep their laptops closed for the duration of the lecture. Results of the study demonstrated that students in the open laptop condition, who engaged in multiple tasks throughout the lecture, performed significantly worse on traditional measures of memory for lecture content. These results are hardly surprising, and by extension, similar studies find that multitasking inhibits performance in a variety of occupational settings as well. The conclusion? Attention is the triumph over chaos.

Hembrooke, E., & Gay, G. (2003). The laptop and the lecture: The effects of multitasking in learning environments. *Journal of Computing in Higher Education, 15*(1), 46-64.

Weekly Checklist:

- ☐ **Web Module to watch: Attention**
- ☐ **Readings: Chapter 6**
- ☐ **Avenue Quiz 7**

Upper Year Courses:

If you enjoyed the content in this week's module, consider taking the following upper year courses:

- PSYCH 2H03 Human Learning and Cognition
- PSYCH 2E03 Sensory Processes

Attention – Outline

Unit 1: Introduction to Attention

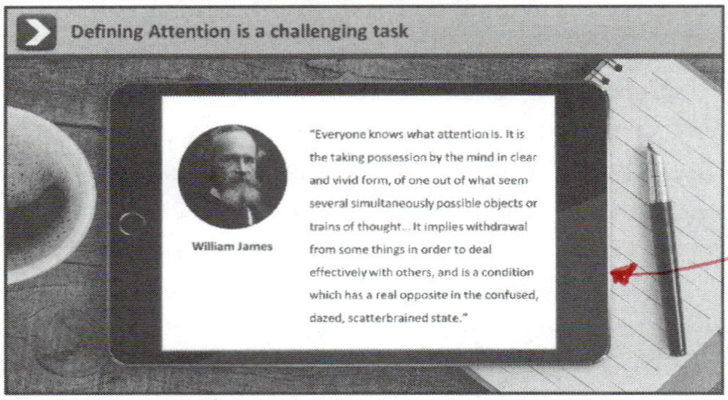

The concept of attention encompasses a broad array of topics that can be difficult to define.

William James on attention: it was hard for psychologists to give one solid definition for attention, but William James gave this definition

Selection: attending to an object to select it apart from the unattended objects

Selecting information to attend to: concious ability to attend to information that is relevant to our goals

The role of irrelevant stimuli: acts as noise that makes it difficult to identify and attend to important information

Unit 2: Automatic and Controlled Attention

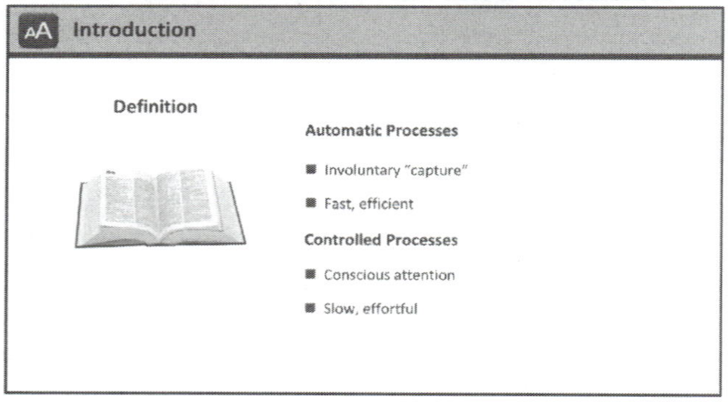

Two essential processes determine where attention is directed.

Automatic processes: are triggered involuntarily by external events, which often triggered the capture of attention
•operate in fast, efficient manner

Controlled processes: guide attention voluntarily and conciously to objects of interest
•operate more slowly because they are assumed to require more cognitive effort

****Our Attentional resources are limited and must be controlled carefully****

Unit 3: The Spotlight Model

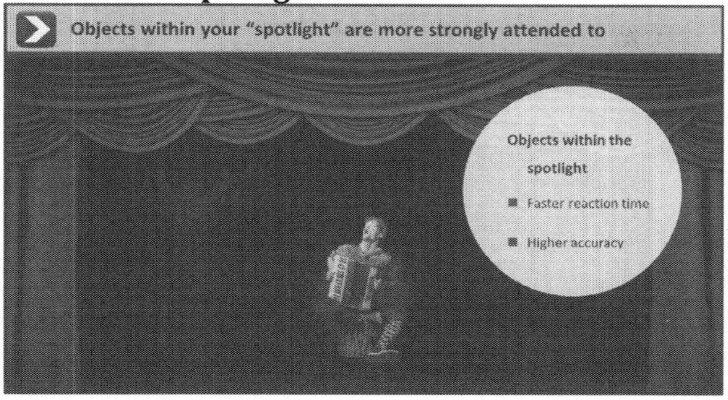

Psychologists use models to gain a well-rounded understanding of attention.

The Spotlight Model: attentional spotlight focuses on only part of the environment at a time

• When your attention moves around your field of vision, objects fall within the spotlight, our process preferentially meaning you can respond to objects faster and with greater accuracy

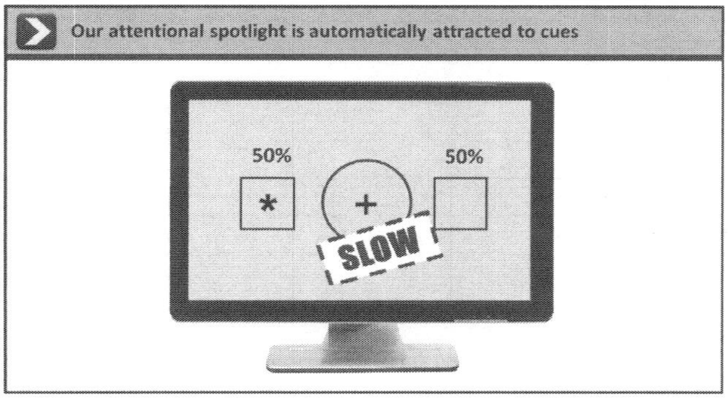

Cueing paradigms can be used to measure changes in attention.

Target appears in flashed box: participants tend to respond more quickly

• flashing box automatically attracts the attentional spotlight to the queved location, if target appears in the queve the attention will amplify the perceptual processing of that target

Target appears outside of flashed box:

• target will be detected more slowly because attentional spotlight will be directed away from actual target location

Unit 4: Filter Models

Information → Filter —further processing→

The Cocktail Party Effect: subjects were asked to listen to two different messages played from a single loudspeaker at the same time

• subjects tried to repeat one message but not the other in a shadowing task

• revealed ability to seperate the based on physical characteristics; gender of speaker, direction, pitch, or speed

Filter Model: shifts away from distractions and only allows important information through

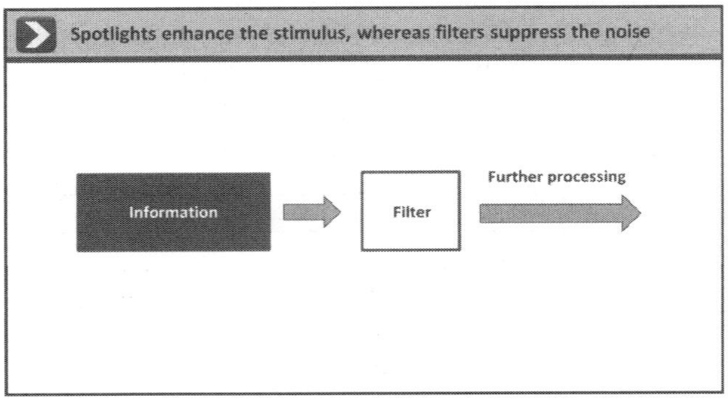

on single flower ↳

Difference between the spotlight and filter models:

- spotlight model suggest attention would enhance the processing of visual information from the single flower relative to grass
- filter model suggests attention helps us to ignore or block the visual information from the grass, allowing mainly the single flower to continue on for further processing

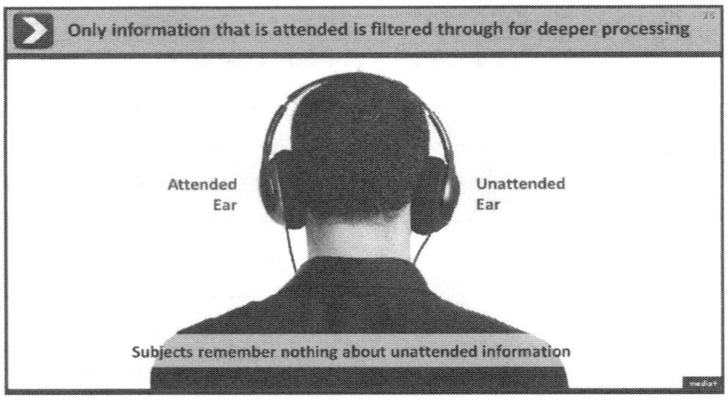

Broadbent's Single Filter Model: attentional filter selects important information on the basis of physical characteristics and allows that information to continue on for further processing

Dichotic listening paradigm: different message in each ear, you have to shadow the message by repeating only one message

- easy to remember attended message, no information processed in unattended ear
- rarely noticed large changes in unattended ear

Evidence supporting Broadbent's model: not surprising because attentional filter allows only information arriving through the attended ear to proceed to deeper processing

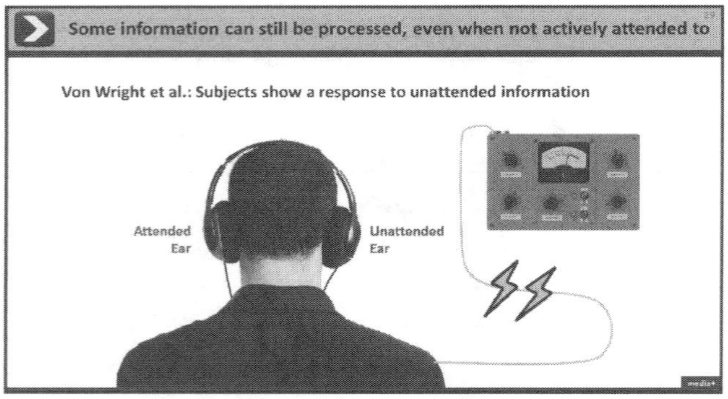

Limitations of Broadbent's model: it assumes that there is absolutely not additional processing of unintended signals

- breakthrough: occurs when participants are able to remember important information in an unintended stream

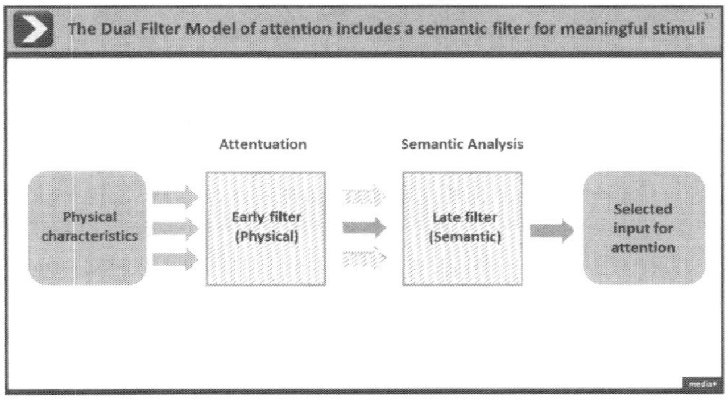

Triesman's Dual Filter Model: one physical and one semantic,

- first passes through physical filter, evaluated based on intensity or pitch (physical cues), weighs the importance of incoming stimuli, then passes it onto semantic filter
- as it passes through the semantic filter it's evaluated for meaning, takes into account the weights assigned by the physical filter, considers the deeper meaning and relevance of the stimuli and chooses which information will attend to while other info is discarded

Unit 5: The Stroop Task

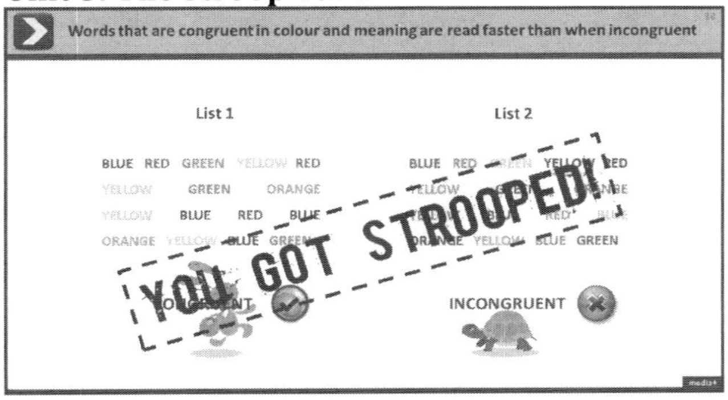

The Stroop Effect is a popular phenomenon that demonstrates the limitations of our attentional processes.

Congruent stimuli: the word and the colour are matched

Incongruent stimuli: the word and the colour displayed in do not match

Typical results: performance is much faster for congruent than incongruent items

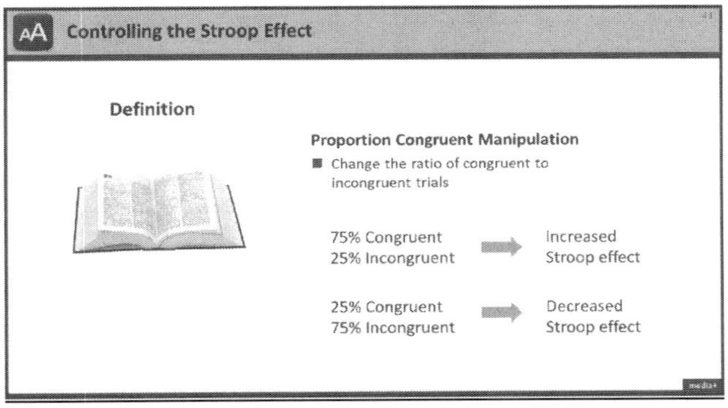

Using the Stroop Effect to measure processes associated with attention: task requires you to attend to information on the task relevant dimension

Results from various proportion congruent manipulations: changes ratio of trial type, more congruent = increased Stroop effect, more incongruent = decreased stroop effect

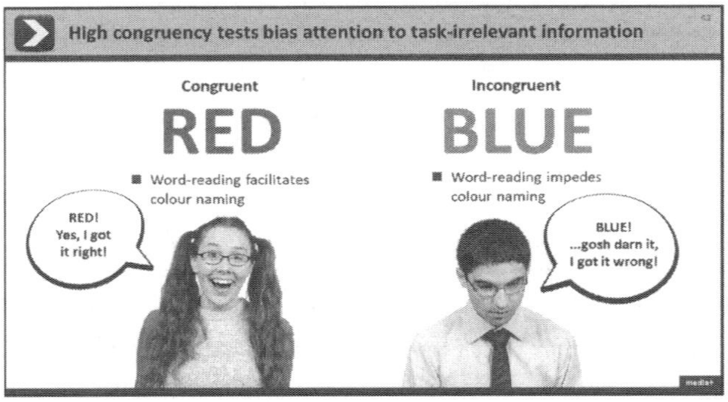

Describe how consciously adopted strategies can influence the Stroop Effect:

- the words match the colour and you adopt a strategy where you consciously attend to just the words and this leads to increased reaction times, when you recieve stimuli you were expecting
- when you receive stimulus you were not expecting like the word in a different colour, you might still focus on the name being the irrelevant dimension and performace will suffer
- drop your concious attention away from font color processing to word processing leads to increased stroop effect

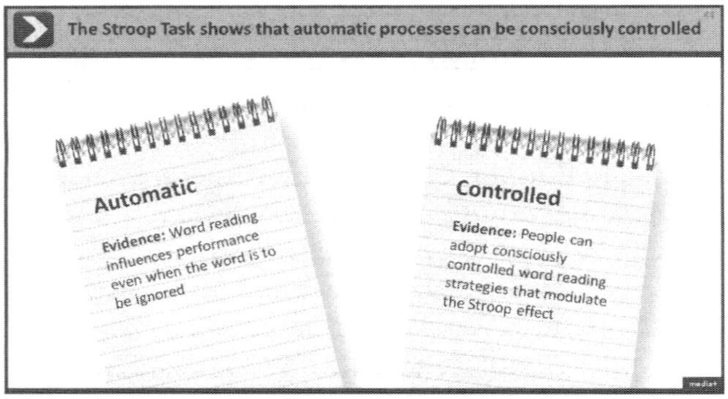

Describe how the Stroop Task can inform us about automatic and controlled processes:

- word reading is a relatively automatic process that occurs in absence of voluntary intention
- proportion congruent manipulation demonstrates people can gain concious control over an automatic process

Unit 6: Visual Search

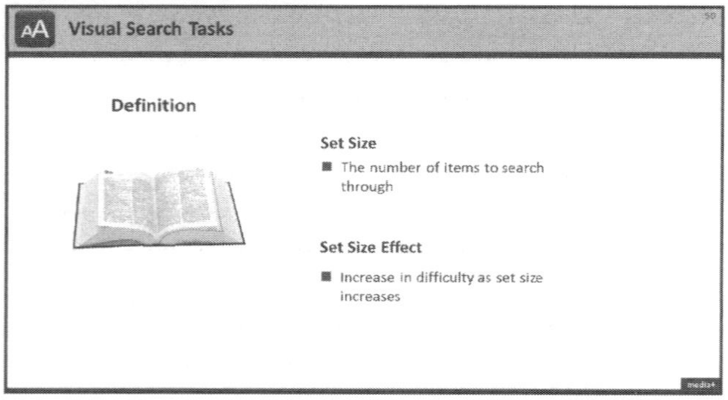

Visual search tasks mimic everyday tasks that require attention.

Set size: increase the number of items you search through

Set size effect: increases in difficulty as set size increases

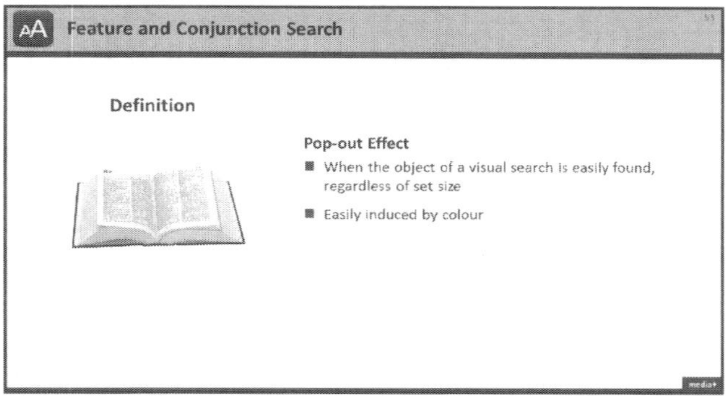

Single feature search: only have to look for one particular feature to identify the target

Conjunction search: identifying a target that is defined by two or more features

Pop-out effect: when object of a visual search is easily found, regardless of set size

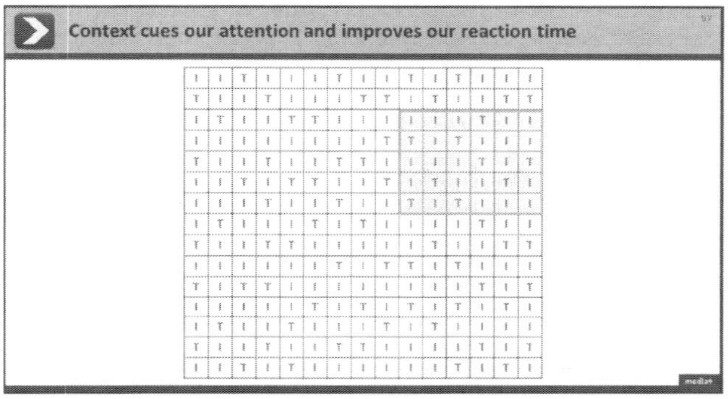

Describe the role of context in everyday search tasks:

- context cues: can come from any number of sources, but in general we gain it from knowing something about our world
- can integrate context cues by designating spots for everything you own

Unit 7: Conclusion

Conclusion

- attention allows you to select and ignore specific information from a sea of noise
- attentional errors can lead to minor everyday inconveniences
- chronic attentional errors can play a role in psychological problems like attentional deficit, hyperactivity, anxiety, insomnia, depression and OCD

Attention – Courseware Exercise

Debbie was driving down busy Main Street to work one morning. As she traveled, she tried to keep her attention focused on the road, but a red Thunderbird convertible, a few lanes over, suddenly caught her attention. She lost focus and began to veer into the next lane. Despite the fact that she had already passed several other red cars that morning, this one caught her eye since it was the same car her father drove.

Can this situation be explained using the spotlight model of attention? Explain why or why not.

____

____

____

____

Can this situation be explained using Broadbent's single filter model of attention? Explain why or why not.

____

____

____

____

Can this situation be explained using Triesman's dual filter model of attention? Explain why or why not.

____

____

____

____

Attention – Review Questions

1) Describe the difference between automatic and controlled processes of attention.
    a. What is the advantage of using an automatic process?
    b. What is the advantage of using a controlled process?

2) Describe the spotlight model of attention.

3) Describe the spatial cueing paradigm.

    Answer the following questions regarding the spatial cueing paradigm:

    a. In Experiment #1, the target appears in the cued location for 26/30 trials. How will this affect response times? What type of attention does this demonstrate?

    b. In Experiment #2, the target appears opposite the cued location for 26/30 trials. How will this affect response times? What type of attention does this demonstrate?

    c. In Experiment #3, the target appears in the cued location for 16/30 of trials. How will this affect response times? What type of attention does this demonstrate?

4) Describe the difference between Broadbent's single filter theory and Triesman's dual filter theory.
    a. What is breakthrough? Why was it important for the development of attention theory?

5) Describe the basic Stroop attention task.
    a. What does the Stroop task tell us about attention?

6) Describe a basic visual search experiment.
    a. What is the difference between feature and conjunction search?
    b. How is the pop-out effect related to the set size effect?
    c. Describe the relevance of contextual cueing.

Attention – Quiz Question

In which of the following would it take participants the longest to find the target?

a. If participants are required to find a red triangle among 150 red squares. (33%)
b. If participants are required to find a red triangle among 70 purple and blue triangles. (3%)
c. If participants are required to find a blue square among 70 blue triangles and green squares. (57%)
d. If participants are required to find a green circle among 150 blue and yellow circles. (7%)

This is an actual question from a previous Memory & Attention Avenue Quiz that many students struggled with. Fortunately, we are going to go through this question together to identify what sort of errors students were making and how to avoid them in the future. To do so, we will look at each answer option individually and identify why it is correct or incorrect.

In this question, students were asked to apply the concepts they learned about visual search tasks to determine which scenario would be the most difficult search and, thus, take the longest to complete.

a. This option was a popular choice, as participants must search through 150 items to find the target, as opposed to only 70 in option C. However, this option describes a single feature search, where participants are only looking for a triangle in a field of squares. As was described in the web module, conjunction searches are more difficult than single feature searches and thus take longer to complete. Therefore, this option is incorrect.
b. It is easy to determine that this option is incorrect because of the pop-out effect. The target red triangle is the only red item in the field, which would make it easier to spot.
c. This option describes a conjunction search, where participants not only have to look for a blue target in a field of blue and green, but also a square in a field of squares and triangles. As was described in the web module, conjunction searches are more difficult than single feature searches, taking longer to complete. Thus, this is the option is the best choice. (**Correct!**)
d. It is easy to determine that this option is incorrect because of the pop-out effect. The target in this option is the only green item in the field, allowing it to "pop out" even in a field of 150 items.

This leaves us with **option C** as the correct answer.

Key Terms

Automatic Processes	Feature Search	Spotlight Model
Broadbent's Single Filter Model	Filter Model	Stroop Task
Conjunction Search	Pop-Out Effect	Triesman's Dual Filter Model
Contextual Cueing	Set Size	
Controlled Processes	Set Size Effect	

Attention – Bottleneck Concepts

Spotlight vs. Filter Models
Single Filter Model vs. Dual Filter Model
Spatial Cueing Paradigm
The Stroop Effect

The Stroop Effect

The Stroop Effect was discovered in an experiment where participants were presented with a list of colour words written in different coloured inks. Their task consisted of naming the colour of the ink that the words were written in while ignoring the actual word that the letters spelt out. Two types of stimuli were presented throughout this experiment: (1) Congruent words, where the colour of the word matched the word itself, and (2) Incongruent words, where the colour of the word differed from the word itself. The Stroop Effect describes the observation that people take longer to name the colour of the ink in incongruent words than in congruent words. This is because in the case of incongruent words, the word itself interferes with the colour-naming task, while in congruent words, the actual word facilitates the colour-naming task. Students often find it difficult to understand the effects of manipulating the proportion of congruent and incongruent words in a block of trials. The Stroop Effect occurs when an individual mistakenly identifies the colour presented in the word dimension, rather than the colour of the ink. When a high proportion of congruent words and a low proportion of incongruent words are presented, the Stroop Effect is increased — the participant requires more time than usual to name the ink color of incongruent words. This occurs because a high proportion of congruent words leads participants to read the word itself to complete the colour-naming task. However, since participants are consciously paying attention to the words, when an incongruent word appears, it especially hinders performance on naming the ink colour of the word.

A useful analogy to understand the Stroop Effect can be drawn from examining a driver's interaction with the GPS system in his car. If an individual always relies on the GPS to navigate to his final destination, he is more likely to get lost if the GPS fails. Similarly, if there are more congruent words, and the participant relies on the word itself to name the ink colour, then they are more likely to be affected when the actual word does not match the ink colour. On the other hand, when a high proportion of incongruent words is presented during a block of trials, the participant will actively avoid using the actual word to help the colour naming task. Since the subject is consciously trying to ignore the word, an incongruent word does not affect the subject as severely and the Stroop Effect is decreased.

To prevent yourself from getting confused, ask yourself whether you would be more or less surprised if an incongruent word was presented during the Stroop Task experiment. Sometimes it helps to imagine yourself in the situation that is described in the question. If there are more congruent words, an incongruent word would surprise you more, increase the time you require to perform the colour-naming task, and result in a bigger Stroop Effect.

Testing your Understanding

1) Which of the following lists of words in a Stroop Task experiment would result in the GREATEST Stroop effect?

a) 100% congruent words
b) 75% congruent words and 25% incongruent words
c) 50% congruent words and 50% incongruent words
d) 100% incongruent words

2) It has been noted that people suffering from attention-deficit hyperactivity disorder (ADHD) do significantly worse on Stroop tasks (i.e. are more affected by the Stroop Effect) than the average person. Why might this be the case?

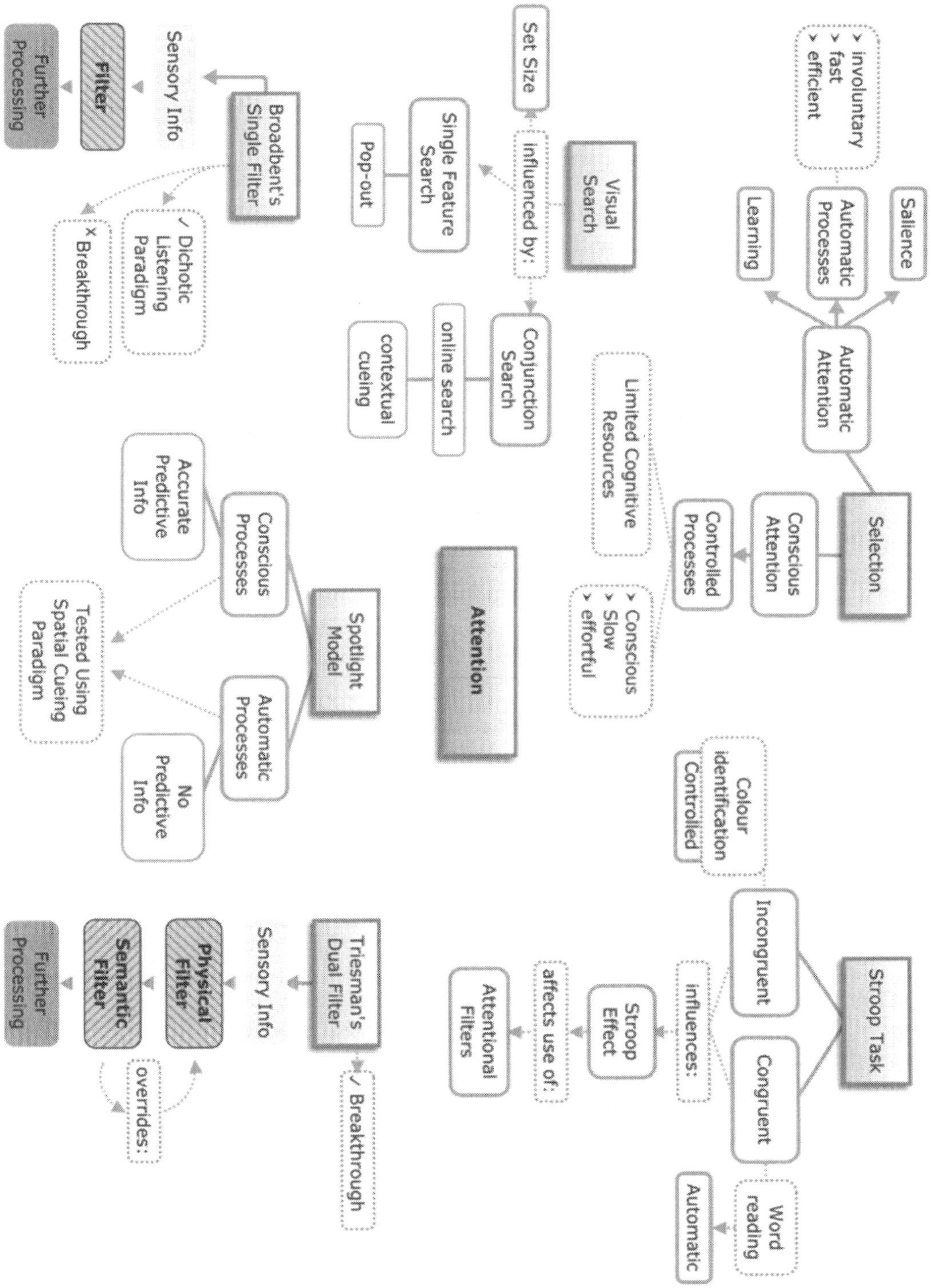

Attention
Selection
Automatic Attention
Salience
Automatic Processes
Learning
› involuntary
› fast
› efficient
Conscious Attention
Controlled Processes
Limited Cognitive Resources
› Conscious
› Slow
› effortful
Stroop Task
Incongruent
Congruent
Colour identification
Controlled
Word reading
Automatic
influences:
Stroop Effect
affects use of:
Attentional Filters
Visual Search
influenced by:
Set Size
Single Feature Search
Pop-out
Conjunction Search
online search
contextual cueing
Spotlight Model
Conscious Processes
Accurate Predictive Info
Automatic Processes
No Predictive Info
Tested Using Spatial Cueing Paradigm
Broadbent's Single Filter
Sensory Info
Filter
Further Processing
✓ Dichotic Listening Paradigm
× Breakthrough
Triesman's Dual Filter
Sensory Info
Physical Filter
Semantic Filter
Further Processing
overrides:
✓ Breakthrough

Automatic Processes
Attention

MAC
IntroPsych

Broadbent's Single Filter Model
Attention

MAC
IntroPsych

Conjunction Search
Attention

MAC
IntroPsych

Contextual Cueing
Attention

MAC
IntroPsych

Controlled Processes
Attention

MAC
IntroPsych

Feature Search
Attention

MAC
IntroPsych

Filter Model
Attention

MAC
IntroPsych

Pop-Out Effect
Attention

MAC
IntroPsych

A model of attention in which a filter selects important information based on physical characteristics and allows only that information to continue on for further processing.
Example: When looking in a crowd for a friend wearing a blue shirt, all people wearing a different coloured shirt would not pass through your filter. This helps direct your attention toward locating your friend.
Personal Example:

When external events involuntarily "capture" one's attention.
Example: When hearing a loud noise, one may automatically direct their attention to its source, even if they did not intend to attend to the noise.
Personal Example:

In a visual search, the expected position of a target is known which helps search more efficiently and find a target more quickly.
Example: If you are meeting a friend in a large lecture hall, they may advise you that they are sitting on the right side of the lecture hall and wearing a blue shirt with a bright pink hat.
Personal Example:

A visual search for a target that is distinguished from distracters on the basis of multiple features, such as a combination of shape, size or colour. A conjunction search takes longer than a feature search.
Example: Finding a green T amongst green L's and red T's.
Personal Example:

A visual search for a target that is distinguished from the distracters on the basis of one feature, such as colour, shape, texture or size.
Example: Finding a green T amongst many green L's.
Personal Example:

When one guides their attention voluntarily and consciously to an object of interest.
Example: When studying for a psychology exam, one may actively focus on their psychology notes while music is playing in the background.
Personal Example:

A visual search task that is rapid regardless of set size. This occurs when there is a specific feature in the target that highly contrasts the features in the rest of the set.
Example: A neon yellow square will pop-out in a set size full of red squares.
Personal Example:

A model suggesting attention works by filtering distractions and allowing only important information through. The model suggests that attention helps to ignore distractions and allow the object of interest to continue for further processing.
Example: If you wanted to attend to a flower, the filter model would suggest that attention helps you ignore the grass around the flower and allow the flower to continue for further processing.
Personal Example:

Set Size Effect
Attention

MAC IntroPsych

Spotlight Model
Attention

MAC IntroPsych

Stroop Task
Attention

MAC IntroPsych

Triesman's Dual Filter Model
Attention

MAC IntroPsych

MAC IntroPsych

MAC IntroPsych

MAC IntroPsych

MAC IntroPsych

A model of attention which suggests that an attentional spotlight enhances processing of objects within the spotlight.
Example: When searching for your friend in a large lecture hall, you will find your friend when your spotlight reaches her.
Personal Example:

In a visual search, it is the phenomenon of increased difficulty in finding a target amongst distractors as the number of items in the set increase.
Example: A visual search task in which you are required to find a green T amongst 200 green L's would be more difficult than finding a green T amongst 10 green L's.
Personal Example:

A model of attention in which there are two filters involved in attention. The first is a physical filter that filters based on physical cues such as pitch or intensity. The second semantic filter considers the deeper meaning when choosing what stimulus to attend to.
Example: When listening to multiple musical parts in a song, the early filter may process each musical line. However, the semantic filter will process the meaning taken from the melody.
Personal Example:

A task in which participants are presented with colour words and are asked to name the ink-colour in which the word is presented. Congruent items contain matching word and colour dimensions, such as RED written in ink-colour red. Incongruent items contain mismatched word and colour dimensions, such as BLUE written in ink-colour red.
Personal Example:

MEMORY

"It's not only people who go to a therapist who might implant a false memory or those who witness an accident and whose memory can be distorted who can have a false memory. Memory is very vulnerable and malleable. People are not always aware of the choices they make."
- Elizabeth Loftus, prominent memory researcher

In 2002, police were investigating the case of the Washington Sniper, a serial killer targeting random victims in Washington, DC. Several eyewitnesses came forward claiming that a suspicious white van was spotted near the scene of several of the murders. However, no white van was found to be related to the murders. In fact, the murderer's vehicle was a dark green car. How did this memory of a white van come to be? Intriguing work from Dr. Elizabeth Loftus suggests that our memories are far from perfect and we are even susceptible to false memories. Loftus noted that an early eyewitness had participated in a media interview mentioning a white van. This idea stuck and subsequent eyewitnesses also made the same claim. Consider the following simple experiment run by Loftus. Subjects were told they were going to evaluate an advertisement, fill out several questionnaires and answer questions about a trip to Disneyland. The first group read a generic Disneyland ad that mentioned no cartoon characters. The second group read the same ad and was exposed to a 4-foot-tall cardboard figure of Bugs Bunny that was casually placed in the interview room. No mention was made of Bugs Bunny. The third, or Bugs group, read a fake Disneyland ad featuring Bugs Bunny. The fourth, or double exposure group, read the fake ad and also saw the cardboard rabbit. Thirty percent of subjects in the Bugs group later said they remembered or knew they had met and shook hands with Bugs Bunny when they visited Disneyland and 40 percent of the people in the double exposure group reported the same. The scenario described in the ad never occurred because Bugs Bunny is a Warner Brothers cartoon character and wouldn't be featured on Walt Disney property. Such research suggests that memory is far from an exact replica of reality; it is more accurate to say that memory is a reconstructive process. This has interesting implications for the reliability of eyewitness testimony and leads to more questions about the very nature of memory.

Braun, K. A., Ellis, R., & Loftus, E. F. (2002). Make my memory: How advertising can change our memories of the past. *Psychology & Marketing*, *19*(1), 1-23.

Weekly Checklist:

- ☐ **Web Module to watch: Memory**
- ☐ **Readings: Chapter 7**
- ☐ **Avenue Quiz 8**

Upper Year Courses:
If you enjoyed the content in this week's module, consider taking the following upper year courses:

- PSYCH 3FA3 The Neurobiology of Learning and Memory
- PSYCH 3VV3 Human Memory

Memory – Outline

Unit 1: Introduction to Memory

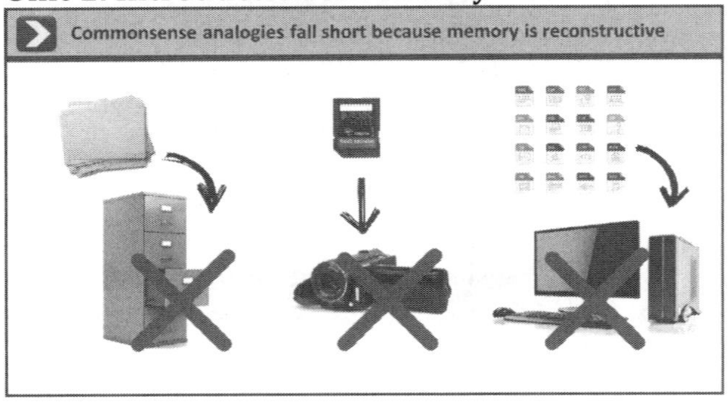

Human memory is reconstructive in nature, making it different than many common forms of externally stored information

Video camera: ______

Filing cabinet: ______

Computer: ______

Unit 2: Basic Terminology

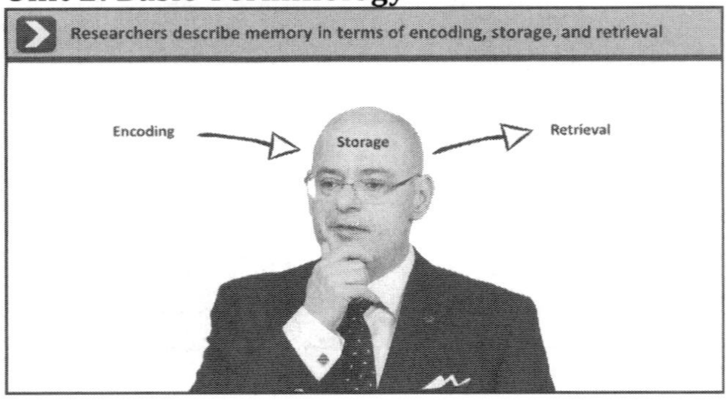

Encoding: describes what information is first being learned

Storage: describes what information is being stored in the brain and how

Retrieval: describes how we access prior experiences to make use of them in the present

Retrieval cues: is any piece of information that is stored in memory
- one piece of information triggers retrieval of another shaping the flow of the conversation
- one piece of information acts as a cue to trigger retrieval of something else stored in memory

Unit 3: Multi-Store Model

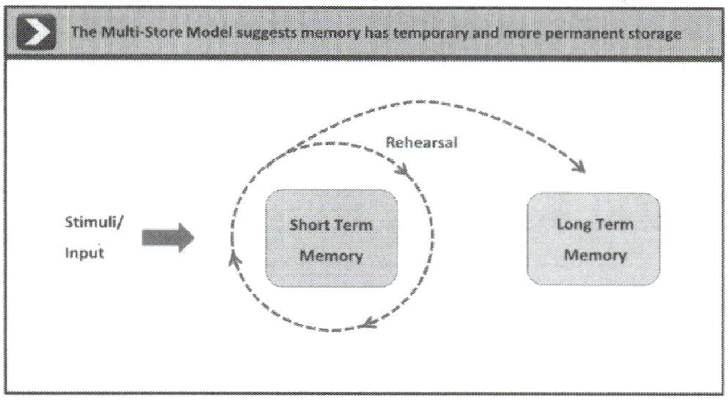

Atkinson & Shiffrin (1968) proposed a distinction between short-term and long-term memory stores

Short-term memory: incoming sensory information is first stored in short-term buffer, holds temporarily in short term memory for in the near future but not permanently

Long-term memory: can come from short term memory to here if it is sufficiently rehearsed

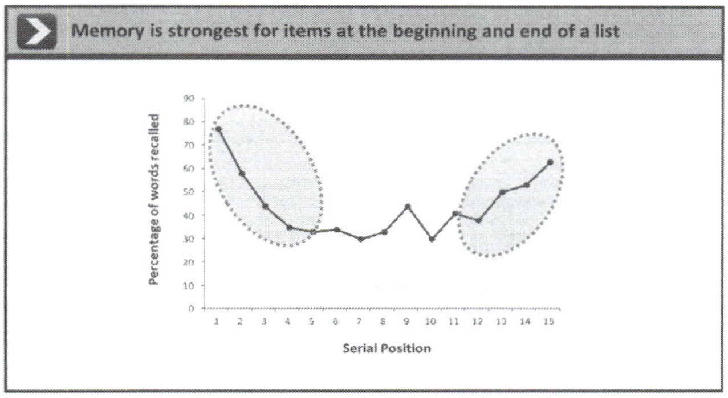

The serial position curve provided evidence for the multi-store model

Primacy effect: memory performance is good for items encoded early in the list
• happens because the items at the beginning of the list will be first to enter short-term memory so will have more opportunity to be rehearsed

Recency effect: last several items have least amount of practice but still more remembered than the middle items
• short term memory holds 7 items so newest items replace old ones, end of list are not replaced by new items so stay in short-term memory

Unit 4: General Principles of Memory

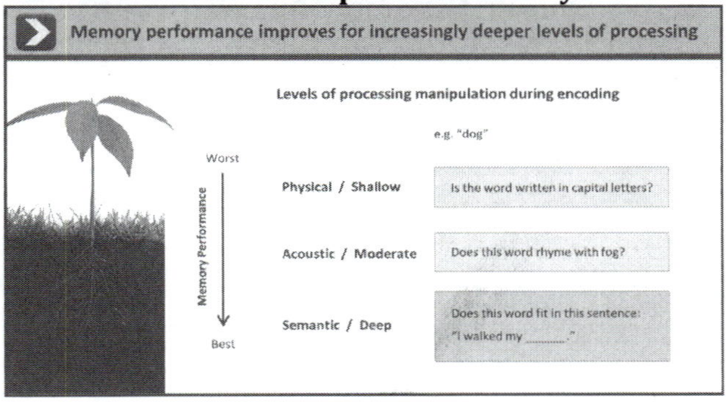

levels of processing principle: the more we try to organize and understand the material, the better we remember it

The level of processing principle suggests that information will be better retained if encoded "deeply" in terms of semantics

Shallow processing: encode physical characteristics, encoding requires little effort, poor memory performance

Deep processing: encode semantic characteristics, encoding requires significant effort, better memory performance

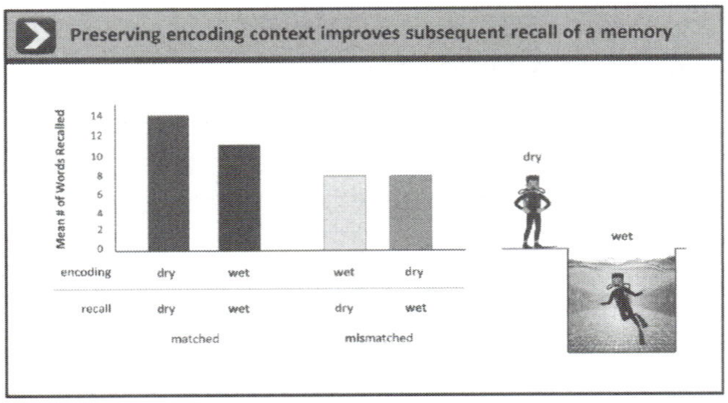

Encoding specificity means that the context during encoding is retained in memory and can later be used as a retrieval cue

Match the context at encoding and retrieval: When context is matched the encoding was much easier and participants could do it rather than the context being mismatched

Unit 5: Forgetting

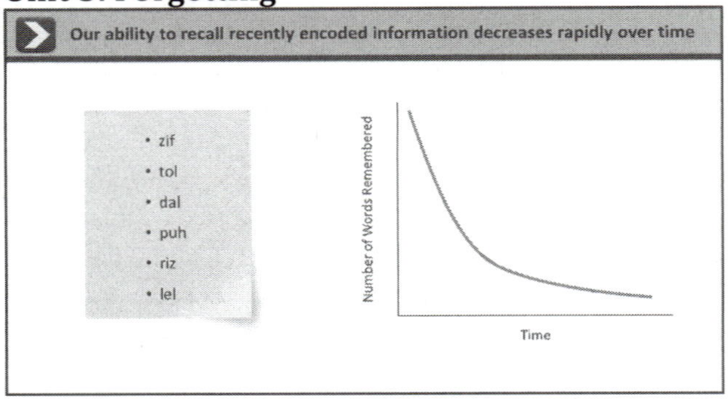

A typical forgetting curve shows the most information is forgotten after encoding, then continues to be forgotten over time

• Ebbinghaus was interested in how long memories could be maintained

Negative acceleration: ability to recall words was best immediately following learning and was able to remember fewer words with longer retention intervals until performance reached an asymptote close to 0

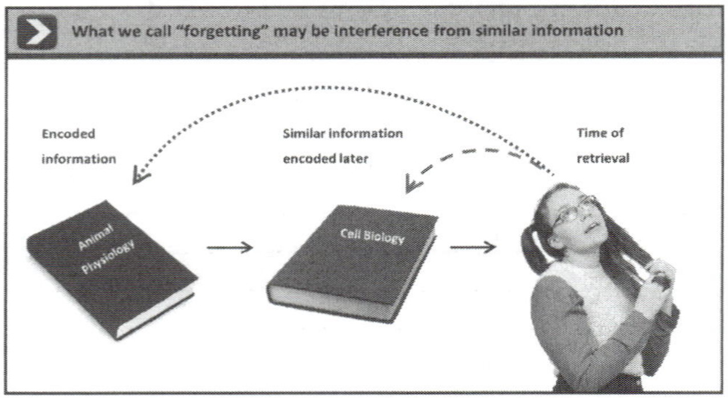

Interference is an inability to access information from memory due to other similar information "competing" for retrieval

interference - inability to access information from memory due to other similar information competing for retrieval

• competition between similar sources, when you go to retrieve relevant information on one topic, information from the other topic might compete for retrieval thus preventing you from remembering what you had hoped to

Unit 6: Memory Illusions and Fluency

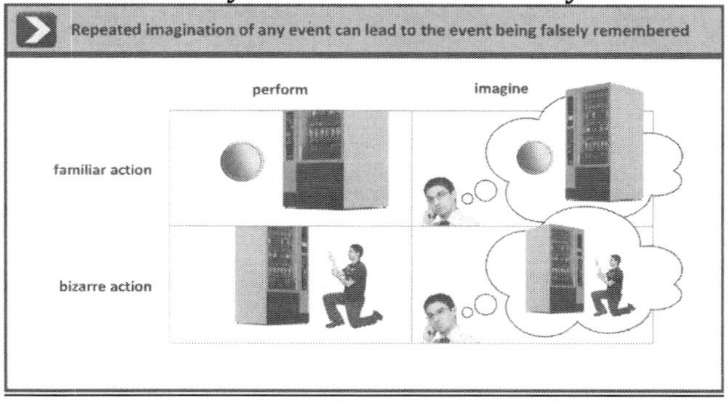

Simply imagining an event can lead to a false memory, even if the event is unlikely or bizarre

- repeatedly imagining bizarre situations can lead to imaginge an event and creating a false memory

Fluency occurs when we feel something familiar, leading to us inferring *why* it feels familiar

Attribution: a judgement that ties together cause with effect

- make an attribution to the processing fluency of the feeling of familiarity which can be tied back to many causes

False Fame Effect:

Unit 7: Conclusions

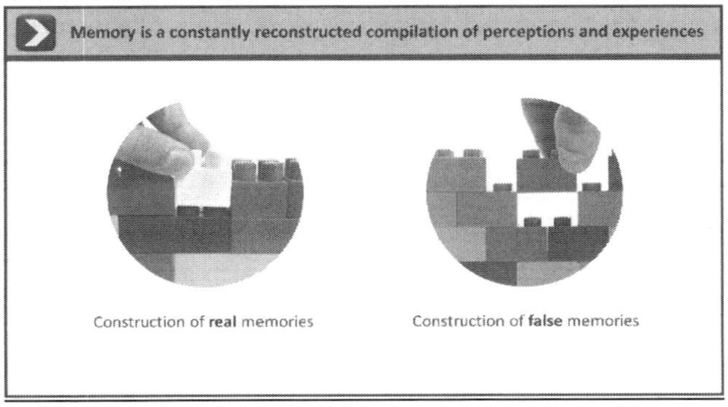

Human memory is reconstructive in nature, meaning we piece together past events rather than retrieving them as intact wholes

- memories are not discrete entities that we store in a memory system
- the act of remembering is an inherent reconstructive process, haphazard piecing together of past experiences that we do not spot when required to remember something
- reconstruction is prone to failure, giving rise to false memories and various fabrications

Memory – Courseware Exercise

Now that you've learned about the serial position curve, it's time for you to try it out for yourself. You will be running your very own memory experiment, replicating the findings of the serial position curve. It will not be a well-controlled experiment, but it is good for demonstrative purposes. (As a bonus, try to think of how you would correctly design this experiment if you were to run it in the lab).

Here is your task:

1. Using PowerPoint or paper, create a slideshow of 10 different words (each word on a different slide).
2. Recruit 3 to 5 friends for your experiment.
3. Have each participant simply sit and view the slideshow quietly.
4. At the end of each slideshow, present them with a list of 20 words (10 will be the words presented in your slideshow, but not in the same order, and 10 will be novel words)
5. Have each participant circle the 10 words that they remember from the slideshow.
6. If you want a more accurate measure from each participant, repeat this procedure a few times per participant with new word slideshows.
7. Now, tally up each participant's results. Use the table below to do so. For instance: if the participant circled the word that was presented first, put an X under that serial position for that block of data.
8. Next, calculate the overall mean accuracy for each serial position across all participants.

Block	**Accuracy by Serial Position**									
	1	**2**	**3**	**4**	**5**	**6**	**7**	**8**	**9**	**10**
Example	X	X	X					X	X	
1										
2										
3										
4										
5										
6										
7										
8										
9										
10										
Mean										

(In the example, the participant correctly remembered the words presented 1st, 2nd, 3rd, 8th, and 9th)

Finally, plot your mean accuracy results in the graph below to see if they resemble the serial position curve.

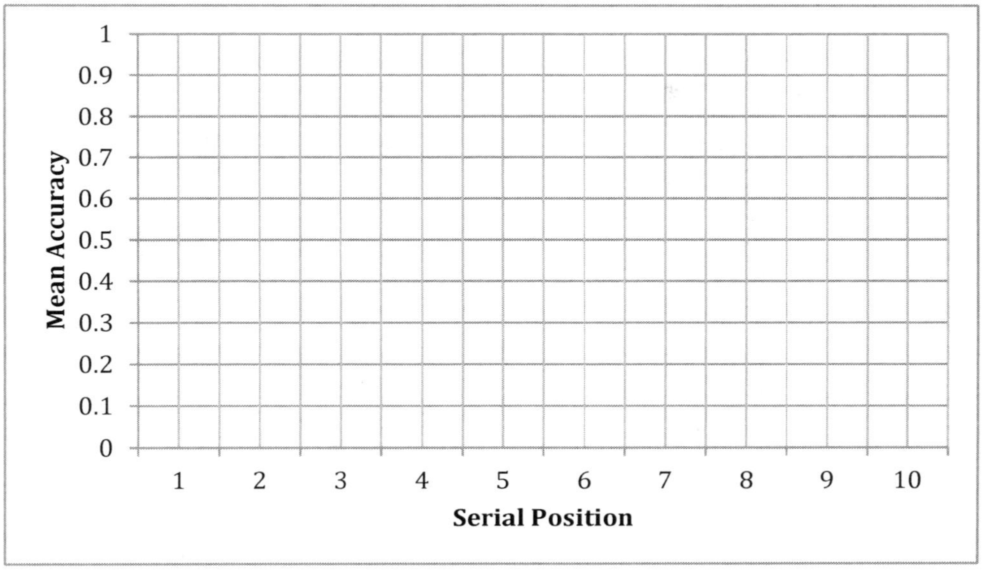

Do the results of your experiment resemble the serial position curve? If so, explain the main characteristics of the curve (2) and why this serial position effect is occurring.

If your results differ from those shown in the module for the serial position curve, explain how they differ and identify any factors in your experimental design that may have been affecting your results.

____

____

____

____

____

____

____

Memory – Review Questions

1) Describe Ebbinghaus' contribution to memory research.
    a. Draw the forgetting curve (include axes).

2) Describe and draw the multi-store model of memory.

3) What is chunking? What is the benefit of chunking?

4) Read the following scenarios and determine how each affects primacy or recency in memory recall.

    a. You have been studying all day for a midterm, right up until the moment you leave for the testing room. On your way to the midterm, you call your friend to discuss plans for the evening.

    b. Your TA leads a simple game in hopes of learning all the names of the students in your tutorial: The first person must say his or her own name. Then, the next person must say the first person's name and their own name. The next person must say the names of the two people before and their own name. This continues around the circle until each student has gone and it's the TA's turn to recite every name. You are surprised to see that she is actually best at recalling the first few names!

    c. In an experiment, a researcher has subjects view a list of words. One group of subjects is allowed to view the list for 30 seconds while the other group is allowed to view it for 2 minutes.

    d. Your friend refuses to talk to anyone in the hall while waiting to write exams. Instead, he studies his notes right up until the exam begins.

5) What does encoding specificity suggest about memory? Describe some experimental results that suggest the presence of encoding specificity in memory.

6) Describe Jacoby's experiment on "becoming famous overnight". What do the results suggest about memory encoding?

Memory – Quiz Question

Which of the following would be most effective at manipulating the serial position curve?

a. Increasing presentation time increases recall of all the words, so the curve becomes flat. (9%)
b. Increasing the list size will diminish the primacy effect, but not the recency effect. (7%)
c. Presentation of a distractor following the encoding phase will conserve the shape of the curve, but equally decrease the recall of all words. (14%)
d. Presentation of a distractor following the encoding phase will decrease the recall of words presented at the end of the list. (70%)

This is a question used on the Memory Avenue Quiz that evaluated students' understanding of the serial position curve. In order to succeed on this question, students should have reviewed what they knew about the serial position curve and its important features such as the primacy and recency effects. Let's examine each of the options to determine where students may have gone wrong:

a. This option reflects a common misunderstanding about the serial position curve. The serial position curve depicts memory performance based on that item's position in the list (beginning, middle or end). Increasing the presentation time allows for more repetition of a word, which helps the word be stored in long-term memory. Therefore, it will not flatten the curve, it will increase recall only for items presented at the beginning of the list. As a result, this option is incorrect.
b. This option reflects a common misunderstanding about the serial position curve. Increasing the list size, such as presenting 50 words instead of 20, will not diminish the primacy effect.
c. This option requires a thorough understanding of why the primacy and recency effects occur. The primacy effect occurs because the first words on the list have more time to be rehearsed, allowing them to move from short-term to long-term memory where they finally remain. The recency effect occurs because the last words on the list have not been replaced in short-term memory by new information. Information in short-term memory is often replaced since it can only hold 7±2 chunks of information. Once you understand these phenomena, it is clear to see that the presentation of a distractor following the encoding phase will *not* affect those words that have moved to long-term memory. As a result, this option is incorrect.
d. Following the logic above (c), the presentation of a distractor following the encoding phase will *not* affect those words that have moved to long-term memory but *will* replace the most recently presented words from short term memory, thereby decreasing recall of words presented at the end of the list. As a result, this option is correct. (**Correct!**)

This leaves us with **option D** as the correct answer.

Key Terms

Attribution	False Memory	Recall Test
Chunking	Fluency	Recency Effect
Cue	Levels of Processing Model	Recognition Test
Encoding Specificity	Multi-Store Model	Serial Position Curve
False Fame Effect	Primacy Effect	

Memory – Bottleneck Concepts

Primacy Effect vs. Recency Effect
Encoding Specificity
False Fame Effect
Attributional View of Memory

False Fame Effect

To understand this concept, we must first understand how fluency and attribution play a role in false memories. Fluency is the ease with which information is processed. Typically, familiar pieces of information are more easily processed. For example, it is easy to understand a scientific concept if you have encountered it before. Usually, when something is fluent, you can explain why it is more easily processed (e.g. the name, Dr. Joe Kim, will be fluent to you because he is your psychology professor). An example that you may encounter involves re-reading your course notes. When re-reading, you may mistake fluency with understanding. You may think, "gosh, reading my notes on attention seems so easy" and incorrectly conclude that your ease must mean, "man, I remembered this so well and must also understand it well". The process of explaining why a piece of information is processed with great fluency is known as attribution. You are linking the ease of processing to a cause. Sometimes, however, you cannot explain or remember why something or someone seems familiar or fluent. For example, why does that individual in a coffee shop look familiar to you? You can still make an attribution (e.g. that person might be in one of my classes, or they are wearing the same shirt as one of my friends etc.), but that attribution may be incorrect and lead to a false memory.

Fluency and attribution can also be used to explain the false fame effect. Two groups of participants (A & B) read and pronounced a list of non-famous names. Group A was given a second list of names 24 hours later and were asked to give each name a fame rating. On this list were famous names, somewhat famous names, non-famous names from the list presented the day before, and novel non-famous names. Group B also received this second list; however, it was given to them immediately following the reading and pronunciation task. Interestingly, groups A and B rated the names similarly, except for one thing. Group A rated the non-famous names from the first list to be more famous than Group B. This is known as the false fame effect. This phenomenon can be explained through fluency and attribution. Since both groups had seen the non-famous names on the first list, the names would seem familiar and fluent to them. Participants from Group B, having just read the names, were able to make the correct attribution and say that the fluency occurred because they had just read the names. However, Group A, after a 24-hour delay, were more likely to forget where they had seen the name before. Thus, they were more likely to make an incorrect attribution and conclude that the name seemed familiar because it was somewhat famous. This effect can play out in many instances in your everyday life; take a look at the examples below and see if you can think of your own.

Test your Understanding:

1) Alicia was writing a multiple choice MacIntroPsych exam and noticed one of the response options contained the term "Encoding Attribution". This term seemed familiar but she could not remember where she had encountered it. Nevertheless, since she seemed to recognize it, she thought maybe that was the correct answer. She later found out that it was an incorrect response.

a) Explain why Alicia incorrectly selected Encoding Attribution as her answer. Use the terms fluency and attribution in your answer.

b) Has this happened to you before? What are some techniques to prevent incorrect attribution from occurring?

2) Paul introduces you to his friend Ryan whom you have never met before. In which of these scenarios would you be most likely to say that you've met Ryan before?

a) You saw a photo of Ryan on your friend's phone a week before meeting Ryan.
b) Ryan looks like a friend you just bumped into at the supermarket.
c) Another friend showed you a picture of Ryan last night.
d) You have never seen a photo of Ryan before.

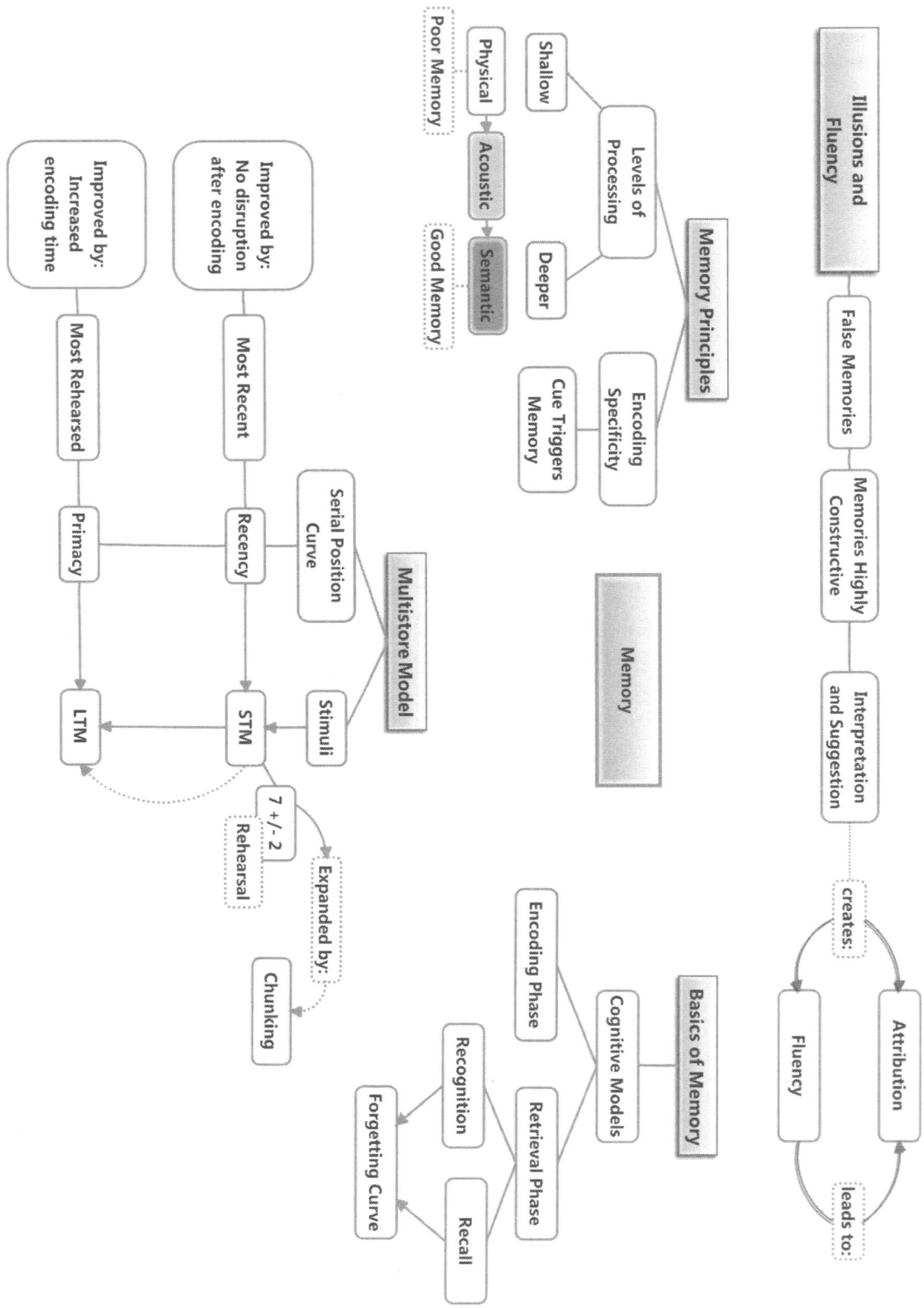
Memory
Illusions and Fluency
False Memories
Memories Highly Constructive
Interpretation and Suggestion
creates:
Attribution
Fluency
leads to:
Memory Principles
Levels of Processing
Shallow
Deeper
Physical
Acoustic
Semantic
Poor Memory
Good Memory
Encoding Specificity
Cue Triggers Memory
Basics of Memory
Cognitive Models
Encoding Phase
Retrieval Phase
Recognition
Recall
Forgetting Curve
Multistore Model
Serial Position Curve
Stimuli
Recency
Primacy
STM
LTM
Most Recent
Most Rehearsed
Improved by: No disruption after encoding
Improved by: Increased encoding time
7 +/- 2
Rehearsal
Expanded by:
Chunking

Attribution
Memory

MAC IntroPsych

Chunking
Memory

MAC IntroPsych

Cue
Memory

MAC IntroPsych

Encoding Specificity
Memory

MAC IntroPsych

False Fame Effect
Memory

MAC IntroPsych

False Memory
Memory

MAC IntroPsych

Fluency
Memory

MAC IntroPsych

Levels of Processing Model
Memory

MAC IntroPsych

Reorganizing information by grouping smaller items into larger packets, allowing more information to be remembered. By chunking, individuals can remember more significant information within the short-term memory capacity of 7 +/- 2 chunks.
Example: If each item is actually a meaningful combination of 3 numbers, then approximately 21 numbers can be remembered within those 7 items.
Personal Example:

Judgments that tie together a cause and effect.
Example: If you see someone you recognize, the effect is the feeling of fluency or familiarity. Upon feeling the effect of fluency, you use attribution to investigate the cause for this effect, or how you know the individual.
Personal Example:

The finding that memory recall is better when retrieval takes place under similar conditions to encoding. It demonstrates that our internal and external environment affects our memory.
Example: According to this theory, if you were to write an exam (retrieval) in the same room as your lectures (encoding), test performance may be improved because you are retrieving the information in the same environment where you encoded it.
Personal Example:

A signal that can be used to trigger the retrieval of a memory.
Example: Stephen's dad would always wears red shirts on Sundays when they watched football together. Years later, Stephen sees a man of similar stature to his father wearing a red shirt on a Sunday, and remembers the times they watched a football game on TV.
Personal Example:

When an individual recalls a false past experience that is remembered as real. As time passes from the initial description of the experience, subjects become more likely to believe the experience is true.
Example: A subject may be told to recall the time when they were lost in a park as a child. At first, they may not believe it truly happened, but over time they are likely to believe that this is a true memory.
Personal Example:

The finding that subjects who read a list of both recently learned and famous names will incorrectly identify some of the newly learned names as famous after a 24-hour delay. Due to increased processing fluency, these names would seem familiar to the participant, who would then incorrectly assume that the names were famous.
Personal Example:

A memory model, which states that the more deeply a concept is processed, the better memory performance becomes.
Example: When memorizing the word "car", a shallow level would be remembering that the word was spelled in capital letters (CAR). A deeper level would be to understand the word in a context, such as "The car is driving on a highway similar to the ones my grandfather used to drive home on".
Personal Example:

The ease with which an experience is processed. Familiar experiences are generally processed more fluently than are novel experiences.
Example: You likely process a familiar song with more ease than a brand-new song in a foreign language that you have not previously heard.
Personal Example:

Multi-Store Model
Memory

MAC IntroPsych

Primacy Effect
Memory

MAC IntroPsych

Recall Test
Memory

MAC IntroPsych

Recency Effect
Memory

MAC IntroPsych

Recognition Test
Memory

MAC IntroPsych

Serial Position Curve
Memory

MAC IntroPsych

MAC IntroPsych

MAC IntroPsych

The finding that memory performance is better for items encoded earlier in a list because they are more likely to transfer to long-term memory.
Example: If you were to repeat a list of words and add a successive word each time, the word at the beginning of the list will be repeated the most and will thus have the highest chance of transfer to long-term memory.
Personal Example:

The assumption that memory is composed of both short-term and long-term storage systems. Incoming information is first stored in a short-term memory buffer and then transferred into long-term memory following active rehearsal of that information, or it is lost.
Personal Example:

Memory performance is better for items encoded later in a list because they remain in the short-term memory stores, since new items do not replace them.
Example: Only remembering the last few digits of a new phone number.
Personal Example:

A memory test in which a subject is asked to read a list of items, and after a time delay, freely generate as many items they can remember from the list.
Example: A subject reads a list of 10 animal words and two days later is asked to write down as many words they can remember from the list.
Personal Example:

A U-shaped curve describing the recall performance of each item in an ordered list of words, indicating that recall is worst for items placed in the middle of the sequence.
Example: When learning a new unit in a course, information at the beginning and end of the unit will be recalled more easily than information from the middle of the unit.
Personal Example:

A memory test in which a subject is asked to read a list of items and then after some time to read another list of items and determine whether each item is "new" or "old" (i.e. whether it was present in the initial list).
Example: A subject may be required to read a list of 14 names. After two days, they return and read a new list of 14 names and are required to determine whether these names were present in the list they read two days earlier.
Personal Example:

FORMING IMPRESSIONS

"The psychological opposition of irreconcilable ideas, held simultaneously by one individual, created a motivating force that would lead, under proper conditions, to the adjustment of beliefs to fit prior behaviour instead of changing behaviour to express beliefs – the sequence conventionally assumed."
-Leon Festinger on cognitive dissonance

Group membership is often steeped in ritual. Although hazing is now banned on most university campuses, new university students are still referred to as "frosh" until they attend their first class. Having passed this threshold, the new members join the larger university community. Although such a tradition may be fairly innocuous, the rites of passage for membership in other groups can involve more severe rituals. After completing 10 training jumps, US Marine paratroopers receive their golden wings, a metal badge with two half-inch pins. During the blood pinning ceremony, the pin is thumped into a marine's chest. A controversy was sparked when amateur videotapes aired on news reports showing the ritual in full. The tapes depicted dozens of marines taking turns punching, pounding and grinding the gold pins into the bloody chests of new initiates who scream in pain. One video plainly showed a senior officer watching as his men are being abused. Although blood pinning has officially ended, rites of passage are not likely to be completely eliminated. Hazing rituals are viewed by senior group members as an integral part of the tradition. Even initiates who have gone through the ritual insist it is an important part of bonding. A practical solution may be to shift the focus to regulation. As summarized by General John Shalikashvili (Chairman of the Joint Chiefs of Staff at the time), "We are always going to try to fix human behaviour, but we are not always going to have 100% success."

Gleick, E. (1997, Feb. 10). Marine blood sports. *Time, 149*(6), 30.

Festinger, L., & Carlsmith, J. M. (1959). Cognitive consequences of forced compliance. *The Journal of Abnormal and Social Psychology, 58*(2), 203.

Weekly Checklist:

- ☐ **Web Module to watch: Forming Impressions**
- ☐ **Readings: Chapter 8**
- ☐ **Avenue Quiz 9**

Upper Year Courses:

If you enjoyed the content in this week's module, consider taking the following upper year courses:

- PSYCH 2C03 Social Psychology
- PSYCH 3CB3 Attitudes and Persuasion

Forming Impressions – Outline

Unit 2: Attribution Theories

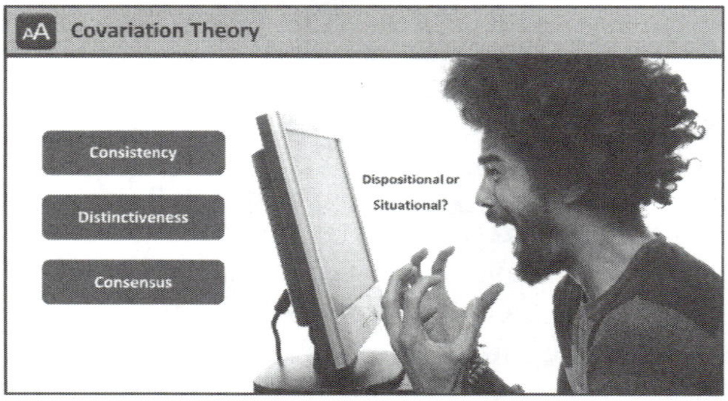

The Covariation Theory determines if we will attribute someone's behaviour to their disposition or their situation.

Consistency: does the individual usually behave this way in this situation? if yes then you wonder if it is Chris who is the issue

Distinctiveness: does the individual behave differently in different situations; if yes then behavior is from situation, if no the behavior is from disposition

Consensus: do others behave the same in this situation? if yes then it is situational, if no then response is due to individuals particular disposition

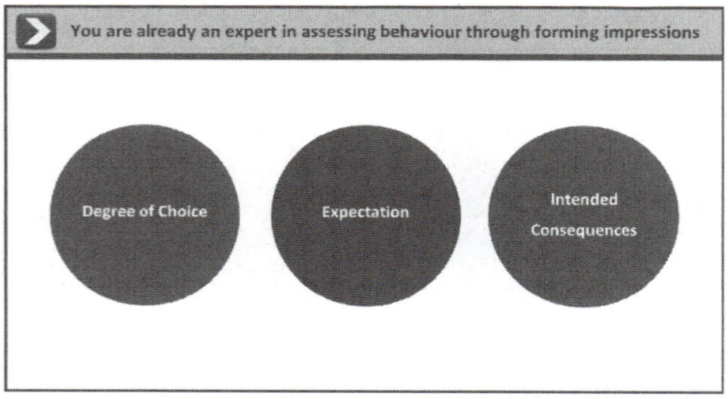

The Correspondent Inference Theory suggests that we attribute others' behaviours based on three variables.

Degree of choice: the amount of freedom the actor had in choosing their opinion or behaviour

Expectation: the occurence of a particular behaviour for a specific actor

Intended consequences: the goals and motivations of an actor underlying their behaviour

Unit 3: The Fundamental Attribution Error

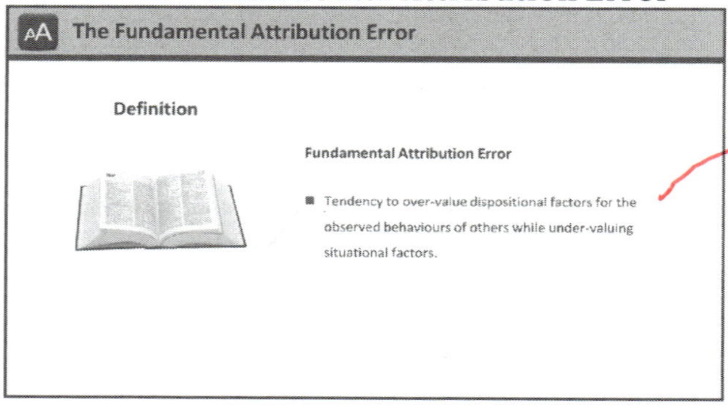

The Fundamental Attribution Error describes our tendency to attribute others' behaviours to dispositional factors.

• your interpretation of the behavior of others

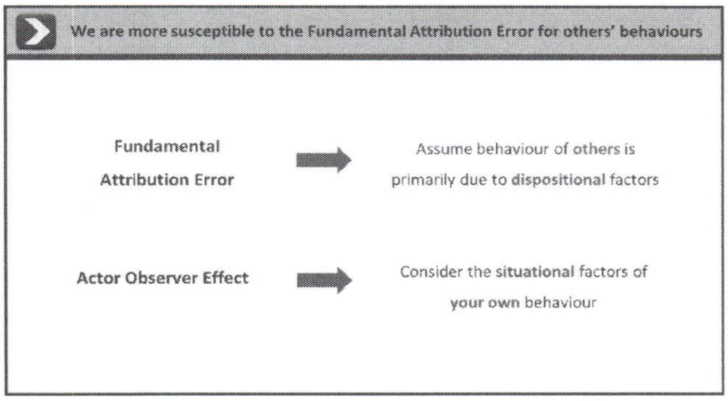

Being aware of situational pressures that influence our behaviours, we attribute our actions to our situation.

Actor/Observer Effect: much more aware of situational influences, this difference in how you perceive your behavior and that of others.

Supporting evidence from teen drivers: teens attributed their own driving to situational factors, attributed their friends driving to personal factors (fun or showing off)

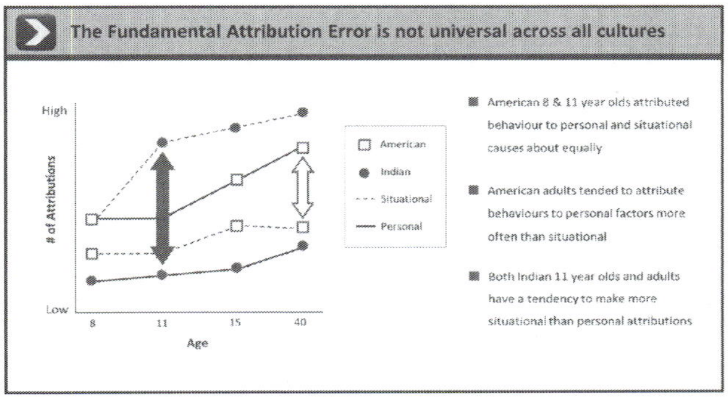

Cultural differences in FAE for young children:
US → attributed behaviour to personal and situational causes about equally
Indian → make more situational than personal attributions

Cultural differences in FAE for teens and adults:
US → attribute behaviours to personal factors more often than situational
Indian → make more situational than personal attributions

Attributions made by Olympic athletes from different cultures: US → attribute winning to their determination and talent, Japanese → attribute winning to the success of the coaching team and organization

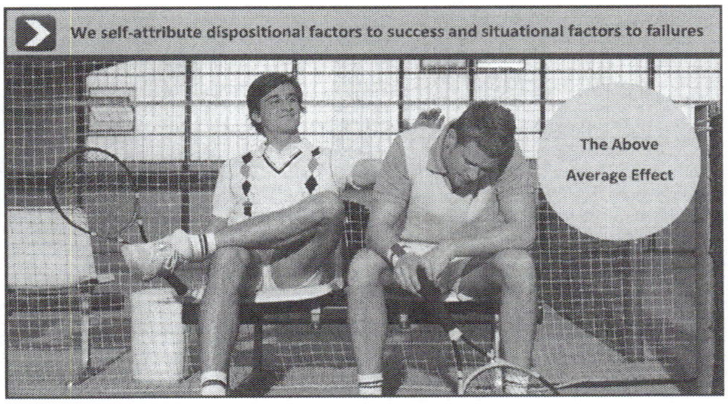

The Self-Serving Bias allows us to perceive ourselves favourably in numerous situations.

Above Average Effect: the bias in your perception may lead you to think you are above average on many things that may be important to you; above average attractiveness, intelligence and social skills

self-serving bias: perceive dispositional causes for your success but situational causes for your failures

Describe how the Fundamental Attribution error, the actor observer effect, the self-serving bias, and the above average effect are connected.

Actor-observer effect draws on FAE by suggesting we tend to be more cognizant of situational factors driving our own behaviors, ideas then give rise to self-serving bias by describing how we attribute success to dispositional and failure to situational
• the above average effect describing how we tend to view ourselves favourably

Unit 4: Cognitive Heuristics

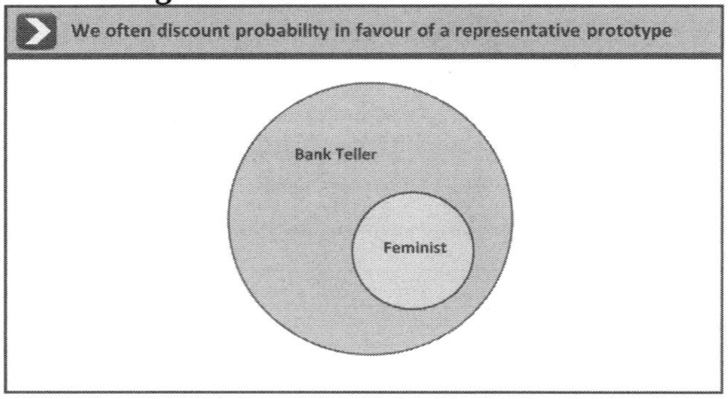

Along with helping us make quick decisions, heuristics are also used to make social judgements.

Representativeness Heuristic: classify people by considering how well their behaviour fits a certain prototype

The bank teller example: by probability you would choose first statement but because of description you seemed to choose second

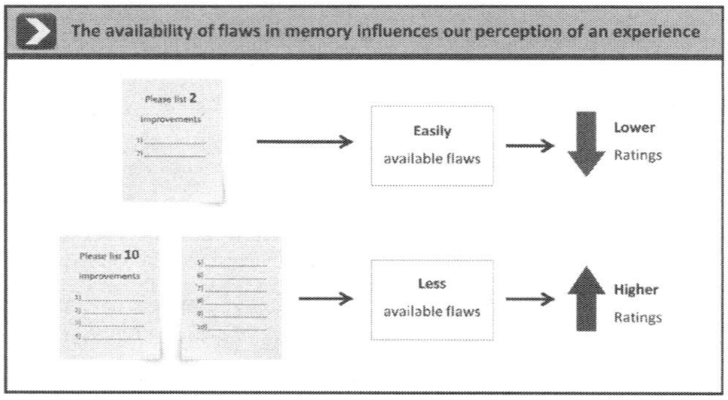

Availability Heuristic: more positive memories are more readily available in your memory

The course evaluation example: have more positive result because more motivated in class (first sem), will have very few memories from second class, although both teachers were good, you had different experiences

Unit 5: Relationships

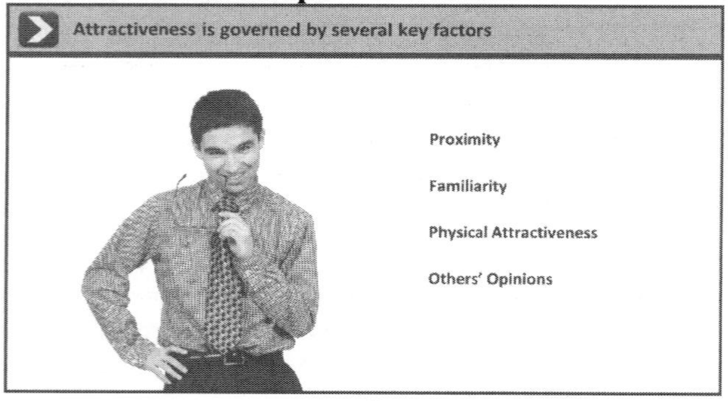

A combination of four factors can predict the degree of attraction between two individuals.

- someone who is attractive to you leaves you with a positive impression and you are likely to desire their company

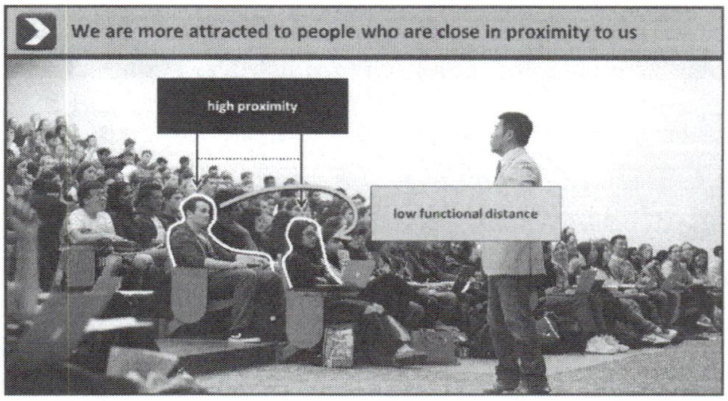

Proximity: more likely to be attracted to or become friends with those you live or work closely with

Functional distance: how often two individuals get to interact

How does anticipating an interaction with someone influence their attraction ratings?
increase ratings if they anticipated having an interaction with someone

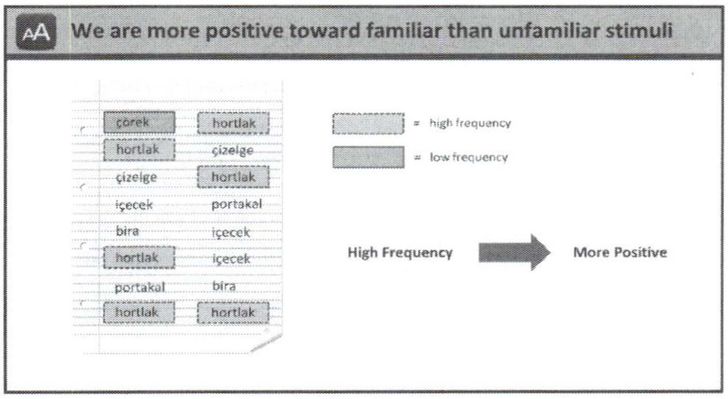

Familiarity:

The Mere Exposure Effect: a tendency to perceive previous stimuli as more favourable

Describe the foreign words experiment:
without understanding words with high and low frequency, high frequency got a more positive response while low frequency was a more negative response

Why do we rate a mirror image of ourselves as being more attractive than a correct image?
because you are more familiar with a mirror image

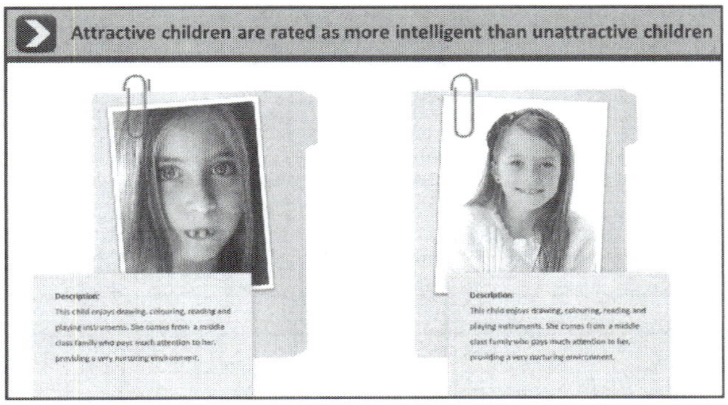

Physical attractiveness: on the presumption that what is beautiful is also good, more physically attractive people are often judged as nicer people

How does an individual's attractiveness impact their ratings in other domains?
- more attractive people are seen as warmer, nicer, sensitive people
- halo effect: tendency for people to attribute more positive characteristics to those that they have already positive impressions of

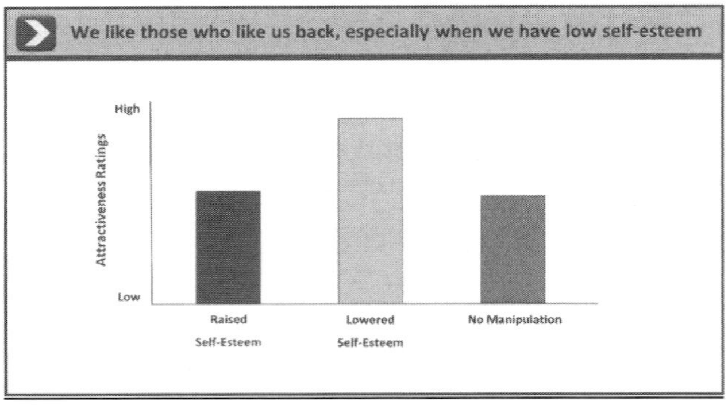

Others' opinions:

Describe the effect of self-esteem on being attracted to those who find us attractive:

someone liking you when your self esteem is low has a lasting impression

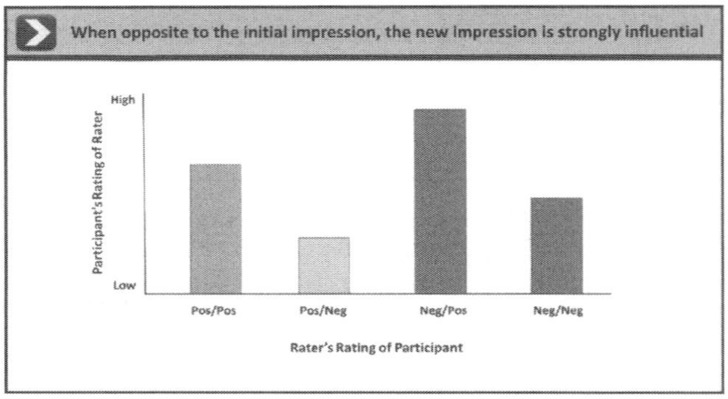

How do others' opinions of us influence our opinions of them?

Unit 6: Conclusion

Conclusion

- decisions use same heuristics as any other decision and are vulnerable to error

Forming Impressions – Courseware Exercise

It is Sarah's first day at McMaster University and she is desperate to make a good impression in hopes of making new friends. Using the principles you've learned in the Forming Impressions module, describe four strategies that Sarah can use to present herself favourably to a new classmate.

1) Principle: ______________________________

   Strategy: ______________________________

   ____

2) Principle: ______________________________

   Strategy: ______________________________

   ____

3) Principle: ______________________________

   Strategy: ______________________________

   ____

4) Principle: ______________________________

   Strategy: ______________________________

   ____

In using these strategies, Sarah has become friendly with two girls at her school. Monica is in Sarah's psychology class, a subject that Sarah enjoys and excels at. Sarah knows Maria from her physics class, a mandatory course with an awful professor—a course she'd rather not be taking. Recently, Sarah won 2 tickets to a concert from a local radio station. In choosing which friend to bring, Sarah decides on Monica because she'll be more fun to go to the concert with.

What heuristic is Sarah making use of and why is it possible that her assumption is incorrect?

____

____

____

____

Forming Impressions – Review Questions

1) According to correspondent inference theory, which three factors influences our analysis of others' behaviour? Consider how the three factors influence behaviour attribution.

2) Using the three factors associated with covariation theory, determine if the male student's behaviour (below) is situational or dispositional:

   Yesterday, you walked into your Biology lecture a few minutes late and observed a male student standing at the front of the lecture hall bragging to the whole class about all his accomplishments and avid devotion to community involvement. When you take your seat beside your friend, she tells you that her friend speaking at the front is a really great, humble guy who would be the best candidate for president of the student's union.

3) a. What is the Fundamental Attribution Error?

   b. Answer the following question regarding FAE:

   Cheryl, a Canadian bank-teller, is out for lunch with her 9-year-old son Matthew and her new co-worker Meili who recently immigrated from China. While waiting to order, they overhear their waitress speaking rudely to her other customers. How would each Cheryl, Matthew and Meili interpret the behaviour of the waitress?

   a. **Cheryl and Matthew** are most likely to assume that the waitress has had a bad day; **Meili** is most likely to assume that the waitress is just a rude person.
   b. **Cheryl** is equally likely to assume that the waitress has had a bad day or that she is just a rude person; **Matthew** is most likely to assume that the waitress has had a bad day; **Meili** is most likely to assume the waitress is just a rude person.
   c. **Cheryl** is most likely to assume the waitress has had a bad day; **Matthew and Meili** are most likely to assume the waitress is just a rude person.
   d. **Cheryl** is most likely to assume that the waitress is just a rude person; **Matthew** is equally likely to assume that the waitress has had a bad day or that she is just a rude person; **Meili** is most likely to assume the waitress has had a bad day.

   c. What accounts for cross-cultural differences in FAE?

4) How do the availability and representativeness heuristics apply to forming impressions of others?

5) List four factors that play an important role in our liking of others. Describe each factor.

Forming Impressions – Quiz Question

Katherine has been watching a lot of television to find examples of correspondent inference theory. As she channel surfs, she witnesses many different behaviours. In which case has Katherine correctly analyzed behaviour according to the correspondent inference theory?

a. President Obama is supporting the legalization of marijuana and Katherine thinks that he is so passionate that his position on the matter must be his own. (39%)
b. Homer Simpson is wearing glasses and acting very intelligent, and Katherine thinks that his attire and behaviours lack consistency with Homer's usual self. (21%)
c. Walter White is yelling at one of his friends in his house, at work and at a restaurant, which Katherine feels represents his true behaviour being present across a variety of situations. (13%)
d. Dexter Morgan finds a man tied down on a table and, instead of helping him, Dexter hits him on the head. Katherine feels that others would not do the same thing in such a situation. (26%)

This is a question from the Psych 1X03 Forming Impressions Avenue Quiz. In this question, students are asked to apply the three aspects of **correspondent inference theory** and to differentiate these from the three variables used in **covariation theory**. In correspondent inference theory, the variables used to analyze behaviour are *degree of choice*, *expectation*, and *intended consequences.* In covariation theory, the variables are *consistency, distinctiveness,* and *consensus.* Now, let's look at each option in turn:

a. This option suggests that Katherine believes President Obama's position in this debate is his own. This reflects the variable *degree of choice* in **correspondent inference theory**, because she believes that he was not forced to argue for the legalization of marijuana and chose this position. Degree of choice *is* a variable in correspondent inference theory and thus A is the correct answer. (**Correct!**)
b. This option applies the variable of *consistency* in **covariation theory**, because Katherine thinks that Homer does not often behave in this manner in his daily life. Since the question requires us to consider correspondent inference theory, this option is incorrect.
c. This option describes *distinctiveness* in **covariation theory**, by asking the question "Does Walter yell at his friends in a variety of situations or just in this situation?" Katherine can determine that this behaviour is not distinct for any one situation. Katherine might later conclude that this is Walter's disposition. However, since distinctiveness is related to the covariation theory, this option is incorrect.
d. Here, Katherine analyzes Dexter's behaviour using the *consensus* variable of **covariation theory** by asking "Would others behaviour similarly in this situation?". Since others would not behave similarly in this situation, Katherine might conclude that this is Dexter's disposition. However, since the question requires us to consider correspondent inference theory, this option is incorrect.

We can see that only **option A** uses an aspect of correspondent inference theory to analyze behaviour. The other three options use variables from covariation theory, which is not what the question has asked for! Thus **A** is the only correct option.

Key Terms

Above Average Effect	Correspondent Inference Theory	Other's Opinions
Actor/Observer Effect	Covariation Theory	Physical Attractiveness
Attribution Theory	Distinctiveness	Proximity
Consensus	Familiarity	Self-serving Bias
Consistency	Fundamental Attribution Error	

Forming Impressions – Bottleneck Concept

Fundamental Attribution Error
Availability Heuristic vs. Representativeness Heuristic
Correspondent Inference Theory vs. Covariation Theory
Mere Exposure Effect

Availability Heuristic vs. Representativeness Heuristic

Both of these heuristics may seem similar at first, but there are clear differences between them. To start, a heuristic is a decision-making shortcut we use to help us make quick decisions or impressions about elements in our surroundings. The availability heuristic, when used in the context of forming impressions, represents how we often use the most readily available information when forming an opinion about others. For example, if your group of friends aren't fond of a particular class and regularly complain about its difficulty, you will immediately think of these negative opinions when asked about the class. You would probably develop an impression that the class is terrible and difficult based of the information most readily available to you.

The representativeness heuristic, on the other hand, describes our assumptions of people or things based on an internal representation that we have of certain groups. Stereotypes are a form of the representativeness heuristic. For example, when you see a well-dressed student on campus, you might assume that they belong to the school of business because in your mind, all business students dress well. When trying to differentiate between the two, ask yourself, "Is the person using the most readily available information about a topic/person to make their judgment? Or are they making conclusions based on an internal representation of what they think of that topic/person?"

Test your Understanding:

1) Is the following situation an example of the availability or representativeness heuristic? Why?

a) Philip was Karly's online TA for the physiology course Karly took in first year. A year later, Karly met Philip at the Charity Ball and found out that he was her TA in first year. Meeting Philip for the first time in person, Karly was surprised to see that he was outgoing and looked like an average guy. She imagined him to have glasses, be reserved, and not come out to social events because he was a TA.

b) A new restaurant opened up down the street from Dave's house. Many of Dave's neighbours told him that the food was exceptional. Later in the week, Dave recommended the restaurant to his friend, Kyle, who wanted to find a good place to eat. The food ended up being mediocre at best. Dave later found out that his neighbours like everything they eat.

2) Explain how the media can promote stereotypes, with reference to the availability and representativeness heuristics.

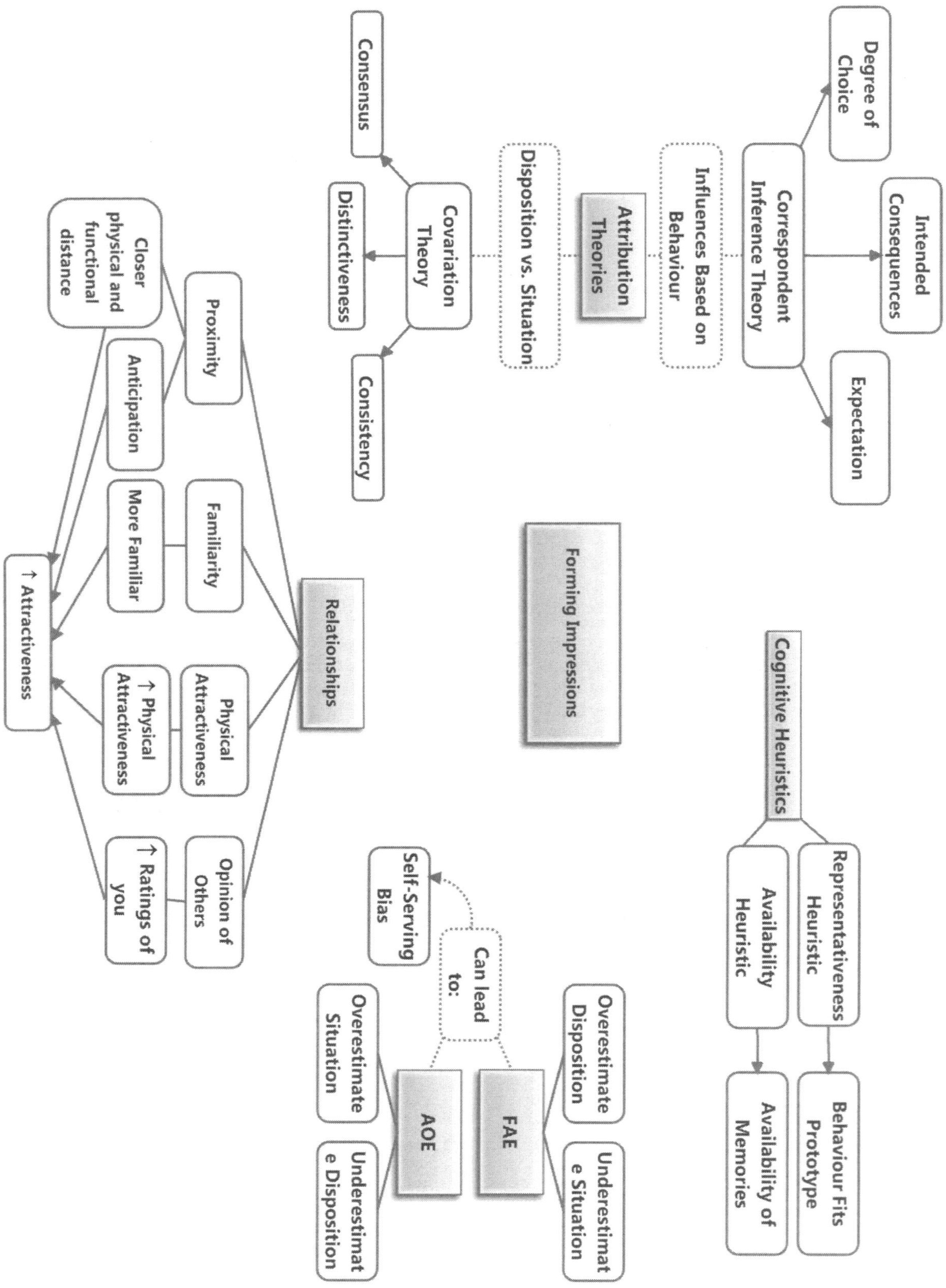
Forming Impressions
Attribution Theories
Correspondent Inference Theory
Degree of Choice
Intended Consequences
Expectation
Influences Based on Behaviour
Disposition vs. Situation
Covariation Theory
Consensus
Distinctiveness
Consistency
Cognitive Heuristics
Representativeness Heuristic
Behaviour Fits Prototype
Availability Heuristic
Availability of Memories
FAE
Overestimate Disposition
Underestimate Situation
AOE
Overestimate Situation
Underestimate Disposition
Can lead to:
Self-Serving Bias
Relationships
Proximity
Closer physical and functional distance
Anticipation
Familiarity
More Familiar
Physical Attractiveness
↑ Physical Attractiveness
Opinion of Others
↑ Ratings of you
↑ Attractiveness

Above Average Effect
Forming Impressions

MAC IntroPsych

Actor/Observer Effect
Forming Impressions

MAC IntroPsych

Attribution
Forming Impressions

MAC IntroPsych

Consensus
Forming Impressions

MAC IntroPsych

Consistency
Forming Impressions

MAC IntroPsych

Correspondent Inference Theory
Forming Impressions

MAC IntroPsych

Covariation Theory
Forming Impressions

MAC IntroPsych

Distinctiveness
Forming Impressions

MAC IntroPsych

An individual is more likely to make the fundamental attribution error when determining causes of others' behaviour rather than their own. As the actor, an individual is better aware of the situational factors contributing to their behaviour. However, when observing others, an individual will assume another's current behaviour is representative of that person. **Example:** An individual is more likely to attribute their own speeding to situational factors such as being late while attributing the speeding of others to dispositional factors such as being aggressive drivers. **Personal Example:**	The tendency for an individual to assume that they are better than the average person and will not face similar challenges or failures. This results in an exaggerated view of one's own abilities. **Example:** Despite being aware of the risks of drunk driving, some individuals may still drive when intoxicated, claiming that, "Other people get into accidents. I won't." **Personal Example:**
The variable in covariation theory that asks how others would behave in the same way in a given situation. **Example:** If other people would agree with Jim's decision to give presents to his coworkers when he was promoted, the behaviour is likely situational. If other people would not agree with his decision and would not repeat the behaviour themselves, then the behaviour is likely dispositional. **Personal Example:**	Judgments that tie together a cause and effect. Example: If you see someone you recognize, the effect is the feeling of fluency or familiarity. Upon feeling the effect of fluency, you use attribution to investigate the cause for this effect, or how you know the individual. **Personal Example:**
An attribution theory proposed by Jones and Davis, stating that we actively analyze a person's behaviour to make inferences or attributions based on three factors. These are the degree of choice, expectation, and intended consequences. **Personal Example:**	The variable in covariation theory that asks whether an individual usually behaves the same way in a given situation. **Example:** If Lisa always comes to work angry and upset, the behaviour is consistent and one could attribute it to dispositional causes. If Lisa usually comes to work smiling and friendly, the angry behaviour is inconsistent and likely to be attributed to situational causes. **Personal Example:**
The variable in covariation theory that asks whether an individual behaves differently in different situations than the given situation. **Example:** Han always makes time to play with his children. If Han makes time to play with and be nice to all children, his behaviour is likely dispositional. If Han frowns and gets upset by other children, his behaviour is likely situational. **Personal Example:**	An attribution theory proposed by Kelley that is used to determine if a person's behaviour is due to situational or dispositional factors. It is based on three variables: consistency, distinctiveness, and consensus. **Personal Example:**

Familiarity
Forming Impressions

MAC IntroPsych

Fundamental Attribution Error
Forming Impressions

MAC IntroPsych

Others' Opinions
Forming Impressions

MAC IntroPsych

Physical Attractiveness
Forming Impressions

MAC IntroPsych

Proximity
Forming Impressions

MAC IntroPsych

Self-Serving Bias
Forming Impressions

MAC IntroPsych

MAC IntroPsych

MAC IntroPsych

The finding that people often overestimate dispositional causes for others' behaviour, while underestimating situational causes. People are more likely to make this error when determining the causes of others' behaviour rather than their own. **Example:** If a cashier is rude to you, you may think that they are generally a very rude person (dispositional). However, their boss may have just let them know that the company was laying off several people, thus putting them in a bad mood (situational). **Personal Example:**	One of the factors influencing attraction. Individuals are more likely to be attracted to people and/or things that are more familiar, even if they have only been seen a few times in the past. **Example:** When judging the sound of a baby name, parents may be more likely to like a name that they have previously heard over a brand new, unusual name. **Personal Example:**
One of the factors influencing attractiveness. Individuals are more likely to be attracted to someone they perceive as being physically attractive. This is done on the presumption that what is beautiful is also good. **Example:** People who are physically attractive are often judged as kinder, warmer and more intelligent. **Personal Example:**	One of the factors influencing attraction. Individuals are more likely to be attracted to those who have already expressed that they like them. This is especially true of individuals with low self-esteem. **Example:** You may be more likely to like someone who has expressed their like for you, especially if it was right after you failed your driver's test. **Personal Example:**
The tendency to perceive yourself favourably. **Example:** Even if everybody in a class gets an 80% or higher on a midterm, you are more likely to attribute your success to your own intelligence, instead of simply saying the test was easy. **Personal Example:**	One of the factors influencing attractiveness. Individuals are more likely to be attracted to or become friends with people they work or live closely with. There is not only high proximity (physical closeness) but also high probability of interaction (functional distance). **Example:** You are more likely to be attracted to the friend you sit beside in class whom you talk to and study with than the person who sits directly in front of you to whom you've never spoken. **Personal Example:**

INFLUENCE OF OTHERS

"I was not surprised that it happened. I have exact, parallel pictures of prisoners with bags over their heads."
- Dr. Philip Zimbardo, comparing the Abu Ghraib prison conditions to his infamous Stanford Prison study.

In this week's web modules, we will explore some fascinating experiments in which subjects under controlled settings could be made to act in strange and sometimes sadistic ways. We like to think that our own behaviour (guided by dispositional factors) would prevent us from acting as many subjects did in these experiments. Are such findings applicable to real world settings? Outside of the lab, can ordinary people be made to act in bizarre ways at the command of another person? The scene was a busy Kentucky Fried Chicken restaurant in an affluent Manchester, New Hampshire neighbourhood. A young supervisor was overseeing his energetic staff through the lunchtime rush when he received a call directly from corporate headquarters. This was unusual in itself, but the message from corporate executive Jeff Anderson was even more unusual. Jeff calmly explained that a toxic chemical had been released from the overhead sprinkler system. He ordered the supervisor to gather all the employees. Over the speakerphone, Jeff explained that everyone must strip down and urinate on each other to neutralize the chemical. To encourage the employees, at one point Jeff said, "I need you to be strong, I need you to be brave and do exactly what I say." Police arrived in the parking lot to witness a strange scene of several naked people, panicking and soaked in each other's urine. In fact, there was no toxic chemical and the employees were never in any danger. Jeff Anderson turned out to be a prankster named "Dex" who had perpetrated several such deceptions and posted them on the Internet. Authorities in several US cities are considering whether Dex should be charged and extradited to face trial.

Verma, S. (2009, Aug. 8). Criminal or comedy? Online anonymity lets cruel pranksters take jokes too far. *Globe and Mail*, 1-2.

Haney, C, Banks, W.C., & Zimbardo, P.G. (1973). Interpersonal dynamics in a simulated prison. *International Journal of Criminology and Penology, 1*, 69-97.

Weekly Checklist:

- ☐ **Web Modules to watch: Influence of Others 1 and 2**
- ☐ **Readings: Chapter 9**
- ☐ **Avenue Quiz 10**

Upper Year Courses:

If you enjoyed the content in this week's module, consider taking the following upper year courses:

- PSYCH 2C03 Social Psychology
- PSYCH 3AC3 Human Sexuality

Influence of Others I – Outline

Unit 2: Presence of Others

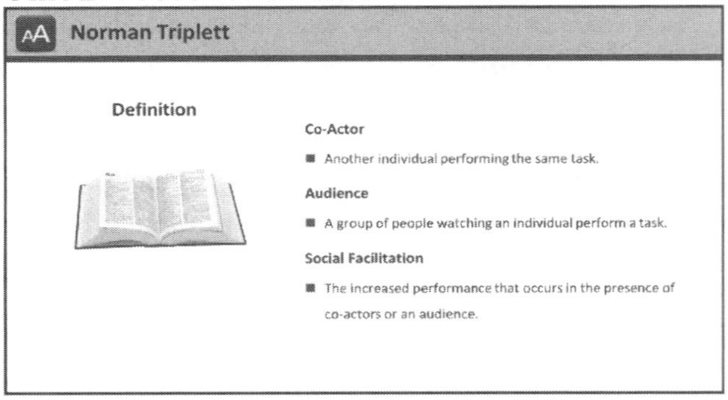

Norman Triplett conducted systematic studies to demonstrate that people behave differently in the presence of others.

Triplett's findings: observed that cyclists raced faster when competing against eachother in a group, compared to racing against the clock or an individual time trial
• noted children would wind fishing rod faster when other children were present

Complications of Triplett's hypothesis: some evidence showed the presence of others could hinder performance on tasks such as learning nonsense syllables

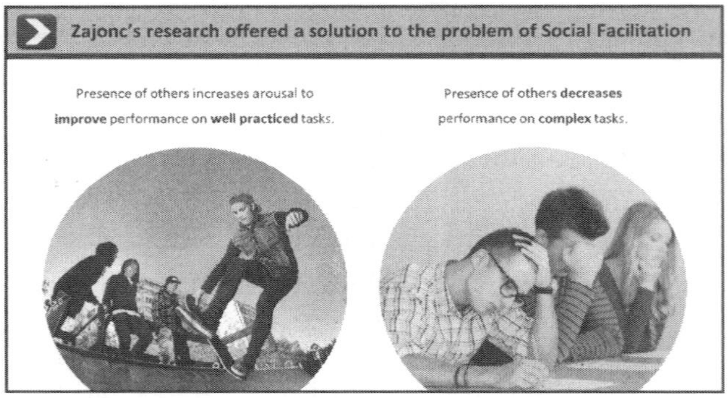

Describe Zajonc's resolution of conflicting data from social facilitation studies: the important factor to consider is that the presence of others increases arousal
• how this heightened arousal effects performance depends on the

Unit 3: Social Learning Theory

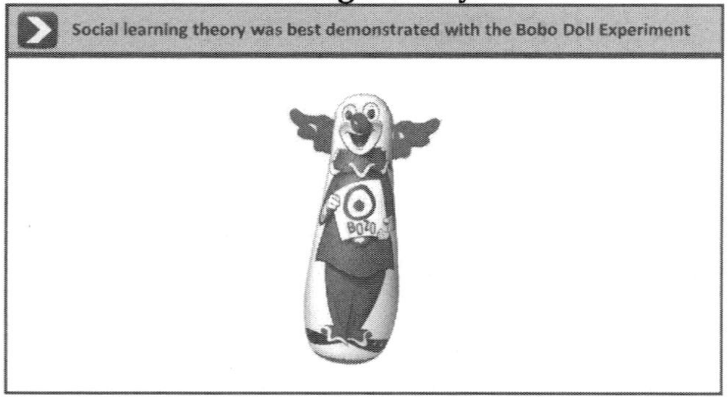

Albert Bandura, a proponent of Social Learning Theory, suggested that we learn our behaviours from those around us.

Describe how Social Learning Theory can be differentiated from conditioning:
because the behaviours you learn from others do not always require explicit reinforcement to develop

What were the main findings from the Bobo Doll experiment and its follow up?
children who previously viewed aggressive play model were much more likely to subsequently display aggressive play to the bobo doll
• aggressive behaviour was spontaneous with no reinforcement

Unit 4: Conformity

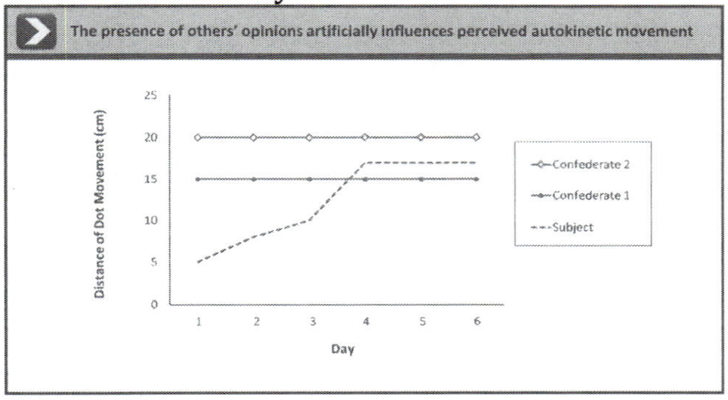

Muzafer Sherif studied norm formation and conformity using the autokinetic effect.

Describe the autokinetic effect: a stationary light in a pitch black room will appear to move about randomly, because as your eyes scan the scene you mistake the movement of the image of your retina as actual motion of the light

Describe Sherif's experimental setup: on day one you are by yourself, on day 2 you are with others in the room and all say how much you think the light moved

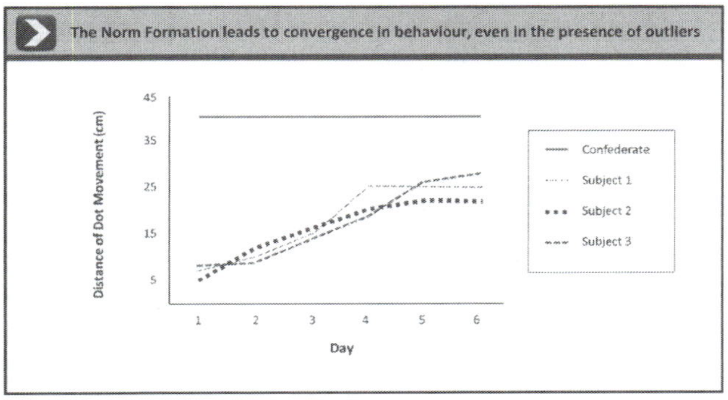

What were the results of Sherif's experiments?
- after several days of testing your responses will gradually converge with the others, despite the different starting points of the individual participants
- norm formation: a powerful effect that can be further manipulated by the experimenter

Solomon Asch furthered Sherif's research by determining why individuals conform to group pressures.

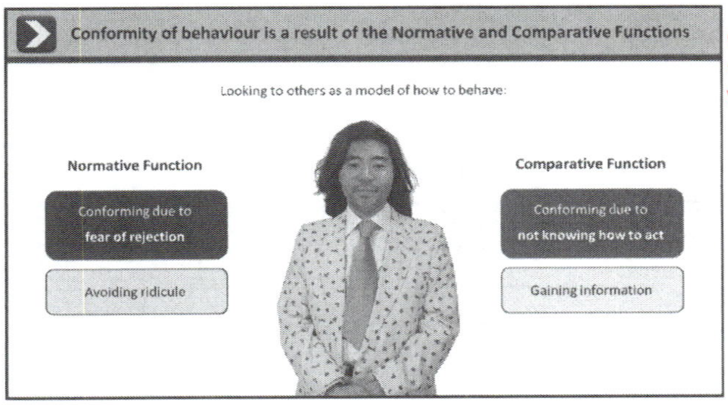

normative function: the role of others in setting standards for our conduct based on a fear of rejection

comparative function: the role of others in providing information about an ambiguous situation

only 1 real participant

Describe Asch's experimental setup: seated in a room with a group of individuals, see one sample line and 3 comparison lines and identify which comparison matched the standard

What were the results of Asch's experiments?
- when confederates chose incorrect answers the participant would change their answer
- 75% of participants conform to an incorrect answer on at least one trial, 37% of the responses conformed to a clearly wrong answer

Describe the difference between normative and comparative functions: comparative describes when we conform because we don't know how to act in a situation and it helps us gain information, normative describes when we conform from fear of rejection

Unit 5: Group Dynamics

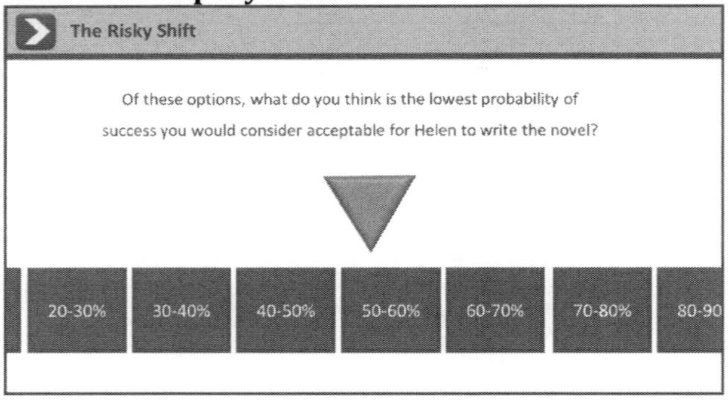

James Stoner systematically studied group decision making to determine how group decisions differ from those made individually.

Describe Stoner's experimental setup: studied that groups were more cautious than individuals
• asking individuals to read a set of hypothetical situations and make risk assessments, the individuals then come together and come to a consensus

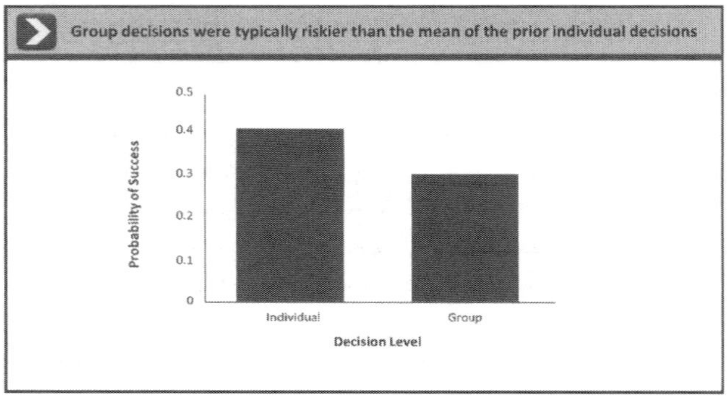

Describe the Risky Shift and the types of situations where it is a concern: group decisions were riskier than the mean decision of the individuals before the group discussion

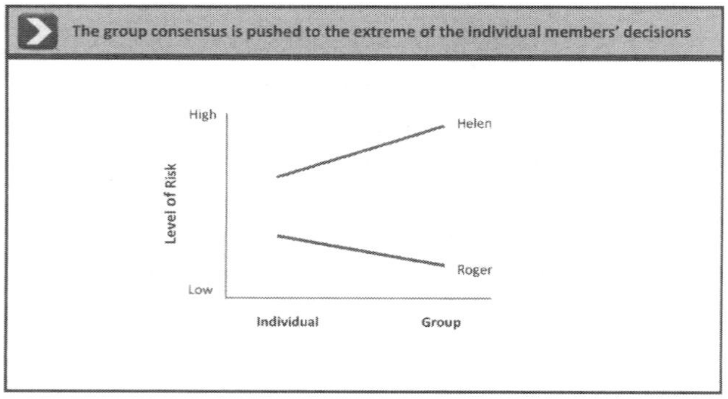

Group Polarization: decision making strengthens the original inclinations of the individual group members

How does the concept of Group Polarization provide a better explanation of group decision making when compared to the Risky Shift? shows that decision making cannot only become riskier, but sometimes also more cautious as a result of the group process

Groupthink

Definition

Groupthink

- A group decision making environment that occurs when group cohesiveness becomes so strong it overrides realistic appraisals of reality and alternative opinions.

Describe Groupthink and its implications:

groupthink: a group decision-making environment that occurs when group cohesiveness becomes so strong it overrides realistic appraisals of reality and alternative opinions.
• people victim to group think believe they are always right and all other groups are wrong
• they censor dissenting opinions and those who disagree are rejected

Groupthink powerfully influences the group's perception of themselves in the world

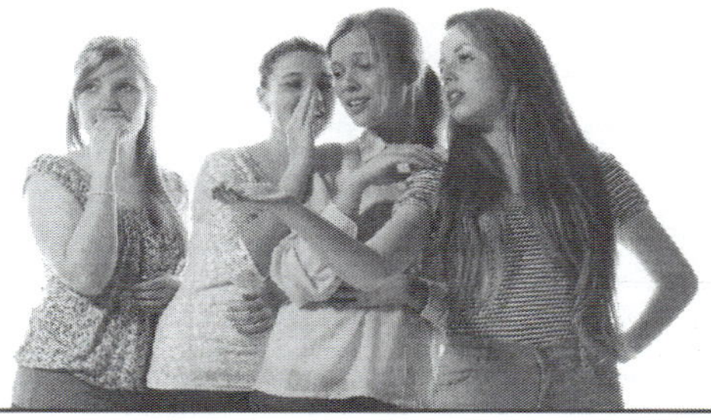

What are some ways in which Groupthink can be prevented?

1. be impartial; group leaders should never endorse a particular position from the outset
2. encourage critical evaluation and allow group members to disagree; assign "devil's advocate", the present counterarguments
3. subdivide the group; come to seperate decisions then reuniting to discuss differences
4. call a second chance meeting to air any lingering doubts

Unit 6: The Bystander Effect

Two Decisions

Definition

Collective Ignorance

- When each individual in a group see nobody responding in a given situation, they conclude that the situation is not an emergency.

Describe supporting evidence for the concept Collective Ignorance and how it influences bystanders: collective ignorance: when each individual in a group see nobody responding in a given situation, they conclude that the situation is not an emergency

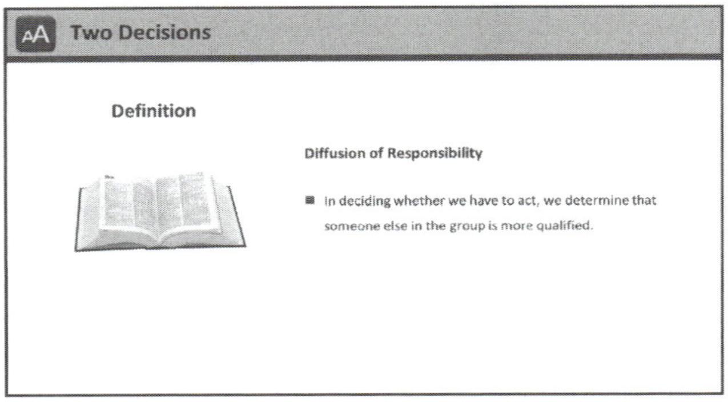

Describe supporting evidence for the concept of Diffusion of Responsibility and its influence on bystanders: if there are many others around, particularly anyone with special skills, you are less likely to act

How can individuals ensure they receive help when needed? the best thing is to be direct

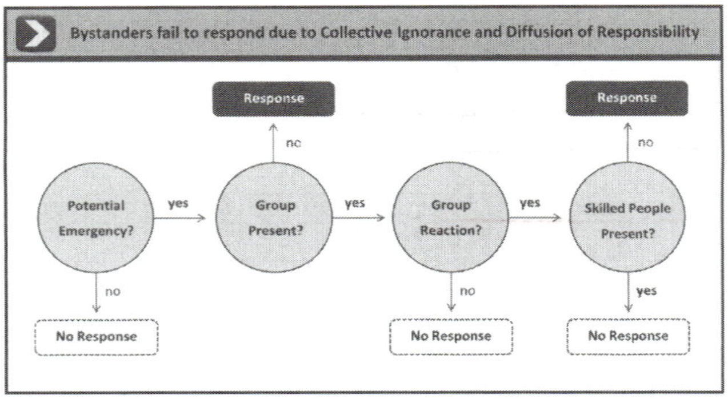

Describe how the concept of Social Loafing is related to Diffusion of Responsibility and provide evidence supporting this phenomenon: Social loafing: individuals seem to be less motivated when working in a group than when working alone

We put in less effort when we think others will "pick up the slack"

- participants made less noise as the group size increased
- we diffuse responsibility in all situations

Influence of Others I – Courseware Exercise

On January 28th 1986, the Space Shuttle Challenger broke apart just after lift-off, resulting in disintegration of the shuttle and the deaths of all crewmembers on board. Though the disaster was due to a faulty O-ring seal, further investigation revealed that NASA's decision-making process had been seriously flawed. The project managers had known about the faulty design 9 years before the launch, but failed to correctly address the problem. Furthermore, NASA engineers had warned their managers that launching on a cold morning, as they did, could be disastrous for the space shuttle. However, these managers failed to act on and report this information to their superiors.

The Rogers Commission Report was created in order to investigate the incident and offer suggestions to NASA for future space missions. You are encouraged to do a bit of extra research on the Challenger disaster and the Rogers Commission recommendations.

Knowing that a large group of people were working on this one project and having learned about the dynamics of group work, what do you think was at the root of NASA's problematic decision-making process?

____

____

____

Plan out a course of action for decision-making that NASA could have taken, incorporating all of the solutions to prevent groupthink that were presented in the web module.

____

____

____

____

____

____

Influence of Others I – Review Questions

1) What did Triplett observe regarding bicycle racers? What theory was proposed?
    a. Why was Triplett's conclusion not enough?
    b. Describe Zajonc's contribution.

2) Why is Bandura's Bobo Doll experiment important?

3) Describe Sherif's study on Norm Formation (basic methods and results).

4) Describe Solomon Asch's famous experiment on conformity.

5) Describe Deutsch and Gerard's modification to Asch's experiment.

6) Outline the difference between the normative and comparative functions of a group.

7) What is group polarization? How does it compare to the risky shift?

8) What do Darley and Latane's results suggest about helping behaviour in groups?
    a. What is diffusion of responsibility and how can it be broken?

9) What is social loafing?

Influence of Others I – Quiz Question

Which of the following is a major difference between collective ignorance and diffusion of responsibility?

a) Collective ignorance is a form of group decision-making that results in a strong opinion without taking into account alternate options, whereas diffusion of responsibility is a lack of response while in a group of individuals to an emergency. (9%)
b) Collective ignorance occurs when analyzing a situation, whereas diffusion of responsibility occurs when choosing whether to respond to a situation. (69%)
c) Collective ignorance involves concluding a situation is not an emergency due to the absence of emergency personnel present, whereas diffusion of responsibility involves not responding to a situation. (18%)
d) Collective ignorance involves ignoring all situations that do not have personal involvement, whereas diffusion of responsibility is placing the blame on others when you failed to respond. (4%)

This is a question from a previous Psychology 1X03 Influence of Others Avenue Quiz. This question is testing students' understanding of collective ignorance and diffusion of responsibility. In order to correctly answer this question, it is important to understand that collective ignorance occurs when an individual is unsure if the situation is an emergency and looks to others for an indication of the appropriate course of action. Diffusion of responsibility, on the other hand, occurs when an individual has determined that the situation is an emergency, but is unsure whether they should get involved or wait for another person to help. If we look at each option in turn, we will see that only one of these options fits that description:

A. This is clearly not describing collective ignorance as we just defined it; in fact, it is more closely describing the risky shift and other aspects of group dynamics. Option A does, however, correctly describe diffusion of responsibility.
B. This option appears to fit our description of these phenomena but, as is often the case in IntroPsych tests it does not use the exact definition, forcing students to draw their own conclusions and apply the concepts. (**Correct!**)
C. This option is a very tempting choice and misleads 18% of students, but there is one aspect of this option that makes it incorrect. When collective ignorance occurs, people in the situation do not base their judgement of whether it is an emergency on the presence of emergency personnel.
D. This is also an obvious misrepresentation of these two phenomena based on our previous definition. It is incorrect.

We can see after examining all the possible choices that **option B** best outlines the differences between collective ignorance and diffusion of responsibility.

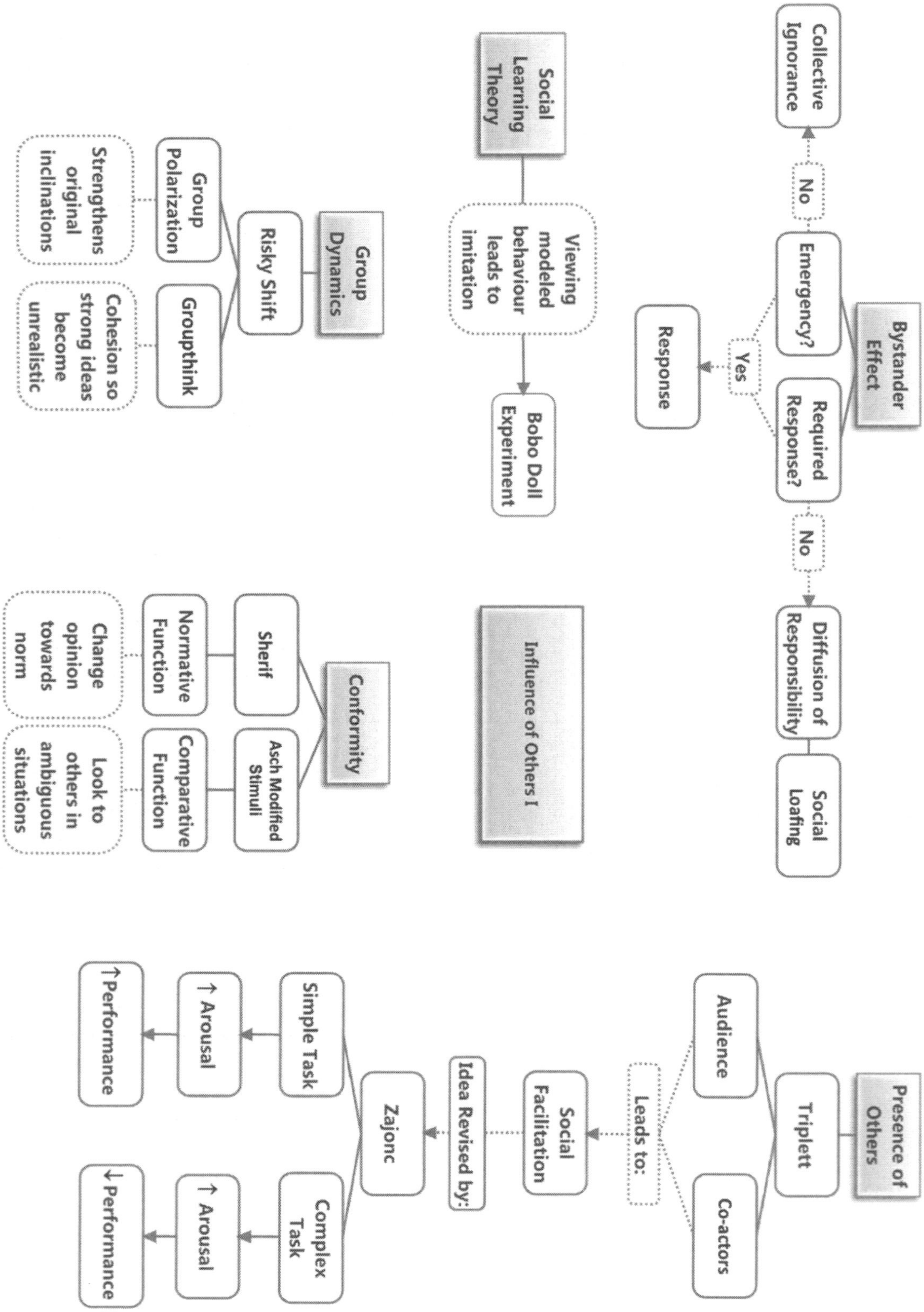
Influence of Others I
Bystander Effect
Emergency?
Required Response?
No
Collective Ignorance
Yes
Response
No
Diffusion of Responsibility
Social Loafing
Social Learning Theory
Viewing modeled behaviour leads to imitation
Bobo Doll Experiment
Group Dynamics
Risky Shift
Group Polarization
Strengthens original inclinations
Groupthink
Cohesion so strong ideas become unrealistic
Conformity
Sherif
Normative Function
Change opinion towards norm
Asch Modified Stimuli
Comparative Function
Look to others in ambiguous situations
Presence of Others
Triplett
Audience
Co-actors
Leads to:
Social Facilitation
Idea Revised by:
Zajonc
Simple Task
↑ Arousal
↑Performance
Complex Task
↑ Arousal
↓ Performance

Influence of Others II – Outline

Unit 2: Obedience

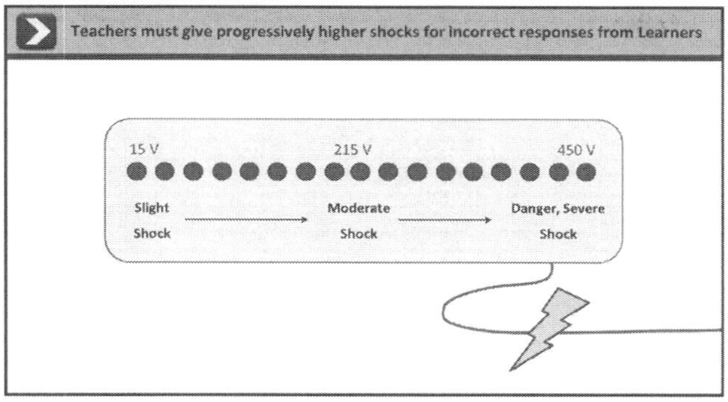

Stanley Milgram's experiment elucidated the effects of authority on human behaviour.

Milgram's experimental setup: experiment explains that the purpose of the study is to examine the effect of punishment on learning

- one participant is the teacher and the other is the learner
- learner is a confederate of the study
- each time learner gives an incorrect answer they are shocked
- learner starts to complain, and that his heart is bothering him
- learner stops responding but you must continue

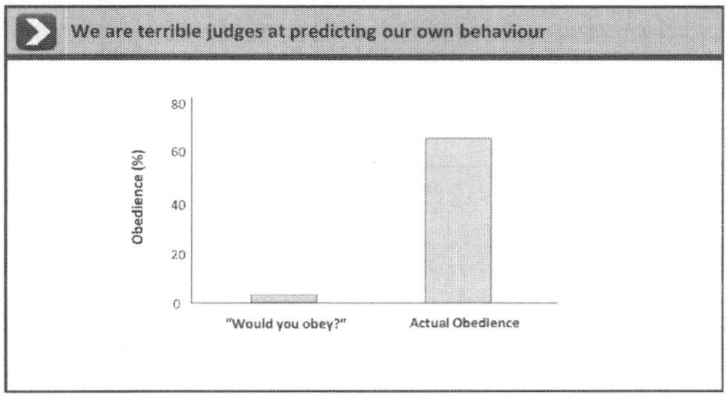

Results from Milgram's original shock experiment: 65% of participants continued to the very end of the experiment

Implications of Milgram's experiment:

- a very strong tendency of obedience to authority, even if this power is limited
- you are not always an accurate judge of how you would behave in a given situation ← 65%

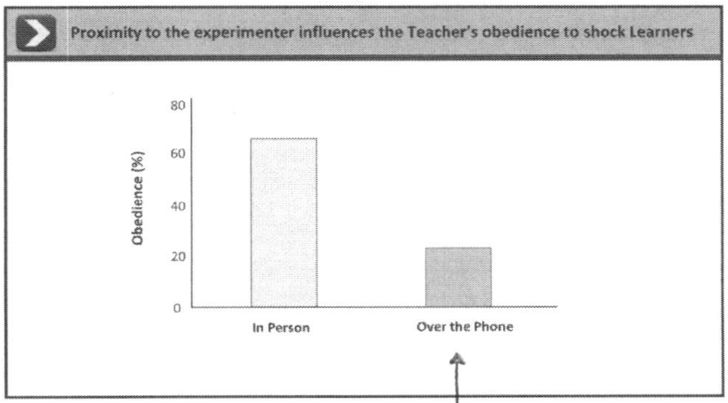

↑ 25% of participants obeyed

How did Milgram change his original design and how did these manipulations impact the results? moved site to a rundown office in a commercial part of town, participants that obeyed dropped from 65% to about 50%

- another variation is a student was the superior, obedience dropped even more here
- one was the learner was in another room but the teacher could see them, or the teacher and learner were in the same room, or the teacher had to place the learners hand on the shock electrode, less participants obeyed in this setting
- experimenter was out of the room and orders were through the phone

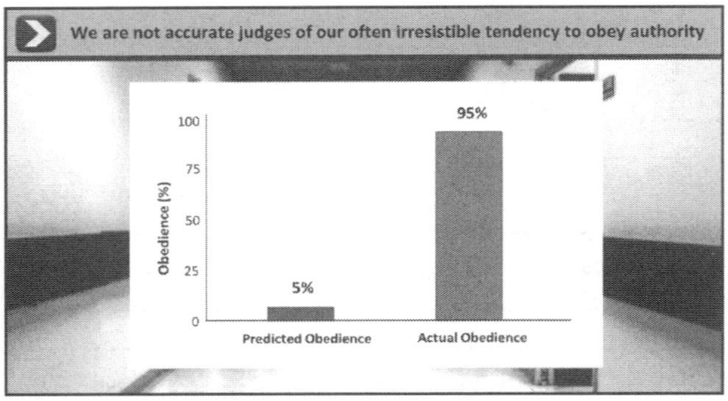

Describe the study by Hofling et al. and how it demonstrates the power of authority in a real world setting: fake doctor called a real nurse saying to administer a large dose of a fake drug to the patient who was also fake. if doing so the nurse would be violating many rules

- 95% nursing students said they would not obey but 21 of the 22 nurses obeyed

Unit 3: Cognitive Dissonance

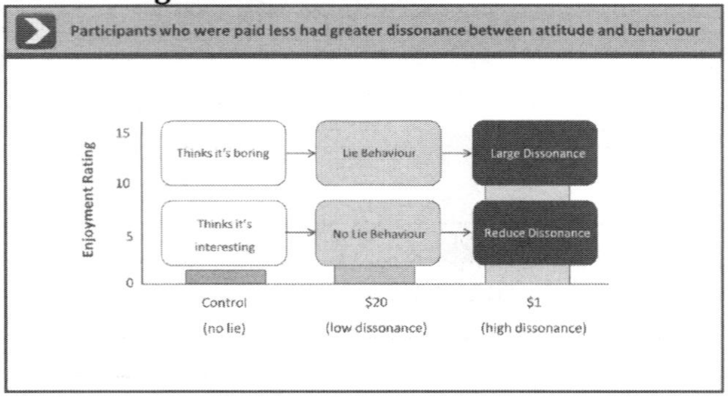

What is cognitive dissonance? a state of psychological discomfort brought on by conflict between a person's attitudes and their behaviour

How did the experiment conducted by Festinger and Carlsmith produce cognitive dissonance in participants? when they tell the next participant it was exciting when they didn't believe that creates an inconsistency between their attitudes and behaviour that produces an uncomfortable feeling called dissonance

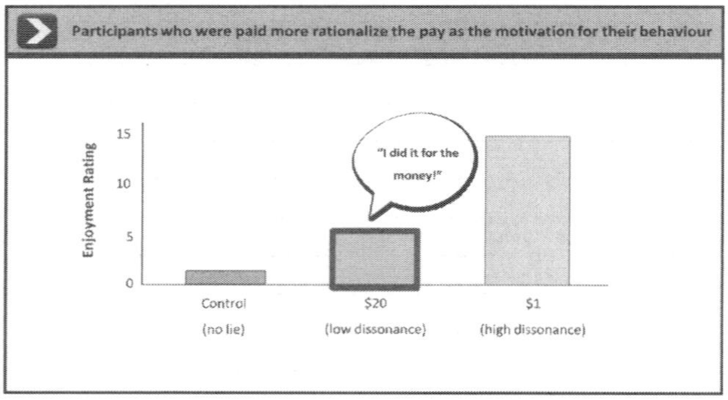

Why did participants receiving less money rate the experiment as more enjoyable? those who got 20$ convinced themselves they lied for the money instead of 1$ participants who could not change their action so instead changed their attitude

What are overjustification effects? the resolution of cognitive dissonance as conflict in behaviour and attitude are justified by some external means

Unit 4: The Stanford Prison Experiment

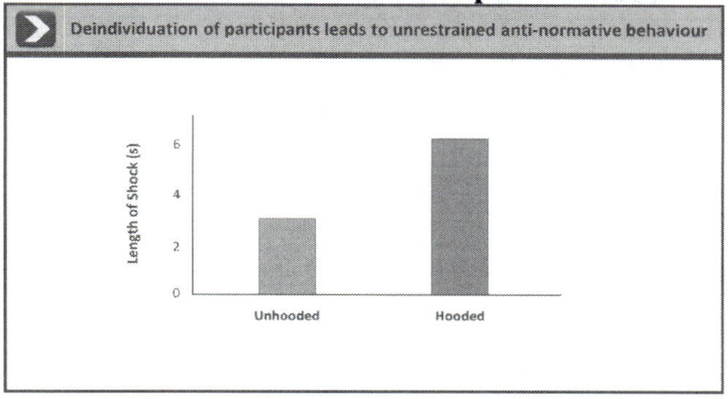

Describe the Stanford Prison Experiment: 24 participants were selected to check on criminal background and cognitive screens for psychopathology, those assigned as prisoners were told some civil liberties would be suspended, participants as guards had to keep order in the prison

In what manner did deindividuation contribute to the results? deindividuation: in a group situation, the loss of a sense of personal responsibility and restraint

- guards were able to lose their sense of personal responsibility resulting in behaviour that wouldn't normally occur

Unit 5: Persuasion

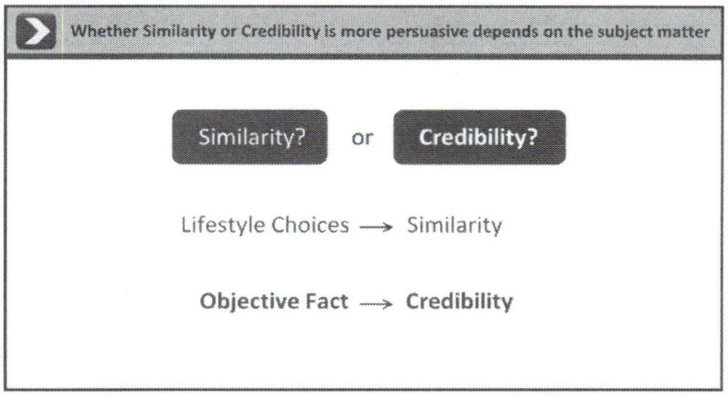

Several factors play a role in determining whether an individual can persuade others to behave in a certain manner.

Describe specific traits that may enhance a communicator's persuasiveness: most persuasive communicators are those with high credibility

- physical attractiveness
- drawn to communicators that look and sound like you

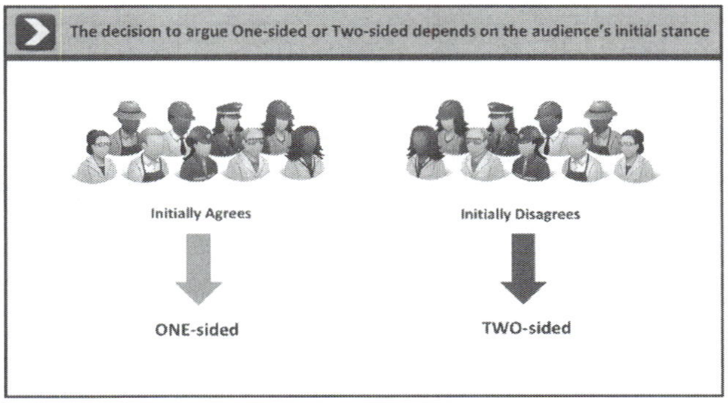

How can an audience's inclinations influence the contents of a persuasive message?

- if your audience initially agrees a 1 sided argument is most effective
- if your audience initially disagrees, a 2 sided argument is most effective
- in a 2 sided argument you acknowledge the opposing opinion, respond the resent arguments for why your position may be better

The Audience

Definition

Central Appeal

- Well reasoned, factual, two-sided arguments.
- Effective for academic audiences.

Peripheral Appeal

- Well presented, easy to understand messages.
- Effective for non-academic audiences.

How do the characteristics of the audience impact the contents of the message?

central appeal - well reasoned, factual, two-sided arguments, effective for academic audiences
peripheral appeal - well presented, easy to understand, effective for non-academic

Unit 6: Techniques in Persuasion

The Foot in the Door Effect

- Assumed identity of an authority figure.
- Established credibility using police jargon.
- Used a gradual escalation of demands to increase compliance - **"Foot in the door effect"**.

Describe the Foot in the Door Effect and evidence supporting this phenomenon:

- foot in door effect: named after door to door salesman who tried to lure in customers with small requests
- a request that seems outrageous in isolation is seen as being less unreasonable if it follows previous requests of escalating magnitude

The Low-Ball Technique

Definition

Low Ball Technique

- An escalation of the terms of an agreement after someone has already agreed to comply.

Describe the Low-Ball Technique and evidence supporting this phenomenon:

low ball technique - an escalation of the terms of an agreement after someone has already agreed to comply

What are some differences between the Foot in the Door Technique and the Low-Ball?

Influence of Others II – Courseware Exercise

You've now learned about persuasion and how people can be convinced by others. This area of psychology has many practical applications, from conflict management to motivational speaking and from politics to marketing.

Imagine that you have been hired to design an advertising campaign for a small business that produces Psychology textbooks for university students. They want to become well-known to increase sales and have thus given you complete creative freedom to help them do so. You first decide to put together a commercial for the company. Using the principles that you learned in lecture, detail your plans for the commercial.

Who is your communicator? What should they look like? Should they be credible or similar? Do they have any important personality traits?

____

____

Consider your message. Should it be one-sided or two-sided? What type of appeal should be used and why?

____

____

Who is your audience? Are you appealing to a specific subpopulation of university students? What salient characteristics of your audience will be important to keep in mind?

____

____

Following the first phase of the advertising campaign, the company has done a bit of market research. Unfortunately, this small company must charge 10% more than a larger rival company. Research showed that 80% of students who bought textbooks from the small company felt some anxiety afterwards at having spent so much when they knew they were on a tight budget. Afraid of losing these customers to the larger company during textbook season next term, the company enlists your help for the second phase of the advertising campaign.

How might you use cognitive dissonance to your advantage and address this issue in your campaign? (hint: you don't want these students to change their behaviour, so you must influence an attitude change)

____

____

____

Influence of Others II – Review Questions

1) Describe Stanley Milgram's obedience experiment setup.
   a. What were the results of this experiment?
   b. What are some possible factors contributing to Milgram's result?
   c. What are the implications of this experiment?

2) In Festinger and Carlsmith's cognitive dissonance experiment, why did the $1 group rate the experiment more positively than the $20 group? Explain using cognitive dissonance and overjustification.

3) Describe the setup of the Stanford Prison Experiment.
   a. What were the results of this prison experiment?
   b. What are the implications of this experiment?

4) What makes a persuasive communicator?

5) Is a two-sided message better than one-sided?

6) What is the difference between central and peripheral appeal? When should either be used?

7) Describe the "Foot in the Door" technique. How is the Foot in the Door related to the Low-Ball technique? Use your own example to illustrate the differences between the two.

Influence of Others II – Quiz Question

Jeffrey is an artist who has created an unusual t-shirt design that may not appeal to everyone. While it does not resemble other popular designs, he would still like to get feedback to use to promote further sales. According to **cognitive dissonance theory**, which of the following marketing schemes would lead to Jeffrey receiving the most positive feedback?

a) Charging $20 per t-shirt with Jeffrey's design, allowing him to make a profit. (37%)
b) Charging $5 per t-shirt with Jeffrey's design, informing customers it's to cover the cost of the t-shirt only. (22%)
c) Giving the first 10 t-shirts away for free in hopes of better reviews. (15%)
d) Paying the first ten individuals $5 to take a t-shirt and provide feedback. (27%)

This question is from a previous Influence of Others I & II Avenue Quiz. It is a question that many students struggled with, so let us examine what the question is asking more closely. Jeffrey is trying to use cognitive dissonance theory to gain *positive* feedback for his t-shirt design. Cognitive dissonance occurs when one's behaviours do not match their attitude and can be anxiety-producing.

Looking at our options, we can see:

A. In this case, the customers must pay $20 for the t-shirt. The behaviour of paying that amount of money indicates that they must like the shirt; therefore, it would create cognitive dissonance if they provided negative feedback for the design—"Why would I pay $20 for the shirt if I didn't like it? It must be amazing!" Therefore, individuals in this situation are most likely to provide positive feedback because of cognitive dissonance. (**Correct!**)
B. In this option, the customer providing feedback is forced to pay for the shirt, but it is a small amount and only covers the cost of the shirt. It is possible, in this case, that the person does not like the shirt very much, but the behaviour of paying $5 is not enough to shift their attitude that they don't like the shirt. Therefore, the customer may not feel too much dissonance when giving mediocre or negative feedback. This is not the best answer.
C. In this option, accepting a free shirt does not mean the person likes the t-shirt design at all. They have not gone out of their way to obtain the t-shirt. Therefore, producing mediocre or negative feedback won't create any cognitive dissonance with their behaviour of accepting a free shirt.
D. This option involves the audience being paid to accept a t-shirt and provide feedback, so they again did not go out of their way to obtain the shirt. Again, there will be no cognitive dissonance between accepting money and providing negative feedback—their attitude cannot be misaligned with being paid to accept a shirt.

As a result, **option A** is the correct answer.

Key Terms

Asch's Stimuli	Comparative Function	Normative Function
Audience	Deindividuation	Overjustification Effects
Bobo Doll Experiment	Foot in the Door Effect	Peripheral Appeal
Bystander Effect	Group Polarization	Persuasion
Central Appeal	Groupthink	Risky Shift
Co-Actor	Low-Ball Effect	Social Loafing
Cognitive Dissonance	Message	Stanford Prison Experiment
Communicator	Milgram Experiment	Zajonc's Resolution

Influence of Others I & II – Bottleneck Concepts

Normative vs. Comparative Function
Cognitive Dissonance
Foot in the Door Effect vs. Low-Ball Effect
The Bystander Effect

Normative vs. Comparative Function

Both normative and comparative functions describe ways in which others can influence our behaviour in a group setting. The normative function comes into play when, due to a fear of rejection, we conform to what others are doing. This may lead us to perform actions and behave in ways that are contrary to our beliefs. The influence of normative function can be evident in fashion trends, peer pressure to consume alcohol and drugs, and listening to certain types of popular music.

The comparative function, on the other hand, happens in ambiguous situations where we do not know what to do. To determine an appropriate response, we often observe others' behaviours and act accordingly. This can be seen when students receive an essay assignment without an explicit page limit. To determine approximately how many pages they should write, students will often resort to asking their peers. In this case, the peers provide information in an ambiguous situation. Importantly, students in this scenario are not conforming due to a fear of rejection. Other examples of the comparative function include: comparing your answers with a group of friends when completing a practice midterm, copying others' dance moves when you are uncertain of your own, and following a crowd during a fire drill because you do not know the location of the fire exit.

To differentiate between the normative and comparative functions, determine whether the subject is following others due to a fear of rejection or because he does not know what to do in that situation.

Test your Understanding

1) Identify if the following situations are an example of the normative or comparative functions and explain why.

a) Students at Creekside High School were asked to vote anonymously between two bands to play at their graduation. Since Karly did not know either band, she asked her friends which band they would vote for and ended up voting for the same band.

b) Trevor has a severe fear of heights preventing him from going on roller coasters at amusement parks. One day, Trevor visited the park with all his friends who were especially excited to ride the roller coaster. Trevor, not wanting to look wimpy and afraid, decided to give the roller coaster a shot.

2) Explain why in Deutsch and Gerard's (1955) manipulation of Asch's stimuli experiment, the researchers demonstrated the comparative function as opposed to the normative function.

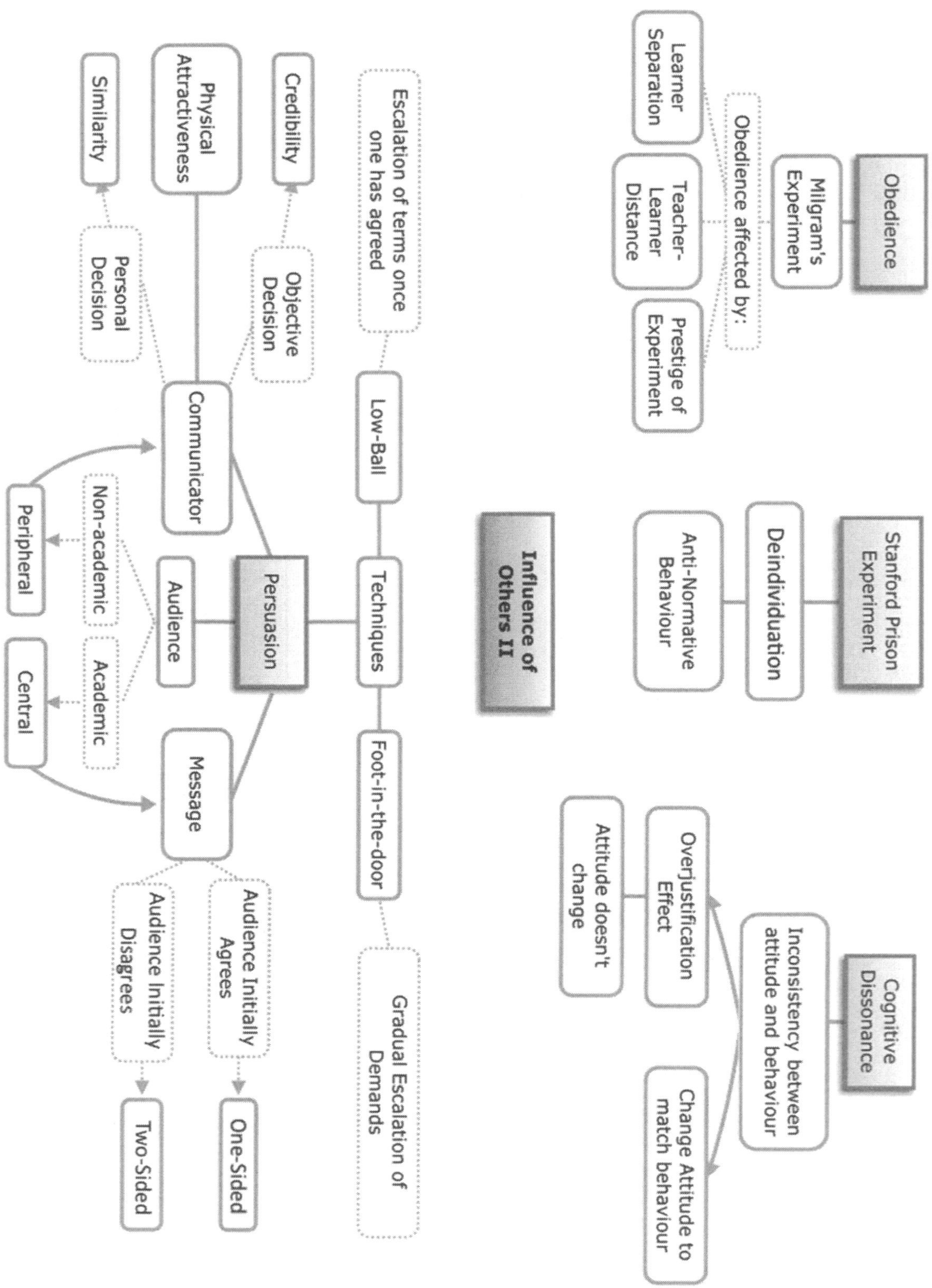
Influence of Others II
Obedience
Milgram's Experiment
Obedience affected by:
Learner Separation
Teacher-Learner Distance
Prestige of Experiment
Stanford Prison Experiment
Deindividuation
Anti-Normative Behaviour
Cognitive Dissonance
Inconsistency between attitude and behaviour
Overjustification Effect
Attitude doesn't change
Change Attitude to match behaviour
Persuasion
Techniques
Low-Ball
Escalation of terms once one has agreed
Foot-in-the-door
Gradual Escalation of Demands
Communicator
Credibility
Objective Decision
Physical Attractiveness
Similarity
Personal Decision
Audience
Non-academic
Peripheral
Academic
Central
Message
Audience Initially Agrees
One-Sided
Audience Initially Disagrees
Two-Sided

Asch's Stimuli
Influence of Others

MAC IntroPsych

Audience
Influence of Others

MAC IntroPsych

Bobo Doll Experiment
Influence of Others

MAC IntroPsych

Bystander Effect
Influence of Others

MAC IntroPsych

Central Appeal
Influence of Others

MAC IntroPsych

Co-Actor
Influence of Others

MAC IntroPsych

Cognitive Dissonance
Influence of Others

MAC IntroPsych

Communicator
Influence of Others

MAC IntroPsych

A group of people watching an individual perform a task, which can enhance or hinder the performance of the actor.
Example: During a concert recital, a famous cello player may find that they perform better in front of a large audience than when by themselves.
Personal Example:

Solomon Asch's experiment in which a participant (among confederates) was required to identify which of three lines matched a standard in length. If all confederates in the experiment gave an incorrect response, the participant would conform and agree despite it being obviously incorrect.
Personal Example:

A phenomenon in which individuals do not offer help to a victim in an emergency situation when they think others are present.
Example: If an individual views someone being harassed when many other people are present, they are less likely to offer help than if they were the only person around.
Personal Example:

An experiment performed by Albert Bandura, in which a child would model an adult's behaviour when playing with a bobo doll. If the adult exhibited aggressive or passive play, the child modeled the same behaviour, without any explicit reinforcement required.
Personal Example:

Another individual performing the same task as someone, often influencing performance through social facilitation.
Example: If an individual is bowling, his or her performance may be increased if they are competing against other bowlers.
Personal Example:

Well-reasoned, factual, two-sided arguments that are effective for intelligent audiences.
Example: When trying to persuade a group of academics, factual and two-sided arguments will be a more successful form of persuasion.
Personal Example:

The person persuading another. The higher the credibility or attractiveness of the communicator, the more likely they are to persuade another individual. Additionally, a communicator who has more in common with an individual is more likely to persuade them.
Example: An attractive communicator of similar age to yourself may be the most persuasive communicator in persuading you to buy a new car.
Personal Example:

A psychologically uncomfortable state that occurs when a person's attitude and behaviour are inconsistent. Cognitive dissonance must be resolved by changing one's attitude as one's behaviour cannot change after the fact.
Example: Christa exercises regularly and is a huge advocate of healthy living. If she were to eat unhealthy foods, she would likely resolve her cognitive dissonance by convincing herself that sticking to a strict, healthy diet is not her main priority.
Personal Example:

Comparative Function
Influence of Others

MAC IntroPsych

Deindividuation
Influence of Others

MAC IntroPsych

Foot in the Door Effect
Influence of Others

MAC IntroPsych

Group Polarization
Influence of Others

MAC IntroPsych

Groupthink
Influence of Others

MAC IntroPsych

Low-Ball Effect
Influence of Others

MAC IntroPsych

Message
Influence of Others

MAC IntroPsych

Milgram Experiment
Influence of Others

MAC IntroPsych

A loss of a sense of personal responsibility, individuality and restraint when put in a group situation. **Example:** In the Stanford Prison Experiment, prison guards would perform anti-normative behaviour in a group situation because the anonymity on both sides meant that individual identifying characteristics could not be used against them. **Personal Example:**	When individuals use information from group members to understand ambiguous situations and make decisions. **Example:** If there is a sign that explicitly says "The water may be unsafe – swim at own risk", but others are in the water, an individual may use the information from the group to make their own decision to go swimming. **Personal Example:**
The finding that group decision-making tends to lead to more extreme or polarized views than the original views of individual group members. By strengthening these original views, the group decision can move in either the risky or cautious extreme. **Example:** An individual interested in canoeing is more likely to develop their interest among a group of individuals who enjoy canoeing. **Personal Example:**	When individuals are more willing to comply with a large request after they have already complied with a smaller request. **Example:** If an individual wanted to ask people to make a donation to their charity, they may initially have asked for them to sign up for an email flyer. **Personal Example:**
An escalation of the terms of an agreement after someone has already agreed. Compliance is secured at a smaller cost, only to later reveal additional costs, making the initial decision seem irreversible. **Example:** An individual may ask their friend to help them carry some groceries. Once they agree to help, they may be asked to help grocery shop, help pay for the groceries, as well as help put them away. **Personal Example:**	A group decision-making environment where group cohesiveness becomes so strong that it tends to override a realistic appraisal of alternative opinions. **Example:** A group of city councillors may strongly believe that recycling should be eliminated from their city because it is expensive. Those who disagree or try to discuss the benefits of recycling will be rejected from the group. **Personal Example:**
An experiment in which a subject was required to shock a confederate learner if they answered a question incorrectly, and progressively increase the shock for each incorrect answer. The experiment measured the willingness of a subject to obey an authority figure when actions conflicted with their personal conscience. **Personal Example:**	The facts used by a communicator to persuade listeners, and a contributing factor in persuasion. They can be framed from multiple perspectives to effectively persuade multiple audiences **Personal Example:**

Normative Function
Influence of Others

MAC IntroPsych

Overjustification Effect
Influence of Others

MAC IntroPsych

Peripheral Appeal
Influence of Others

MAC IntroPsych

Persuasion
Influence of Others

MAC IntroPsych

Risky Shift
Influence of Others

MAC IntroPsych

Social Loafing
Influence of Others

MAC IntroPsych

Stanford Prison Experiment
Influence of Others

MAC IntroPsych

Zajonc's Resolution
Influence of Others

MAC IntroPsych

When overjustification occurs, cognitive dissonance does not happen because the behaviour in conflict with your attitude is justified by some external means.
Example: Jesse gets paid to program code but considers it to be very boring. However, Jesse's behaviour of writing code is overjustified by the fact that he gets paid so he does not need to change his attitude to match his behaviour.
Personal Example:

The role of others in setting norms or standards of conduct based on fear of rejection.
Example: If an individual doesn't enjoy eating pizza but the rest of the group wants to order pizza, they may conform by expressing the desire to have a few slices to avoid rejection.
Personal Example:

The process of causing someone to believe an idea using reasoning or argument, which may affect their future thoughts, actions and choices.
Example: An individual may try to persuade their friends to join them on a trip to the Caribbean by talking about how much they all need the break after a hectic semester.
Personal Example:

Well-presented, easy to understand messages which are effective for unintelligent audiences.
Example: When trying to persuade a less academic audience, quick decision-making techniques based on heuristics are more successful persuasion tactics.
Personal Example:

The finding that individuals are less motivated when working in a group than when working alone.
Example: An individual working on a chemistry group project may not work as hard among four other students compared to if they were working alone.

The theory that group decisions tend to be riskier than the mean decisions of the individuals within that group.
Example: An individual may not want to go cliff jumping on his or her own. However, as a group, everyone may want to.
Personal Example:

The presence of co-actors or an audience will improve performance in a task which an individual finds simple or has experience with. It will decrease performance in a task in which the individual is unfamiliar or finds difficult.
Example: A child may tie his shoes more quickly when his parents are watching but may struggle to complete his math homework that he finds challenging when they are watching.
Personal Example:

An experiment conducted at Stanford University to study the behaviour of normal people under situations of authority. The experiment demonstrated the issues of authority, assignments of control, as well as the ethical concerns of conducting experiments with humans.
Personal Example:

ANSWER KEY

Activities and Practice Questions

Research Methods I – Courseware Exercise

Lighting in Factories 1: 1. No control group. 2. No hypothesis. 3. Possibility of practice effect (since all subjects are put into changing conditions from week to week). 4. Potential for subject biases (since AMC has volunteered to participate in this study). 5. Small sample size.

Lighting in Factories 2: 1. Has a testable hypothesis. 2. Uses random sampling when selecting subjects. 3. Has a control group. 4. Uses a between-subjects design (to avoid the practice effect). 5. Has a large sample size.

1. **Problem**: The experimenter knows which factories will receive which condition. As a result, experimenter bias might occur.
Solution: Use a double blind study, in which neither the experimenter nor the participants know which group each participant belong to.
2. **Problem**: The factories participating in this study are located in different countries. As a result, it is possible that the control groups may differ from the experimental groups in more ways than the independent variable alone.
Solution: Have both a control and an experimental group present in each factory throughout the course of the experiment.

Research Methods I – Review Questions

1. Please consult your TA if you require assistance with this activity.
2. A theory is a *general* set of ideas about the way the world works, while a hypothesis makes *specific* predictions about a phenomenon. A hypothesis is a testable statement that is *guided* by theories.
3. a) **IV**: Breakfast consumption. **DV**: The amount of material learned in lecture or test scores.
b) Between-subjects design. The independent variable is manipulated across two groups of participants. Participants only take part in one condition (they either eat breakfast or they don't). To make this into a within-subjects design, you could have the same group of students eat breakfast before watching the module one week and skip breakfast before watching the following week's module.
c) Random sampling is important for a quality experiment as the sample of participants must accurately reflect the population you are studying. Choosing a sample at random from the entire population reduces the chance that results might be biased towards a specific group.
d) i
4. d

Research Methods II – Courseware Exercise

1. The results from Professor A's class have a larger spread (and thus a larger standard deviation) than the results from Professor B's. This means that in Professor A's class some students scored very well, while others scored very poorly. In Professor B's class, for which the results have a smaller spread, most students obtained very similar scores, despite the average being slightly lower than class A's. This suggests that all students learn similar amounts from Professor B. In contrast, only some students learn a great amount from Professor A, while others learn much less and perform very poorly. These results suggest that professor A's teaching methods only appeal to some, but not all of his students.

2. Using inferential statistics, a t-test can be performed to in order to see if the difference in scores between Professor A's class and Professor B's class is statistically significant. If results are "not statistically significant" they are considered to be obtained by chance—the difference between class scores are not meaningful. If results of the t-test are "statistically significant", that would suggest that there is a real difference in scores between the two classes, which *may* suggest differences in the teaching abilities of Professor A and Professor B. Keep in mind, many other factors could contribute to this difference between the classes apart from teaching ability. Future studies could manipulate specific teaching factors in order to determine the source of the potential difference!

Research Methods II – Review Questions

1. Please refer to the "Using Histograms" in Unit 1, Subtopic 3.
2. **Mean:** 5.6, **Median**: 6, **Mode**: 6
3.

	Advantages	Disadvantages
Mean	-Useful in statistical equations -Most common measure of central tendency	-Influenced by outliers -Exact value may not appear in the data set
Median	-Not influenced by outliers	-Exact value may not appear in the data set
Mode	-Not influenced by outliers -Exact number appears in the data set -Can be used with non-numerical data sets	-Not representative of all data

4. a has the largest standard deviation of 15
d has the smallest standard deviation of 2
5. While a population is the full group of individuals that you are interested in studying, a sample is a subset of that population that you will use in your research. An experimenter would prefer to conduct an experiment on a

sample as conducting an experiment on an entire population (e.g. all undergraduate students) would be too costly and time-consuming and likely impossible. Inferential statistics allow us to use results from samples to make inferences about the overall, underlying population.

6. Statistically significant results suggest that the difference between two or more groups is due to some true difference between them and not random variation or chance.
7. Correlation is a measure of the strength of the relationship between two variables. We must be careful when measuring correlations, as "correlation does not necessarily equal causation". Although variables may be strongly correlated, we cannot definitively state that one causes the other or that the relationship between them is causing the observed effect.

Research Methods – Bottleneck Concepts

a) He obtained a p-value of 0.10. If he is only 90% confident that there is a true difference between the groups, it means there is a 10% chance he could have gotten the results by chance. This means that his results are not significant because his p-value is > 0.05.

b) Brian may increase the likelihood of achieving significant results if he performed the experiment with more participants. With more participants, Brian diminishes the likelihood that a difference is due to chance. He may also consider using more obnoxious noises if he suspects that the construction sounds were not loud enough and did not distract his participants appropriately. By making the noises louder and re-running the experiment, it may be possible to get significant results. There are many other possible answers. If you are unsure about the accuracy of your answer, feel free to ask a TA.

Classical Conditioning – Courseware Exercise

1. Answers may vary. The idea is that you would pair your product with something positive. For example, in the TV commercial, you could pair the presentation of the product with a popular song that evokes positive emotions in your viewers.
2. Answer may vary. Example: Create a contingency between the competitor's product (CS) and a negative song (US). When listening to the negative song, viewers will experience negative emotions (UR). After repeated viewings, a contingency will form between the song and the product and viewers will also experience negative emotions (CR) when viewing the competitor's product in the absence of the song.
3. Answers should follow the this format
   CS: Carbonated beverage
   US: Upbeat song
   CR: Positive emotions
   UR: Positive emotions
   Presenting the carbonated beverage (CS) while playing the popular upbeat song (US) will elicit positive emotions in your viewers (UR). Since the beverage and the song are presented alongside each other, a contingency will form between the two. Eventually, customers will be presented with the beverage in the absence of the song, but will still feel positive emotions (CR), making them want to buy your product to continue to feel the positive emotions!
4. Stimulus generalization is the classical conditioning principle at play in this case. In stimulus generalization, stimuli similar to the original CS (History Presentation) also produce the CR (Fear/Anxiety). Stimulus discrimination restricts the range of CSs that can elicit a CR. It uses an extinction procedure to extinguish the CR in which the CS is presented in the absence of the US (Poor Performance). In this case, students should also be required to perform another oral presentation in a course that is NOT history. The student would then be exposed to the CS (Class Presentations) in the absence of the US (Poor Performance). This would eliminate the fearful response that the child has towards class presentations.
5. Individual answers may vary. Please consult your TA if you require assistance.

Classical Conditioning – Review Questions

1. **The US**: A stimulus that automatically triggers a response in the absence of learning.
   The UR: A response, which is automatically triggered by the US in the absence of learning.
   The CS: A previously neutral stimulus that is paired with the US to form a learned contingency between the two such that presentation of the CS reliably predicts the presence of the US.
   The CR: The response, which occurs in response to the CS once a contingency between the CS and US has been learned. The CR and UR are often similar.
2. Acquisition is the process by which the contingency between a CS and US is formed. The negatively accelerated increasing function suggests that learning a contingency takes many trials and that the majority of learning occurs during the early trials. In subsequent trials learning occurs, but never as much as in the earlier ones.
3.
   a) **US**: Flu. **UR**: Nausea. **CS**: New food. **CR**: Nausea.
   b) **US**: Passionate date. **UR**: Joy. **CS**: Date's perfume. **CR**: Joy.
   c) **US**: Panic attack. **UR**: Anxiety/Fear. **CS**: Airplane. **CR**: Anxiety/Fear.
4. Stimulus generalization occurs when stimuli similar to the CS also produce the CR. In a classical conditioning experiment, a 500Hz tone (CS) is paired with food (US). This leads to salivation (UR) in the participant. Eventually, the presentation of the 500Hz tone (CS) alone will lead to salivation (CR). Once the contingency between the 500Hz tone (CS) and the food (US) has been established, experimenters test for stimulus generalization by presenting the participant with tones of varying

frequencies and measuring the salivation (CR). The strongest CR will be elicited by the original 500Hz tone, but stimuli similar to the original tone CS (i.e. 600 Hz) will also elicit the salivation CR at similar levels. The more different the tone (CS) becomes, the less salivation (CR) is elicited. Stimulus discrimination restricts the range of CSs that elicit a CR. In discrimination training, a CS at the far end of the generalization gradient is repeatedly presented in the absence of the US, which results in the CR to be extinguished. As a result, other tones similar to the original 500Hz still elicit a CR as they did before, but the one for which the CR was extinguished does not. For example, extinguishing the CR to the 600 Hz tone will not alter the CR to the 400 Hz tone.

5. Extinction refers to the loss of a CR when the CS no longer predicts the US. Extinction occurs when the CS is repeatedly presented in the absence of the US so that the CS no longer elicits the CR. In the salivation example, the 500Hz tone would be repeatedly presented in the absence of food. Following an extinction procedure, the CR to the CS gradually fades. But, following a rest period, the CS is presented again and the CR occurs! This is called spontaneous recovery. Spontaneous recovery suggests that extinction involves a *new* inhibitory learned response. The original learned association between the CS and the US is not actually "unlearned". Instead, extinction promotes a learned inhibitory response that competes with the original contingency.
6. Homeostasis is the process of keeping the internal state of the body constant, including but not limited to temperature, glucose, and ion levels. Classical conditioning allows the body to prepare for challenges to homeostasis, such as changes in blood glucose levels after sugar intake.
   US: Sugar intake
   UR: Insulin release (to counter the rise in blood glucose levels)
   CS: Taste of sugary drink (Cola)
   CR: Insulin release (to counter what your body thinks will be a rise in blood glucose levels)
   Eating something that tastes sweet (CS), suggests sugar intake (US). This usually means that blood glucose levels will soon rise. To counter this rise in blood glucose levels and maintain homeostasis, a CR of insulin release occurs.
7. Because drugs are never taken in isolation, chemical changes associated with drug administration are also signalled by environmental cues. The **drug effects** are the **US** and the **counter-adaptations,** which the body undergoes to counter the drug effects and maintain homeostasis, are the **UR**. **Environmental cues** specific to the conditions under which the drug is taken are the **CS** (e.g. rooms, smells or people present). A contingency is formed between these environmental cues (CS) and the drug effects (US). Eventually, the presentation of the environmental cues alone will trigger the **CR** of **counter-adaptations** by the body to counter the drug effects anticipated by the body. When the drug is not present, the CR can feel like withdrawal.

Classical Conditioning – Bottleneck Concepts

1. **US** Drug Effects; **UR** Counter-Adaptations; **CS** Environment; **CR** Counter-Adaptations;
In drug withdrawal, the CS is presented without the US. The CS produces the CR of counter-adaptations which, in the absence of drug effects, causes the body to become abnormal. This may cause discomfort and result in withdrawal.

In drug overdose, a high amount of US is presented without the CS. Since the CS is unavailable, it cannot elicit the CR and the body is unprepared for a high dose of drugs. This situation may cause an unusually elevated drug effect for which the UR alone cannot compensate, leading to overdose.

2. C (**US** Exercise; **UR** Counter-Adaptations; **CS** No Pain No Gain Gym Environment; **CR** Counter-Adaptations). A is correct because in any other gym, there will not be any CR to prepare Gordon to do exercise. Thus, he would likely be able to lift less weight without first warming up. B is correct. C is incorrect because exercise is the US which leads to the *UR*, counter-adaptations. D is correct because if the gym is completely renovated, the environment will no longer be the same. The loss of the CS would prevent Gordon's body from preparing for exercise in advance.

Instrumental Conditioning – Courseware Exercise

1.
   a) **Name**: Reward Training. **Description**: Presentation of a positive reinforcer. **Example**: Every time Billy picks his jacket off the floor, his mother gives him a cookie.
   b) **Name**: Punishment. **Description**: Presentation of a negative reinforcer. **Example**: Every time Billy leaves his jacket on the floor, his mother scolds him.
   c) **Name**: Omission training. **Description**: Removal of a positive reinforcer. **Example**: Every time Billy leaves his jacket on the floor, his mother gives him a "time out". During the time out Billy must sit alone and he is not allowed to play video games with his brothers and sisters.
   d) **Name**: Escape training. **Description**: Removal of a negative reinforcer. **Example**: Every time Billy picks his jacket off the floor, his mother turns off the classical music playing in the house, which Billy does not like.
   e) Billy's mother may be waiting too long between Billy's behaviour and administering the consequence. To ensure that conditioning is effective, the time between the behaviour (Billy leaving his jacket on the floor) and the punishment (Billy's mother scolding him) should be short; otherwise, Billy may do many other things in between leaving his coat on the floor and the

reinforcement and would have difficulty learning which behaviours lead to the consequences.

2.
   a) FR-3
   b) FR-2
   c) Since Carrie will now receive her pay after picking fewer buckets of strawberries, the 'run' part of the pause-and-run graph (corresponding to the y-axis) will become shorter.
   d) FI-1

Instrumental Conditioning – Review Questions

1.

	Similarities	Differences
Classical Conditioning	- both involve the formation of contingencies	- contingency is formed between two stimuli - response is involuntary or unconscious
Instrumental Conditioning	- both involve generalization, discrimination and extinction	- contingency is formed between a behaviour and a consequence - behaviour is voluntary or conscious

2. c
3. b
4. b
5.

Fixed ratio

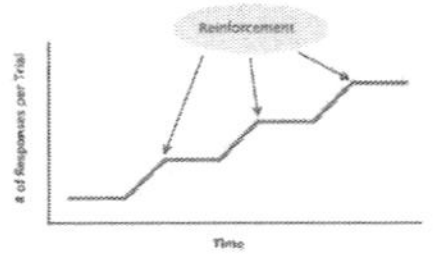

Fixed interval

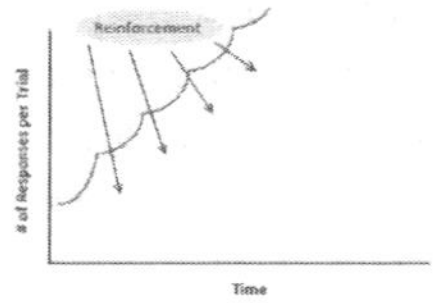

Variable ratio

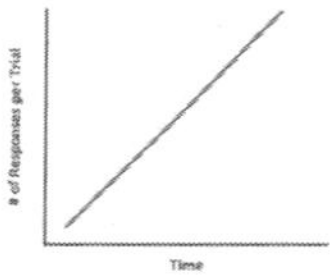

Variable interval

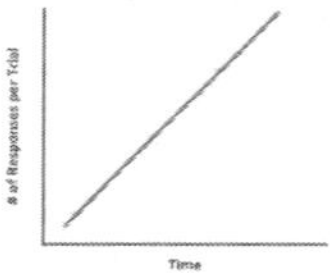

Instrumental Conditioning – Bottleneck Concepts

a) This is an example of instrumental conditioning. Tom has learned the contingency between a behaviour (sticking things into an electrical socket) and a consequence (electrical shock/pain). He knows that sticking things into the socket leads to a negative consequence and voluntarily avoids doing the action again.

b) This is an example of classical conditioning. Francine has learned the contingency between two stimuli, watermelon and food poisoning. The feeling of nausea is involuntary. **US** Food poisoning; **UR** Nausea; **CS** Watermelon; **CR** Nausea

Problem Solving – Courseware Exercise

1. Individual answers may vary. Please consult your TA if you require assistance.
2. Individual answers may vary. Please consult your TA if you require assistance. Also, check this out! "Chimpanzee Problem Solving": http://www.youtube.com/watch?v=ySMh1mBi3cI
3. Individual answers may vary. Please consult your TA if you require assistance.

Problem Solving – Review Questions

1. Deductive reasoning is the process of generating a specific fact from a general theory. Inductive reasoning is the process of generating a general theory from simple facts.
   a. Scientists start with a general theory about the world and use *deductive reasoning* to generate a specific testable hypothesis about the data they expect to obtain. Then through experiments, scientists collect data, using *inductive reasoning* to relate their findings to their general theory in a meaningful way. Therefore, scientists generate testable hypotheses using deductive reasoning and interpret collected data using inductive reasoning.
2. The confirmation bias is our tendency to seek out information that supports our hypothesis. For example, when buying an item of clothing on sale, people often look for similar items in more expensive stores, to convince themselves that they received a good deal.
3. The availability heuristic is our tendency to make decisions based on the information that is most quickly available to us. For example, after watching Shark Week on the discovery channel, you believe that the likelihood of encountering a shark in the ocean is much higher than it actually is. Because of this, you are afraid to swim in the sea on your next vacation.
4. The representativeness heuristic is our tendency to assume that what we are seeing is representative of a larger category we have in our mind. For example, you run into an acquaintance in line for lunch in the cafeteria. Although you can't seem to remember where you know them from, you notice that they are carrying goggles in the side pocket of their backpack. You then assume that you've met them in your chemistry lab, and proceed to talk about your most recent assignment (about which they have no idea!). The goggles could have been for an earth sciences or physics lab, or even an art course. However, you are most familiar with goggles being used for chemistry experiments.
5. James uses the availability heuristic to make a decision not to study. When James thinks of students who get A+

grades, he immediately thinks of his friends who do not study as this is the information that is most readily available to him.

6. Reliability measures the extent to which repeated testing produces consistent results. Validity measures the extent to which a test measures what the researcher actually claims to be measuring.
7. Answer: d
   No one knows! The above options are possibilities that have been proposed, but the primary explanation for the Flynn Effect remains an open question to be answered.
8. Both genetics and the environment play a role in determining IQ. See Unit 4, section "Genetic and Environmental Contributions" for examples.
9. c

Neither child will be able to answer the question correctly. It requires the kind of abstract reasoning that develops later, in the formal operational stage (age 11+).

Problem Solving – Bottleneck Concepts

a) Karen is using inductive reasoning. She starts from a specific case/observation that her two polar-opposite friends, Brian and Patricia, began dating and concludes with a general idea that opposites attract in romantic relationships.

b) Matthew is using deductive reasoning. He starts with the general idea that Wendy only buys clothes when they go on sale, and concludes that there must be a sale at the mall (a specific fact) because she has a new outfit.

Language – Courseware Exercise

Animal example	Regular?	Arbitrary?	Productive?	Is it language?
Waggle Dance	Yes	No	No	No
Bird Song	Yes	No (many bird calls are highly suited for their purpose)	No	No
Washoe	No	Yes	Yes	No
Sarah	Yes	Yes	No	No
Kanzi	No	No	Yes	No
Human Speech	Yes	Yes (with the exception of onomatopoeic terms)	Yes	Yes

Language – Review Questions

1. c
2. b
3. Milestones of Language Development

Age	Milestone
12 weeks	Makes cooing sounds
16 weeks	Turns head towards voices
6 months	Imitates sounds
1 year	Babbles
2 years	Uses 50-250 words; uses two word phrases
2.5 years	Vocabulary > 850 words

   a. The language explosion occurs between about one and a half to six years of age. At this time, vocabulary increases rapidly and most children will have mastered the major aspects of language by the end.
4. In spoken language, segmentation is the process of determining when one word ends and the next begins. The segmentation problem occurs when an individual has difficulty separating the individual words in a speech stream.
   a. An infant's proficiency at speech segmentation predicts their future language ability. There is a strong positive correlation between early speech segmentation and expressive vocabulary at two years of age. Thus, children with large expressive vocabularies have often demonstrated good speech segmentation skills as infants.
5. Universal phoneme sensitivity is the ability of infants to discriminate between any two sounds (phonemes), including sounds from non-native languages.
   a. Evidence for the existence of universal phoneme sensitivity comes from an experiment in which researchers compared English speaking adults, Hindi speaking adults, and infants from English speaking families, on their ability to discriminate between two different /t/ sounds. These sounds are present in the Hindi language, but not in English. Adult English speakers performed worst on this task, whereas infants from English speaking families performed almost as well as the Hindi-speaking adults. Thus, infants can discriminate non-native sounds that are absent from the language of the culture in which they are being raised.
6. <u>Social Learning Theory</u>:
   Supporting Evidence: Without exposure to adequate sources of language, children fail to develop language skills. (Eg. Genie)
   Opposing Evidence: Children's language development is far too rapid and complex to be driven by imitation and repetition alone. In addition, children combine words in novel ways that have never been modeled or reinforced.

Finally, children make language errors that are not heard in adult speech (eg. overextensions and underextensions).
Innate Mechanism Theory:
Supporting Evidence: Children who have been taught to lip read can spontaneously sign, and use innate and automatic grammar when doing so. In addition, young infants show neurophysiological responses to the first language they are exposed to, indicating that their brains are pre-wired to adapt to the sounds and their meanings that are present in their environment. Finally, infants prefer to listen to speech sounds (as opposed to non-speech sounds) indicating that they have an innate predisposition to expose themselves to language.
Opposing Evidence: None listed in the module.

Language – Bottleneck Concepts

1. **C.** Even though the English language does not contain different words for each type of love, Fred is still able to identify which type of love his friend is referring to. This example does not support the Whorf-Sapir hypothesis which would argue that a lack of different words for love would have hindered Fred from differentiating between the various types of love. All other choices support the Whorf-Sapir hypothesis since the absence of a word in an individual's language altered the way in which they perceived the world.

Categories and Concepts – Courseware Exercise

1. Prototype theory could explain the discrepancy in ratings for the object "palm tree". Prototype theory suggests that we categorize objects by comparing them to an internal representation of a category, called a prototype. Prototypes are the average, or "best", member of a category and are formed through personal experience. As a result, prototypes are subjective; they depend on the objects each person has previously encountered and averaged together. Since palm trees do not grow in Canada, they would not have weighed as heavily into forming an average Canadian prototype of a tree. (exemplar theory can also explain this, see answer to #3)
2. The maple tree. It has both high typicality and membership ratings, therefore, not only is it considered a member of the category "trees", it is considered to be a typical, or average, member of the category "trees".
3. Exemplar theory can also explain these results. It suggests that instead of storing *one* internal average of a category, we store *every experience* of that category over our entire lifetime as an exemplar. When categorizing an object, we search through our library of exemplars to find one similar to the current object. Once found, we can then identify the current object as a member of the same category. According to exemplar theory, it's not that the maple tree looks more like their average tree prototype, but that the Canadian subjects have more maple exemplars than palm exemplars. Thus, they are able to retrieve a maple tree exemplar much more quickly and rate it higher in membership and typicality.

Categories and Concepts – Review Questions

1. **Classification**: Categorization allows you to treat objects that appear differently as belonging together. *For example, no matter if they're green or purple, they're still grapes!*
Understanding: Categorizing a scene allows us to understand and react appropriately. *For example, while sitting on a crowded subway, you notice that the elderly woman in front of you is having trouble balancing while standing in the moving car. You immediately understand that she is struggling and offer her your seat.*
Communication: Many of the words in our language refer to categories or concepts! Using the category names allows for efficient communication. *For example, when conversing with one another in the emergency room, doctors and nurses understand each other's medical terminology. Their jargon is confusing for us to understand, but they use it as a part of their regular vocabulary and understand each other easily. E.g., O-neg STAT... means I need O-negative blood immediately!*
2. It is not possible to describe categories with a set of rules. When asked to define a category with a list of necessary and sufficient rules, it is difficult to properly include and exclude items in the category. In addition, it is especially difficult to devise simple rules to define more abstract categories.
   a. Experiments on the use of rules tell us that for simple categories we are quite susceptible to the illusion of the expert. Since categorization is easy for us, we believe it must have a simple rule! In reality, categorization cannot be established through a set of rules. Instead, scientists believe that humans have an internal representation of categories that is independent of the rules we try to define.
3.

	Prototype Theory	Exemplar Theory
Similarities	Used in categorization. Compares a new experience to an internal representation.	
Differences	Suggests that we store one internal average of a category.	Suggests that we store our entire lifetime's worth of experiences.
How does the theory explain the categorization of an "orange" into the category "fruit"?	Prototype theory suggests that we categorize objects by comparing them to an internal representation of the category called a prototype. Prototype are the average or "best" members of a	Exemplar theory suggests that we store our entire lifetime of experiences as exemplars. When viewing an orange, we search through our library of exemplars to find

	category and are formed through personal experience. Thus all of our encounters with oranges have been averaged into our prototype of "fruit".	one similar to it. Since we come across oranges frequently, we are able to categorize it quickly as a type of fruit.

4. Children as young as three are able to understand general categories, as well as category membership. In addition, children also understand the innate properties of a given category (e.g., Racoon into skunk vs. Toaster into teapot).
   a. Evidence that children can apply categories comes from their ability to determine category membership. In the module, Katie learns that her dog likes treats and applies this knowledge to other breeds of dogs as well. She knows that since they are members of the same category, they share similar characteristics. Evidence that children understand categories comes from their understanding of the innate properties of categories. In the modules, it is noted that children understand that you can change the nature of a machine, but that you cannot change the nature of an animal.
5. Evidence that animals can apply categories and concepts comes from research on baboons. Using classical conditioning procedures, baboons have learned to classify objects as either food or non-food, and can do so with 90% accuracy. In addition, baboons are also capable of more abstract categorization and can place objects into the categories "same" and "different" with a high level of accuracy as well.

Categories & Concepts – Bottleneck Concepts

1. In prototype theory, all relevant examples of a category are averaged into a prototypical depiction, which represents the group. All future items are categorized by comparing them to prototypes. Since hundreds of examples contribute to a category's prototype, a few recent examples are unlikely to change the prototype significantly. Therefore, an improvement in the dermatologists' ability to diagnose recently viewed skin diseases should not occur.
2. This phenomenon supports the exemplar theory. Upon his return home, Frederick seemed to think that people in his hometown had a funny accent. Exemplar theory argues that all examples of a category are stored. Therefore, after hearing so many recent examples of the Australian accent, Frederick would first compare what he heard to the Australian accent when trying to categorize what his townspeople were saying. This would make it harder for Frederick to categorize the word, and thus make it seem like the townspeople had a funny accent. On the other hand, in the prototype theory, the recent examples of words said in an Australian accent should be averaged out with a lifetime of examples without that accent. Thus, this new experience would have been unlikely to change the prototype and affect how Frederick categorized words heard back home if the prototype theory applied.

Attention – Courseware Exercise

1. The spotlight model of attention cannot explain this situation. The spotlight model of attention suggests that humans have an attentional spotlight that focuses on part of the environment at one time to the exclusion of the rest of the visual scene. Attention is consciously directed across the visual scene, with objects falling within the spotlight being processed faster and preferentially. Debbie was not consciously attending to the part of the visual scene in which the red car was in, and thus, it was not in her attentional spotlight and should not have be processed.
2. This situation cannot be explained by Broadbent's single filter model of attention. The model suggests that an attentional filter selects important information to be processed on the basis of physical characteristics and allows only that information to continue on for further processing. Information that does not pass through the physical filter is completely eliminated and unavailable for further analysis. In this case, red cars are not relevant to Debbie's physical filter, which is focused on driving a car, and thus should be rejected for further processing.
3. This situation can be explained using Triesman's dual filter model of attention. The model suggests two filters. The first filter attenuates unimportant objects based on physical characteristics, but still allows everything through. The second filter determines what is important based on semantic meaning. Although red cars have been attenuated and are less likely to make it through the second filter, the red Thunderbird has semantic meaning to Debbie and thus makes it through to perceptual processing.

Attention – Review Questions

1. Automatic processes of attention are involuntarily triggered by external events and operate in a fast, efficient and obligatory manner. Controlled processes, however, are slow and effortful. They voluntarily and consciously guide attention to objects of interest.
   a. Because they require less cognitive effort, automatic processes occur quite quickly. They also allow you to process salient information. In addition, frequently practiced tasks can become "automatic" as a result of learning and thus may require less effort over time.
   b. Using controlled processes is advantageous because it allows one to participate in "goal-directed behaviour", which allows you to choose which stimulus warrants your attention.
2. The spotlight model represents an area of enhancement of the visual scene. The "spotlight" area receives enhanced attention, allowing you to react more quickly to cues inside it and identify things within it more accurately. Note, you are still paying attention to things outside the spotlight, but

your reaction to them is slower and less accurate unless you move your spotlight to a new part of the visual scene.

3. The spatial cueing paradigm is an experimental procedure that allows researchers to manipulate the attentional spotlight. In the paradigm, subjects stare at a screen on which there are three boxes. Participants are asked to focus their attention on the middle box (beside which are boxes on the left and right sides). A target will then appear in either the left or right box and subjects are told to identify it as quickly as possible by pressing the designated button. However, before the target appears in one of the boxes, a potential target box briefly flashes, serving as a cue for the subject's attention. The real target will then follow, either in the cued or uncued location.
   a. In Experiment #1, the cue accurately predicts where the target will appear for the majority of trials. Therefore, when an individual notices that the cue is reliable, they will consciously decide to attend to the cue—this demonstrates controlled processing. Consciously controlled shifts of attention can lead to faster responses to targets that appear in the location indicated by the cue than to those that appear opposite to the location of the cue.
   b. In Experiment #2, the cue does not predict where the target will appear for the majority of trials. This demonstrates controlled processing again because the participant will choose to ignore the flash and bring their attention to where they expect the target to be. This will lead to faster responses to targets that appear in the location opposite to the cue than to those that appear in the same location as the cue.
   c. In Experiment #3, the cue provides no predictive information about where the target will appear and so it demonstrates automatic processing. Researchers find that response time occurs more quickly when the target is correctly cued. When the target occurs in the cued location, the subject's attention is already there and thus reaction time is quicker. When the target occurs in the uncued location, the subject must shift their attentional spotlight from the location of the cue to the location of the target, and thus reaction time is longer. These results suggest that the difference in target detection is governed by automatic control of attention

4. Broadbent's single filter model suggests that an attentional filter selects important information to be processed on the basis of physical characteristics and allows only that information to continue on for further processing. Information that does not pass through the physical filter is completely eliminated and unavailable for deeper analysis. In contrast, Triesman's dual filter model suggests two attentional filters. The first filter attenuates (or lowers the weight of) unimportant objects based on physical characteristics, but still allows everything through. The second filter determines what is important based on semantic meaning and chooses what information will be attended to. Information that does not get through this second "semantic filter" is then discarded.
   a. "Breakthrough" is when relevant information from an unattended channel is heard, such as someone calling your name at a busy party. It is relevant, as its existence led to the revision of Broadbent's single filter model and the creation of Treisman's dual filter model, in which the additional semantic filter explains why breakthrough can occur.

5. In the Stroop Task, participants are presented with a colour word and asked to name the ink-colour in which the word is presented. Items can be congruent (matching word and colour dimensions) or incongruent (mismatching word and colour dimensions). Researchers measure how long it takes for a participant to correctly identify the ink colour while ignoring the word dimension. Performance is found to be faster on congruent items.
   a. The Stroop task requires you to attend to information in the task relevant-dimension and ignore information in the task-irrelevant dimension. The difference in performance between congruent and incongruent trials acts as an empirical measure of processes involved in selective attention. On congruent trials, the word and its colour match so that reading facilitates colour naming performance. On incongruent trials, the word and its colour do not match and reading interferes with colour naming performance.

6. In a visual search task, subjects look for an object amongst an array of distractors, e.g., find a red triangle among an array of red squares.
   a. In a feature search, the subject looks for one particular feature to identify the target. For example, finding a square in a group of circles is a feature search, i.e., lines. In a conjunction search, the subject looks for two or more features to identify the target. For example, finding a green T in a set of red and green Is and red Ts is a conjunction search, i.e., colour and shapes.
   b. This occurs when there is a specific feature in the target that highly contrasts the features of the rest of the set. A pop out effect occurs quickly, *regardless* of set size.
   c. Contextual cueing is when the expected position of the target serves as a cue to decrease the difficulty of a visual search. It is relevant; making search tasks both quicker and easier.

Attention – Bottleneck Concepts

i. **B.** A higher percentage of congruent words will lead to an increased Stroop Effect. Participants will be using the actual word to help name the ink colour. Thus, when an incongruent word appears, participants will also use the word to name its ink color. However, since the word and its corresponding ink color do not match, their strategy will actually interfere with their ability to perform the task. Statement C is incorrect because a 50-50 chance of congruent and incongruent words will not encourage participants to adopt a particular strategy. Therefore, an incongruent word won't be especially surprising or cause the **greatest** Stroop Effect. A is not correct because the Stroop Effect **only** occurs when incongruent words are present. D is also incorrect because an entire array of incongruent words will cause participants to adopt a strategy to actively ignore the word itself, thus decreasing the Stroop Effect.

ii. The Stroop task requires a person to focus their attention on naming the color of the ink used to type a word, while ignoring the word itself. However, it is the actual word which automatically captures an individual's attention. It has been hypothesized that people with ADHD do worse because they are either unable to ignore the interfering word and color information or they cannot direct attention and effort towards naming the ink color. In more general terms, people suffering from ADHD may be less able to direct conscious attention to tasks or may be less able to inhibit automatic attention processes.

Memory – Courseware Exercise

Individual answers may vary for this activity. Please consult your TA if you require assistance.

Memory – Review Questions

1. Ebbinghaus operationally defined memory as a serial learning task. Using himself as a subject, he memorized word lists and suggested that each word in the list acted as a cue to trigger the memory of the word that followed. Ebbinghaus noticed that his ability to recall words was highest immediately following learning and that over time he was able to remember fewer and fewer words. This led him to create the forgetting curve which describes the increasing rate of memory failure over time.
   a.

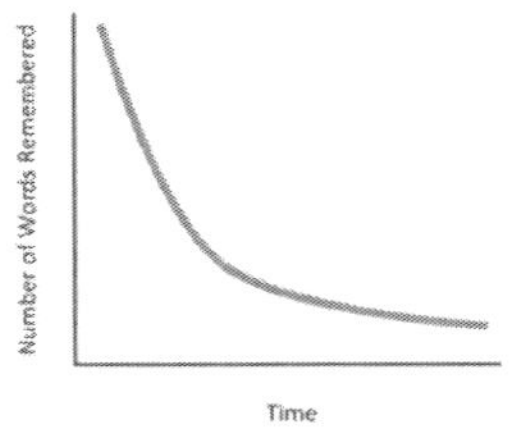

2. The multi-store model assumes that memory is composed of both short- and long-term storage systems. According to the model, incoming perceptual information is first stored in a short-term memory buffer. This information in short-term memory is only available for current tasks, and is not stored permanently in the memory system. Important information encoded in short-term memory can be transferred to the long-term memory system for more permanent and long-term storage. One way to do this is through rehearsal.
3. Chunking refers to the reorganization of information into meaningful packets. Chunking allows more information to be stored in short-term memory. Because it has been observed that only 7+/-2 items can be held in short-term memory at a time, chunking helps store more by containing more information in each of those items.
4.
   a. Recency will be affected by talking on the phone before your test. Although you studied right up until leaving for the midterm, talking to your friend will have used up your short-term memory capacity, thus diminishing the effect of recency on recall for test information.
   b. Primacy is responsible for the fact that your TA remembers the first names most clearly. Your TA was able to rehearse the names at the beginning of the game the most, enhancing recall of these names as they are rehearsed enough to transfer into long-term memory stores.
   c. Primacy will be affected by this manipulation. Those who are able to view the words for 2 minutes will have better recall for the words at the beginning of the list because they had more time to rehearse and transfer these items into long-term memory. Those who only had 30 seconds to view the list of words would not have had the same opportunity to rehearse and have these words transferred to long-term memory.
   d. Recency will be enhanced. Your friend will have better recall for the last items he studied, as these will remain in his short-term memory since he was not distracted by conversations before the exam. Distractions would have used up his limited short-term memory capacity.
5. Encoding specificity is the finding that recall is better when retrieval takes place in similar conditions to encoding. Encoding specificity suggests that both our internal and external environments are encoded and affect our memory. Specific aspects of our original experience influence our memory performance in the future by acting as cues for the event or item being recalled. Memory performance thus depends both on how we encode items *and* the encoding context.
   In a study by Godden & Baddelley, scuba divers were asked to encode a list of words while on land or underwater. To follow, the divers were asked to recall the words from the list in either the same or a different encoding context. Results demonstrated that subjects were better able to remember items from the list when they were in the same original encoding context during their follow up memory test (e.g., encoded on land and recalled on land).

6. Please refer to the module, Unit 7: Slide 57 & 58 for a description of the experiment. This experiment suggests that misattribution of memory can occur. The false fame effect occurs as a result of processing fluency (familiarity) of a non-famous name that you improperly attributed to being famous.

Memory – Bottleneck Concepts

1. a) The phrase **"**Encoding Attribution" is similar to the terms "encoding specificity" and "attribution" found in this week's module. This is why the term "Encoding Attribution" was fluent to Alicia. Since Alicia did not remember the terms "encoding specificity" and "attribution" from the module, she was not able to correctly attribute the fluency of this novel term. Instead, she incorrectly thought the term had been covered in lecture and chose it as her answer.
2. **A**. In this scenario, Ryan would seem fluent and familiar. Since you saw the picture a week ago, which was a greater length of time compared to the other scenarios, you would most likely have forgotten where you saw Ryan and incorrectly attribute the fluency to having met Ryan before.

Forming Impressions – Courseware Exercise

1. Individual answers may vary, however, they should include the 4 factors of attraction: Proximity, physical attractiveness, familiarity, and others' opinions. If you require assistance, please consult your TA.
2. Sarah is making use of the availability heuristic. Sarah is using the relative availability of positive memories from her psychology class compared to the more negative memories from her physics class. Sarah relates the available positive memories with Monica and rates Monica as a more fun friend than Maria. However, Maria could be a very fun person outside of physics class!

Forming Impressions – Review Questions

1. Degree of choice, expectation, and the intended consequences of behaviour.
2. **Consistency**: Does this individual usually behave this way in this situation? The situation in question is him giving a speech to be president of the student union. Without being explicitly told, we can assume that he behaves the same way each time he gives a speech. Therefore, the answer is yes; he consistently behaves this way in the situation.
   Distinctiveness: Does the individual behave differently in different situations? Yes. Because your friend seems to know him and thinks he is a nice, humble guy, it is likely that he usually behaves differently in other situations.
   Consensus: Do others behave similarly in this situation? One can assume, yes. Others who are running for president would also tell of their accomplishments and community involvement.
   Based on the answers to these questions, you can assume that the male student's behaviour is situational, not dispositional.
3.
   a. The Fundamental Attribution Error (FAE) is our tendency to overvalue dispositional factors for the observed behaviours of others while undervaluing situational factors. We are more likely to make an FAE for others than for ourselves.
   b. d – Please refer to the module, Unit 3: Slide 22 & 23
   c. Generally, FAE is diminished in collectivist societies (such as China or India) where there is less focus on individual behaviour and more on relationships and roles in society. Western societies however, are generally individualistic and focus on the individual. Therefore, they are more likely to attribute behaviour of others to dispositional causes over situational causes.
4. Using the representativeness heuristic, one can classify people depending on how well their behaviour fits with a certain prototype (this can lead to stereotyping). Using the availability heuristic, one can decide how likely it is for a person to possess a certain trait by considering how easy it is to come up with examples of that person (or someone similar) acting a certain way.
5. **Proximity**: Refers to both physical and functional difference. You are more likely to become attracted to a person if you see and interact with them often.
   Familiarity: We tend to feel more positively about people and/or things that we have seen before.
   Physical Attractiveness: We presume that "what is beautiful is also good".
   Others' Opinions: You like people...who like you! Or, people who didn't like you at first, but grew to like you.

Forming Impressions – Bottleneck Concepts

1. a) This is an example of the representativeness heuristic. Karly made assumptions about Philip because she knew he was a TA. She possessed an internal representation of what TAs look like and how they act and referenced that when encountering her TA.
   b) This is an example of the availability heuristic. Dave used the most available information to him to form an impression of the restaurant. He heard the positive comments from his neighbours and just assumed that the restaurant had good food.
2. For some people, the media may be the primary source of information about things or people. This means that whatever is shown in the media may be the most readily available information for consumers. Through the availability heuristic, people may incorrectly form an impression of certain things and even certain groups leading to stereotypes of those around us. The media may also promote representations of certain groups that are

internalized by viewers and lead to the development or reinforcement of stereotypes. Consider the constant media coverage on terrorism, stemming from the Middle East, following 9/11. Some individuals allowed this information to colour their view of Middle Eastern individuals and incorrectly stereotype them all as terrorists.

Influence of Others I – Courseware Exercise

1. Groupthink was at the root of NASAs problematic decision-making process. Groupthink occurs when group cohesion is so strong that it overrides realistic appraisals of reality and alternative options.
2. Your solution should include the following: be impartial, use critical evaluation, allow group members to disagree, subdivide the group into smaller ones, call a second chance meeting before implementing a final decision.

Influence of Others I – Review Questions

1. Triplett observed that cyclists raced faster when competing with each other in a group than when they raced against the clock in individually timed trials. This phenomenon, in which the presence of co-actors or an audience leads to enhanced performance, is called social facilitation.
   a. The presence of others does not always improve performance. Sometimes it actually hinders it!
   b. Zajonc suggested that the presence of others increases your arousal. The way in which this heightened arousal affects your performance depends on the specific task to be performed. For simple tasks in which you are well-practiced, performance is enhanced. For complex tasks in which you have little practice, performance is hindered.
2. Bandura's experiment is important as it demonstrated social learning theory; you learn appropriate behaviours by modeling or imitating the behaviours of others.
3. Individuals sat alone in a dark room, observing a stationary light on a wall. Despite it being immobile, the autokinetic effect made the light look like it had moved a small amount. Participants were asked to estimate how much the light moved. The next day, participants sat in the same conditions, except this time two other subjects were present in the room. All participants were asked to provide their estimates of how much the light moved out loud in front of the group. Following a few more days in the same conditions, participants' responses gradually converged, despite the fact that they all had given different estimates on the first day. Even when a confederate of the experimenter sat in with the subjects and gave a very large estimate of the light's movement on the wall, the group's responses still converged to a large number, incorporating this confederate's response as well.
4. Asch's participants were seated in a room with a group of confederates. They were told that they would see one sample line and three comparison lines and that then they would be required to identify which of the comparison lines matched the standard. As the experiment proceeds, confederates start to agree on answers that are clearly wrong. When it is the actual subjects' turn to answer, the majority also conformed to the incorrect response! This experiment demonstrates the normative function.
5. Deutsch and Gerard's modification to Asch's experiment demonstrates the comparative function; we look to the actions of others to provide information about an ambiguous situation. Subjects performed the same task as in Asch's experiment, but this time in cubicles with anonymous identities. Before a subject was to respond, lights lit up on their screen that indicated the results of other participants in the experiment. Although anonymous and free of the potential to be ridiculed, subjects still went along with the rest of the group, even on incorrect answers. Conformity occurred mostly when answers were less clear. Because subjects doubted their own perceptions, they went along with those of the group suspecting that others may be right.
6. Both the normative and comparative functions outline the roles of others in setting standards for our conduct. In the normative function, conduct is based on fear of rejection, whereas in the comparative function, conduct is modelled after the actions of others in an ambiguous situation.
7. Group polarization occurs when group decision-making strengthens the original inclinations of the individual group members. If the individuals were originally inclined to a low level of risk, the group would make an even less risky decision; however, if the individuals were originally inclined to a high level of risk, the group decision would be even riskier than the individuals would have tolerated. The risky shift refers to the idea that some group decisions as a whole have riskier outcomes than when those same decisions are made by individuals alone (because of group polarization).
8. Darley and Latane's experiments demonstrated collective ignorance. When each individual in a group sees nobody responding in a given situation, they conclude that the situation is not an emergency. When subjects were alone, they were more likely to report smoke seeping into a room than if others were in the room, and this likelihood of reporting the smoke decreased as the number of people in the room increased.
   a. Darley and Latane's experiments also demonstrated diffusion of responsibility. In deciding whether we have to act, we determine that someone else in the group must be more qualified. To break diffusion of responsibility, it helps to be direct. Choose an individual out of the group and place the responsibility of a task on them.
9. Social loafing is a special case of diffusion of responsibility, in which individuals are less motivated when working in a group than when working alone.

Influence of Others II – Courseware Exercise

1. The communicator should have high credibility, but also be close in age to a university student. Perhaps a young, attractive PhD student studying psychology.
2. Your audience is intelligent (they are psych students aren't they!?), therefore use a central appeal. Because the students may not initially agree that they should buy the textbook, you should present a well-reasoned and factual two-sided argument.
3. Your audience is university students. The subpopulation of students that you are appealing to are those studying psychology.
4. In this campaign, you should attempt to have the students justify the behaviour of buying the textbook. The students' behaviour (buying a more expensive textbook) does not match their attitude (feeling anxiety over spending more money when their budget is tight). Therefore, you want them to feel that the textbook is so amazing that paying the extra 10% was worth it and that they are glad they didn't buy a far inferior textbook. The justification you employ to relieve cognitive dissonance should be: "well this textbook is much better anyways".

Influence of Others II – Review Questions

1. Please refer to Unit 2: Slide 4 - 6 for a full description of the experiment.
   a. It was found that the majority of subjects (65%) continued on to the end of the experiment, even delivering a shock labelled "high shock voltage" to a patient with a heart condition.
   b. The prestige of the experimenter and environment, as well as the physical separation between the teacher and the learner could have contributed to the results. In addition, the proximity of the experimenter to the learner could have also played a role.
   c. Many lessons can be learned from Milgram's experiment. We learned that humans have a very strong tendency to obey authority. In addition, we do not always accurately judge how we would behave in a given situation. Finally, this experiment also made us deeply reconsider ethics when conducting experiments on human subjects.
2. Subjects who were given $1 to lie about the experiment had cognitive dissonance because their attitude (the experiment was boring) did not line up with their behaviour (telling the next subject the experiment was fun). To relieve this dissonance, they need to make their attitude and behaviour line up. Because their behaviour could not be changed (they had already lied), they had to change their attitude and therefore rated the experiment as being more fun. Those subjects given $20 on the other hand, could justify their lying behaviour by saying that they only lied for the money, thus relieving cognitive dissonance without changing their attitude toward the experiment. As a result, their attitude that the experiment was boring remained and they rated it lower.
3. Please see Unit 4: Slide 32 for details.
   a. This study did not run the entirety of its two-week course. Instead, it was halted after only 6 days as subjects assigned as guards were acting sadistically towards subjects assigned as prisoners (prisoners also became severely depressed).
   b. The experiment demonstrates the power that circumstance and assigned role can have on human behaviour. It also demonstrates how deindividuation may result in dangerous behaviour.
4. The most persuasive communicators are those with high credibility. In addition, both physical attractiveness and how relatable or similar the communicator is also play a role. For decisions of lifestyle choices, a more similar communicator is more persuasive, while for factual decisions, a more credible communicator is most persuasive. Persuasive communicators also speak in a more straightforward, concise manner and maintain better eye-contact.
5. It depends on the audience! A two-sided message is better if your audience initially disagrees with your opinion. A one-sided message is more effective if your audience is already in favour of your message.
6. In a central appeal, a well-reasoned, two-sided argument is presented. This type of appeal often works best when addressing an academic audience. In a peripheral appeal, a well-presented, easy to understand message is presented. Peripheral appeal is often more effective for unintelligent audiences.
7. The Foot in the Door technique refers to a situation in which a gradual escalation of demands increases obedience. Just as the Foot in the Door technique results in a gradual escalation of demands, the low-ball technique does too! However, in the case of the low-ball technique, compliance is secured at a smaller cost, only to later reveal additional costs, while making the original decision seem irreversible.

   Foot in the Door: For example, suppose a vacuum salesman comes to your door. He convinces you to let him in and test the vacuum on your carpet. He later convinces you that his vacuums are the best and you agree to buy the basic model for $300 even though you already have a good vacuum and weren't planning on getting a new one. Once you sit down to sign the papers, he shows you the features that you are missing out on if you only buy the basic model. He convinces you to buy the upgraded model for $450. Finally, he demonstrates the use of some additional vacuum attachments to make cleaning much easier and you agree to pay another $150, bringing your total to $600.

   Low Ball: The same vacuum salesman comes to your door and easily persuades you to purchase a vacuum for only $300 (this time you actually needed one)! When you sit down to sign the papers, he informs you that you will need to pay additional charges of $100 for a customer-care package, $50 for necessary vacuum bags, $50 for shipping and $100 in duty charges as the vacuum will be shipped from the USA. Because he secured your compliance at a lower rate at the beginning, you now feel that your original decision is irreversible and agree to pay $600 for your new vacuum

Influence of Others – Bottleneck Concepts

i. a) There was no fear of rejection because the vote was anonymous and no one would know who Karly voted for. She ended up voting for the same band as her friends because she did not know anything about either of the two bands. Karly's friends provided her with information in an ambiguous situation. This is an example of the comparative function.

b) Trevor went on the roller coaster due to a fear of rejection from his friends. This is an example of the normative function.

ii. Deutsch and Gerard had participants seated in their own cubicles, allowing them to provide anonymous answers. Participants also saw lights indicating the confederates' answers before they inputted their own response. Quite often, the subjects would go along with the confederates' incorrect answers, especially when the correct answer was ambiguous. Since participants' answers were anonymous, fear of rejection was not a significant factor. Therefore, the normative function did not come into play. Instead, this scenario is an example of the comparative function. The situation in Deutsch and Gerard's experiment created an ambiguous situation where two answers seemed possible, leading subjects to refer to others' responses to determine the correct response.

GLOSSARY OF TERMS

A

Above Average Effect: The tendency for an individual to assume that they are better than the average person, and that the challenges and failures of the average person are not ones they will experience. *E.g. Despite the increased awareness about the risks of drunk driving, some individuals may still drive when intoxicated, claiming that, "Other people get into accidents. I won't." (Forming Impressions)*

Accent: A manner of pronunciation unique to an individual, geographical location, or nation. It occurs both between and within languages. It may be influenced by location and dominant speech patterns in the environment in which an individual is raised. *(Language)*

Acquisition: In classical conditioning, it is when a contingency is formed between a CS (conditioned stimulus) and US (unconditioned stimulus) following repeated presentations of one after the other. *E.g. A researcher repeatedly rings a bell before presenting food for a dog. Now, when the dog hears the bell, he salivates in anticipation of food. (Classical Conditioning I)* In instrumental conditioning, it is when a contingency has been learned between a behaviour and a consequence. *E.g. When you were a child, you learned that being polite led to positive consequences and now, as an adult, you are still polite in hopes of positive consequences. (Instrumental Conditioning)*

Actor/Observer Effect: A proposed explanation of the fundamental attribution error, stating that an individual is more likely to make the fundamental attribution error when determining causes of others' behaviour rather than their own. As the actor, they are better aware of the situational factors contributing to their behaviour; but when observing others, they only have the current situation and assume that what you see is typical of that person. *E.g. Drivers may be more likely to attribute their own speeding to situational factors such as being late while attributing the speeding of others to dispositional factors such as they are bad drivers or aggressive people. (Forming Impressions)*

Addiction: In terms of classical conditioning, when a stimulus, often a drug (US), elicits some sort of drug effect (UR). Over time after continued use, the environment which the drug is taken in (CS) will be able to trigger compensatory responses (CR) which prepare the body for the effects of the drug, attempting to maintain homeostasis in the body. *(Classical Conditioning)*

Arch of Knowledge: A diagram used to illustrate the different mechanisms of reasoning in problem solving. Specific facts are found at the base of the arch, while general theories are found at the top of the arch. The general theories govern how all the facts at the bottom are related using deductive reasoning. More specific facts can be determined through experimentation, which may contradict or supplement the general theories. Therefore, broader theories can be altered through inductive reasoning. *(Problem Solving)*

Asch's Stimuli: An experiment performed by Asch, in which a participant (among confederates) was required to identify which of three lines matched a standard in length. If all the confederates in the experiment gave an incorrect response, the participant would conform socially and agree with the incorrect answer despite the obviousness of the mistake. *(Influence of Others I)*

Attraction: In attraction research, this term refers to having a good impression of someone or something and desiring their company. It does not refer exclusively to sexual attraction. *E.g. To say you are attracted to your best friend whom you see often is to say that you have a good impression of that person. (Forming Impressions)*

Attribution: Judgments that tie together causes and effects. *E.g. If you see someone you recognize, the effect is the feeling of fluency or a feeling that the person is familiar. Upon feeling the effect of fluency, you use attribution to investigate the cause for this effect, or how you know the individual. (Memory & Forming*

Impressions)

Audience: A group of people watching an individual perform a task, which can enhance or hinder the performance of the actor. *E.g. During a concert recital, a famous cello player may find that he performs better in front of a large audience than when rehearsing in front of his cat. (Influence of Others I)*

Automatic Processes: When external events involuntarily "capture" one's attention. *E.g. When hearing a loud bang, one may automatically direct their attention to the source of the noise, even if they did not intend to attend to the noise. (Attention)*

Autoshaping: When a behaviour can be learned without explicit training by an experimenter. *E.g. When the cat is in the puzzle box trying to escape, its random behaviour will eventually lead it to pull the rope without any explicit instructions to do so. Over time, it will be able to consistently do this on its own. (Instrumental Conditioning)*

Availability Heuristic: The tendency to make decisions based on the information that is most quickly available to us. *E.g. You may believe that typical lottery winnings are in the millions of dollars because these are most often publicized in the news; however, most winnings are actually a few dollars. You believe this because this information is most readily available to you. (Problem Solving)*

B

Between-subjects design: An experimental design in which an independent variable is manipulated across *separate* groups of participants, in order to observe the change in the dependent variable. One group of subjects receives the experimental manipulation while the other acts as a control group. Each participant or group of participants will take part in only one of two or more conditions. *E.g. When testing the effects of caffeine on alertness, researchers test the ability to recall lecture information in students who drink coffee versus those who do not drink coffee. (Research Methods I)*

Blinding: When participants do not know whether they belong to the experimental or control group, or which treatment they are receiving. *E.g. When comparing the effect of drinking caffeinated or decaffeinated coffee before bedtime, the participants would not know which type of coffee they are drinking. (Research Methods I)*

Bobo Doll Experiment: An experiment performed by Bandura, in which a child would model an adult's behaviour when playing with a toy called a bobo doll. If the adult exhibited aggressive play, the child modeled the same behaviour. If the adult exhibited passive play, the child modeled the same behaviour. No explicit reinforcement was required. *(Influence of Others I)*

Broadbent's Single Filter Model: A model of attention in which a filter selects important information on the basis of physical characteristics and allows only that information to continue on for further processing. *E.g. When looking into a crowded room for a friend wearing a blue shirt, all people wearing shirts of a different colour would not pass through your filter. Your filter would allow you to only focus on the people wearing blue to help direct your attention toward locating your friend. (Attention)*

Bystander Effect: A phenomenon in which individuals do not offer help to a victim in an emergency situation when they think others are present. *E.g. If an individual views someone being harassed when many other people are present, they are less likely to offer help than if they were the only person around. (Influence of Others I)*

C

Categorization: The process by which objects or ideas are recognized, understood, and differentiated by grouping them into different subtypes, each of which has some underlying criteria, with some sort of general rule. *(Categories and Concepts)*

Causation: The suggestion that one variable caused an effect to occur in another variable. A strong correlation alone is insufficient to determine whether or not causation exists occurred between two variables. *E.g. A researcher may observe a positive correlation between hat sales and ice cream sales. However, hat sales do not cause more ice cream sales. They both may be caused by a confounding variable, an increase in temperature due to warmer summer months. Therefore, an increase in temperature is causing hat sales and ice cream sales to increase. (Research Methods II)*

Central Appeal: Well-reasoned, factual, two-sided arguments which are effective for intelligent audiences. *E.g. When trying to persuade a group of academics, factual and two-sided arguments will be a more successful form of persuasion. (Influence of Others II)*

Chunking: Reorganizing information by grouping smaller items into larger packets in order to allow more information to be remembered. Chunking can allow individuals to remember more significant information within the short-term memory capacity of 7 +/- 2 chunks. *E.g. If each item is actually a meaningful combination of 3 numbers, then approximately 21 numbers can be remembered within those 7 items. (Memory)*

Classical Conditioning: Learning a contingency or association between a particular signal and a later event that are paired together in time and/or space. *E.g. The first famous example involves Ivan Pavlov's dog, who learned a contingency between the ringing of a bell and the arrival of food. When the dog heard the bell, it would begin to salivate. (Classical Conditioning)*

Co-Actor: Another individual performing the same task as someone, often influencing performance through social facilitation. *E.g. If an individual is bowling, his or her performance may be increased if they are competing against other bowlers. (Influence of Others I)*

Cognitive Dissonance: A psychologically uncomfortable state that occurs when a person's attitude and behaviour are inconsistent. Cognitive dissonance must be resolved by changing one's attitude as one's behaviour cannot change after the fact. *E.g. Christa exercises regularly and is a huge advocate of healthy living. One day, when at home by herself, she orders two large pizzas and finishes them. In order to resolve the resulting cognitive dissonance, she convinces herself that sticking to a strict, healthy diet is not one of her main priorities. (Influence of Others II)*

Communicator: The person persuading another. The higher the credibility or attractiveness of the communicator, the more likely they are to persuade another individual. Additionally, a communicator who has more in common with an individual is more likely to persuade them. *E.g. An attractive communicator of similar age to yourself may be the most persuasive communicator in persuading you to buy a new car. (Influence of Others II)*

Comparative Function: When individuals use information from group members to provide information in ambiguous situations and to make decisions. *E.g. If there is a sign that explicitly says "The water may be unsafe – swim at own risk", and yet there are others in the water, an individual may use the information from the group to make their own decision to go swimming. (Influence of Others I)*

Compensatory Responses: A natural bodily response to maintain homeostasis by compensating for an oncoming or ongoing change. *E.g. If an individual enters a very hot room, their body temperature will increase. They will then begin to sweat to cool their skin through the evaporation of water, thus helping lower their body temperature back to homeostatic levels. (Classical Conditioning)*

Concrete Operational Stage: The third of Piaget's stages of development, from ages 7 – 12. It is the stage at which the child has mastered all the tasks from the preoperational stage. However, they have difficulty thinking in abstract terms, which means that they have difficulty reasoning using hypotheses. *E.g. A child in this stage might understand the conservation of mass but couldn't understand something more abstract, such as algebra. (Problem Solving)*

Conditioned Response (CR): The response that occurs when presented with the CS once a contingency between the CS and US has been learned. *E.g. James has to get regular allergy shots (US) that cause him fear (UR). If the doctor he sees each time wears a distinct lemon perfume (CS), he may form a contingency between the smell of lemons (CS) and his allergy shot (US). If so, the next time he smells lemons (CS), he will begin to feel fear (CR), even if he isn't at the doctor's clinic. (Classical Conditioning)*

Conditioned Stimulus (CS): When paired with the US, creates a learned contingency where the CS (conditional stimulus) reliably predicts the US. *E.g. Every winter, James works at a restaurant with a bell on the door that rings (CS) every time the door opens. When the door opens, the restaurant becomes very cold (US) and James shivers (UR). The next day, James is at a warm spa where he hears a bell ring (CS) and begins to shiver (CR). (Classical Conditioning)*

Confirmation Bias: Our tendency to seek information that supports our hypothesis. One way to overcome the confirmation bias is to actively seek and collect information that may disprove our hypothesis. *E.g. If an individual is opposed to oil drilling in the Arctic, they may naturally tend to collect information about the negative impacts of offshore oil drilling. However, there are also financial, economic, societal and governmental benefits to initiatives like oil drilling that this individual may not consider. (Problem Solving)*

Conjunction Search: A visual search for a target that is distinguished from distracters on the basis of multiple features, such as a combination of shape, size or colour. A conjunction search takes longer than a feature search. *E.g. Finding a green T amongst green L's and red T's. (Attention)*

Consensus: The variable in covariation theory that asks how others would behave in the same way in a given situation. *E.g. If other people would agree with Jim's decision to give presents to his coworkers when he was promoted, the behaviour is likely situational. If other people would not agree with his decision and would not repeat the behaviour themselves, then the behaviour is likely dispositional. (Forming Impressions)*

Conservation: The ability to understand the constant mass or volume of an object using multiple representations. *E.g. A child in the concrete operational would understand that regardless of whether you break a cookie into two or three pieces, you still have the same amount of cookie. (Problem Solving)*

Consistency: The variable in covariation theory that asks whether an individual usually behaves the same way in a given situation. *E.g. If Lisa always comes to work angry and upset, the behaviour is consistent and one could attribute it to dispositional causes. If Lisa usually comes to work smiling and friendly, the angry behaviour is inconsistent and likely to be attributed to situational causes. (Forming Impressions)*

Contextual Cueing: In a visual search, the expected position of a target is known which helps search more efficiently and find a target more quickly. *E.g. If you are meeting a friend in a lecture in a large lecture hall, they may advise you that they are sitting on the right side of the lecture hall and wearing a blue shirt with a bright pink hat. (Attention)*

Contingency: An association formed between two stimuli after acquisition has occurred. If the presentation of one stimulus reliably leads to the presentation of another stimulus, a contingency can be formed. *E.g. In Pavlov's dog example, a contingency is formed between the sound of the bell and the presentation of food. (Classical Conditioning I)*

Continuous Reinforcement: A schedule of reinforcement in which reinforcement will always follow a particular behaviour. These are infrequent in the real world. *E.g. A dog trained to sit is given a treat every time she obeys (Instrumental Conditioning)*

Control Group: The group in an experiment which does not receive the experimental manipulation to the independent variable and therefore the group to whom the experimental group is compared. *E.g. When testing the effects of caffeine before bedtime on sleep, the control group would not drink any coffee. Researchers would then compare how long it took for these participants to fall asleep, to the group who did drink coffee before bedtime. (Research Methods I)*

Controlled Processes: When one guides their attention voluntarily and consciously to an object of interest. *E.g. When studying for a psychology exam, one may actively focus on their psychology notes while music is playing in the background. (Attention)*

Correlation: A measure of strength of the relationship between two variables. Remember, correlation does not equal causation. *E.g. A researcher may observe a positive correlation between hat sales and ice cream sales. However, hat sales do not cause more ice cream sales. They both may be caused by a confounding variable, an increase in temperature due to warmer summer months. (Research Methods II)*

Correlation Coefficient (r): Measures the degree to which two variables are correlated. Its value tells us the strength and direction of the correlation. Can be any value greater than or equal to -1, and less than or equal to +1. *E.g. Age and height in children have a strong, positive correlation with a value close to r=+1 which means that as age increases, height increases. (Research Methods II)*

Correspondent Inference Theory: An attribution theory proposed by Jones and Davis, stating that we actively analyze a person's behaviour to make inferences or attributions based on three factors. These are **the degree of choice** (whether or not an individual chooses to act a specific way), **expectation** (how likely it is one would behave in a specific way in that situation), and **intended consequences** (what motivation the person may have to behave a certain way because of the resulting consequences). *(Forming Impressions)*

Covariation Theory: An attribution theory proposed by Kelley that is used to determine if a person's behaviour is due to situational or dispositional factors. It is based on three variables: consistency, distinctiveness and consensus. *(Forming Impressions)*

CS-: A signal that reliably predicts the absence of an event (US). *E.g. A green light at a traffic intersection indicates that there will be no traffic from perpendicular lanes, signalling that it is safe to drive ahead. (Classical Conditioning)*

CS+: A signal that reliably predicts an event (US). *E.g. At a railway crossing, the signal of flashing red lights and train bells reliably predicts an oncoming train. (Classical Conditioning)*

Cue: A signal that can be used to trigger the retrieval of a memory. *E.g. Stephen's dad always wears red shirts on Sundays when they watched football together. Many years after he moves away, Stephen sees a man the same height and weight as his father wearing a red shirt on his Sunday, and remembers the times they watched a football game on TV. (Memory)*

D

Data: Quantifiable values which measure the outcome of a test. *E.g. When testing the effects of caffeine on alertness, the data would be represented by the number of minutes that each participant required to fall asleep. (Research Methods I)*

Deductive Reasoning: Arriving at a specific fact based on a general theory. *E.g. If you know that dogs are generally friendly, you will be able to deduce that because your neighbour's new pet is a dog, he is likely friendly. (Problem Solving)*

Deindividuation: A loss of a sense of personal responsibility, individuality, and restraint when put in a group situation. *E.g. In the Stanford Prison Experiment, prison guards would perform anti-normative behaviour in a group situation because the anonymity on both sides meant that individual identifying characteristics could not be used against them. (Influence of Others II)*

Dependent Variable: The variable that researchers observe but do not change during an experiment. The researchers change the independent variable and measure the effects (if any) on the dependent variable. *E.g. When testing the effects of caffeine on alertness, the experimenter observes the amount of time required for each participant to fall asleep (dependent variable) by manipulating coffee consumption (independent variable). (Research Methods I)*

Descriptive Statistics: Describes data in a way that summarizes at a glance the overall results of an experiment. This includes summary statistics such as histograms, measures of central tendency (mean, median, and mode), and measures of variability (standard deviation). *(Research Methods II)*

Discrimination: Restricting the range of CSs that can elicit a CR. *E.g. A certain sound (CS) signals that a phone has received a text message (US) which leads to the individual checking their phone (UR and CR). If another similar sound is repeatedly presented without the arrival of a text message, then the individual would stop expecting a text message in response to the similar sound. (Classical Conditioning)*

Discriminative Stimulus (SD): In instrumental conditioning, it is a cue that signals when a contingency between a particular response and reinforcement is available. *E.g. When a dog is asked to roll over by its owners, it may be rewarded with a treat. However, a vet may not necessarily reward a dog for rolling over. The contingency between the behaviour (rolling over) and the reinforcement (a treat) is only valid in the presence of the owners (discriminative stimulus). (Instrumental Conditioning)*

Distinctiveness: The variable in covariation theory that asks whether an individual behaves differently in different situations than the given situation. *E.g. Han always makes time to play with his children, no matter how busy, and this behaviour could be attributed to dispositional or situational causes. If Han makes time to play with and be nice to all children, his behaviour is likely dispositional. If Han frowns and gets upset by other children, his behaviour is likely situational. (Forming Impressions)*

Double-blind Study: An experiment in which neither the experimenter nor the participants know which treatment a particular group of participants is receiving. *E.g. When comparing the effects of drinking caffeinated or decaffeinated coffee before bedtime, neither the participants nor the experimenter would know which type of coffee the participants are drinking. (Research Methods I)*

Drug Tolerance: With each successive drug trial, the drug effects become less and less effective, especially when the drug is taken in the same environment each time. This occurs because the environment reliably triggers compensatory responses, even before the drug has been taken, thus requiring more of the drug to be administered to achieve the same effects. *(Classical Conditioning)*

E

Encoding Specificity: The finding that memory recall is better when retrieval takes place under similar conditions to encoding. It demonstrates that our memory is affected by our internal and external environment. *E.g.*

According to this theory, if you were to write an exam (retrieval) in the same room as your lectures (encoding), test performance may be improved because you are retrieving the information in the same environment where you encoded it. (Memory)

Escape Training: The removal of a negative reinforcer following a behaviour in order to increase the frequency of that behaviour. *E.g. If you are consistently getting sunburned while tanning at the beach, you may learn to wear sunscreen to prevent yourself from getting burned further. (Instrumental Conditioning)*

Exemplar Theory: The theory that suggests we categorize new objects by comparing them to all the objects we have encountered in our past experiences. *E.g. When seeing a breed of dog that you have never seen before, you recognize that it is a dog by comparing it to all other dogs you have seen in the past. This involves realizing that this new animal shares similarities with them, such as a distinct nose, a tail that wags and the ability to bark. (Categories and Concepts)*

Experimental Group: A group of participants which receives the manipulation of the independent variable, in order to test the effect on the dependent variable. *E.g. When testing the effects of caffeine on alertness, the experimental group would receive regular caffeinated coffee and their alertness would be measured by the time it takes participants to fall asleep. (Research Methods I)*

Experimenter Bias: Actions made by the experimenter, unintentionally or deliberately, to promote the result they hope to achieve. *E.g. When testing the effects of caffeine on alertness, the experimenter may spend more time talking to the experimental group than the control group, thus keeping them engaged and alert in ways not caused by drinking coffee. (Research Methods I)*

Extinction: In classical conditioning, it is the loss of the CR when the CS no longer predicts the presentation of the US. This occurs after repeated trials of presenting the CS without the US. Therefore, the CS no longer leads to the CR. *E.g. If James was repeatedly exposed to the smell of lemons (CS) without receiving his allergy shot (US) and experiencing fear (UR), he would no longer experience fear (CR) when smelling lemons (CS). (Classical Conditioning)*

F

False Fame Effect: The finding that subjects who read a list of both recently learned and famous names will incorrectly identify some of the newly learned names as famous after a 24-hour delay. Due to increased processing fluency, these names would seem familiar to the participant, who would then incorrectly assume that the names seemed familiar because they were famous. *(Memory)*

False Memory: When an individual recalls a fake experience that is remembered as a real experience from that individual's past. As time passes from the initial description of the experience, subjects become more likely to believe the experience is true. *E.g. A subject may be told to recall the time when they were lost in a park as a child. At first, they may not believe it truly happened, but over time they will be more likely to believe that they really did get lost in a park as a child. (Memory)*

Familiarity: One of the factors influencing attraction. Individuals are more likely to be attracted to people and/or things that are more familiar, even if they have only been seen a few times in the past. *E.g. When judging the sound of a baby name, parents may be more likely to like a name that they have previously heard over a brand new, unusual name. However, with more exposure to the name, they may also come to like the unusual name. (Forming Impressions)*

Feature Search: A visual search for a target that is distinguished from the distracters on the basis of one feature, such as colour, shape, texture or size. *E.g. Finding a green T amongst many green L's. (Attention)*

Filter Model: A model that suggests attention works by filtering distractions and allowing only important information through. The subtle difference between a filter model and a spotlight model of attention is that the spotlight model suggests that attention enhances processing of an attended object while filter models suggest that attention helps to ignore other distractions and allow the object of attention to continue for further processing. *E.g. If you wanted to attend to a flower, filter model would suggest that attention helps you ignore the grass around the flower and allow the flower to continue for further processing. (Attention)*

Fixed Interval: An instrumental conditioning schedule of reinforcement in which reinforcement is delivered after a constant period of time. *E.g. Employees of many companies are paid for every two weeks of work, a fixed interval schedule of reinforcement. (Instrumental Conditioning)*

Fixed Ratio: An instrumental conditioning schedule of reinforcement in which reinforcement is delivered after a constant number of responses. *E.g. In the case of an individual who works on a specific contract, they will be paid after a specific number of tasks have been completed. For instance, an agent for an actress may only receive payment for every 5 auditions he books. (Instrumental Conditioning)*

Fluency: The ease with which an experience is processed. Familiar experiences are generally processed more fluently than are novel experiences. *E.g. You likely process a familiar song with more ease than a brand-new song in a foreign language that you have not previously heard. (Memory)*

Flynn Effect: The observation that raw IQ scores have continued to increase every year since 1932. It is argued that this increase may be due to a number of factors, such as increased quality of schooling, accessibility to information, increased nutrition and health. *(Problem Solving)*

Foot in the Door Effect: When individuals are more willing to comply with a large request after they have already complied with a smaller request. *E.g. If an individual wanted to ask people to make a donation to their charity, they may initially have asked for them to sign up for an email flyer from the same charity. (Influence of Others II)*

Foreign Accent Syndrome: In very rare cases following serious brain injury or stroke, some individuals sound as though they are speaking their native language with a novel, acquired foreign accent. *E.g. A person with a British accent may then sound like they are speaking English with a Russian accent. (Language)*

Formal Operational Stage: The fourth and last of Piaget's stages of development, occurring at 11+ years of age. It is the stage at which a child has mastered the tasks from the concrete operational stage and is able to think in abstract terms. *E.g. A child in this stage would be able to learn algebra and enjoy fantasy games. (Problem Solving)*

Four Consequences in Instrumental Conditioning: Four mechanisms of describing how reinforcement can be used to influence behaviour. The four consequences are the presentation of positive reinforcement, presentation of negative reinforcement, removal of positive reinforcement, and removal of negative reinforcement. Note: The presentation of negative reinforcement is not the same as the removal of positive reinforcement. *(Instrumental Conditioning)*

Frequency Distribution: A type of graph illustrating the distribution of how frequently a given value or range of values appears in a data set. It is essentially a smooth curve that connects the peak of each bar in a histogram. *E.g. A researcher may create a frequency distribution that illustrates how many students have weights between 120 – 139 pounds, 140 – 159 pounds, 160 – 179 pounds, 180 – 199 pounds and 200+ pounds, respectively. (Research Methods II)*

Functional Fixedness: The difficulty of seeing alternative uses for common objects. *E.g. It is obvious that a flashlight is used to illuminate dark areas. However, it is less obvious or intuitive that you would be able to use it as a paperweight on a very windy day. (Problem Solving)*

Fundamental Attribution Error: The finding that people often overestimate dispositional causes for others' behaviour, while underestimating situational causes. People are more likely to make this error when determining the causes of others' behaviour rather than their own. *E.g. If a cashier is very rude to you, you may think that they are generally a very rude person (dispositional). However, their boss may have just let them know that the company was laying off several people, thus putting them in a bad mood (situational). (Forming Impressions)*

G

Generalization: When a stimulus similar to the CS also produces a CR. *E.g. If a certain sound (CS) signals that a phone has received a text message (US) which leads to the user checking their phone (UR and CR), then another similar sound may also elicit the same response. (Classical Conditioning)*

Generalization Gradient: A graph demonstrating the extent to which similar stimuli elicit the same CR as the CS in a classical conditioning paradigm. It often appears like a bell shaped curved, in which the original CS elicits the strongest response, and as other stimuli became less similar (further away from the CS), the conditional response becomes less strong. *E.g. If a certain sound (CS) signals that a phone has received a text message (US), this sound will lead to the user checking their phone in response to the sound the majority of times it goes off. Similar sounds may also lead to the user checking their phones frequently and as the sounds become less and less similar to the CS, checking responses will decrease. (Classical Conditioning)*

Group Polarization: The finding that group decision-making tends to lead to more extreme or polarized views than the original views of individual group members by strengthening the original inclinations of the individual group members. This can move the group decision in either the risky or cautious extreme. *E.g. An individual interested in canoeing is more likely to develop their interest among a group of other individual who enjoy canoeing. (Influence of Others I)*

Groupthink: A group decision-making environment where group cohesiveness becomes so strong that it tends to override a realistic appraisal of alternative opinions. *E.g. A group of city councillors may strongly believe that recycling should be eliminated from their city because it is too expensive and any person who disagrees and tries to discuss the benefits of recycling will be rejected from the group. (Influence of Others I)*

H

Histogram: Type of graph used to report the number of times a group of values appear in a data set. It forms the basis of a frequency distribution. *E.g. A researcher may create a histogram that illustrates how many students have weights between 120 – 139 pounds, 140 – 159 pounds, 160 – 179 pounds, 180 – 199 pounds and 200+ pounds, respectively. (Research Methods II)*

Homeostasis: The process of keeping the internal state of the body constant, including but not limited to temperature, glucose, and ion levels. *E.g. Sweating is a compensatory response that occurs when the body is becoming too warm and needs to cool down to maintain a constant body temperature. (Classical Conditioning)*

Hypothesis: A testable statement that makes specific predictions about the relationship between the variables in a theory. *E.g. When testing the effects of caffeine on alertness, researchers may hypothesize that drinking coffee keeps participants more alert and therefore, it takes them longer to fall asleep. (Research Methods I)*

I

Illusion of the Expert: The perception that something is simple because we are good at it. *E.g. A math professor may have a hard time communicating with his class of first year students because he explains challenging concepts at a level they do not understand. He may assume that because he can do the math easily, it must be simple enough for first year students to also understand. (Categories and Concepts)*

Implosive Therapy: A mechanism used to treat phobias, encouraging the individual to directly confront the CS that causes them anxiety by repeatedly presenting this CS in the absence of the anxiety-causing US. *E.g. Someone who fell from a ladder as a child and now has a phobia of heights may be asked to ride to the top of the CN tower (which results in exposure to heights without falling), thereby treating the phobia. (Classical Conditioning)*

Independent Variable: The variable manipulated by the scientist. *E.g. When testing the effects of caffeine on amount of time required to fall asleep (dependent variable), the experimenter can manipulate the amount or type of coffee the participants drink (independent variable). (Research Methods I)*

Inductive Reasoning: Coming to a general theory based on a specific fact. *E.g. If you see your neighbour's dog, Spot, is very friendly, you may use inductive reasoning to determine that all dogs or furry four legged creatures are also friendly. (Problem Solving)*

Infant-Directed Speech: The natural tendency for people to use higher pitch and exaggerated tones when speaking to infants, which may help infants learn to segment speech. *(Language)*

Innate Mechanism Theory: The theory that humans are born with instinctual mechanisms to help them understand universal grammar rules which allows them to develop language skills rapidly. *(Language)*

Inferential Statistics: Statistics that allow us to use results from samples to make inferences about overall, underlying populations. *E.g. If you wanted to use your tutorial to determine the distribution of height of all undergraduate students at McMaster, you would make an inference using the distribution of height in your tutorial. (Research Methods II)*

Intelligence: The cognitive ability of an individual to learn from experience, reason well, remember important information, and cope with the demands of daily living. *(Problem Solving)*

Interval Schedule of Reinforcement: A schedule of reinforcement in which reinforcement is provided once some amount of time has passed since the last response was reinforced. *E.g. If a shoemaker is paid for his work every week, then he will receive a pay cheque regardless of how many shoes he has made. (Instrumental Conditioning)*

Inhibition: In classical conditioning, when extinction leads to the learning of a new, inhibitory response to the CS (CS), suggesting the presence of two learned processes (the original learned response to the CS and inhibitory learned response to the CS). *E.g. After extinguishing a fear of bees by repeatedly presenting bees (CS) in the absence of being stung (US), a new inhibitory response to bees is learned rather than the contingency between bees and being stung being unlearned. (Classical Conditioning)*

Instrumental Conditioning: *The overall training paradigm that allows for the* learning of a contingency between a behavior and a consequence. *E.g. A cat may no longer chew wires if it finds itself getting shocked when doing so. (Instrumental Conditioning)*

L

Language: The human capacity for acquiring and using complex systems of communication. There are three criteria to outline a "true" language. Firstly, language is governed by rules and grammar. Secondly, symbols used in language are completely arbitrary. Lastly, language is productive, meaning there are limitless ways to combine words. *(Language)*

Language Acquisition Device (LAD): An innate mechanism, which Noam Chomsky argues is present in humans of all languages, that helps language develop rapidly according to universal grammar rules. *(Language)*

Language Explosion: The point in children's language development where vocabulary increases very rapidly and most children have mastered the major aspects of language. This typically occurs between one and a half to six years of age. *(Language)*

Law of Effect: Behaviours with positive consequences become stamped in. *E.g. reaching for the cookie jar at the top of the fridge is a positive behaviour if the reward is a cookie.* Behaviours with negative consequences are stamped out. *E.g. if you were blamed and punished for stealing the cookies from the cookie jar, then you probably won't repeat the same behaviour. (Instrumental Conditioning)*

Levels of Processing Model: A memory model, which states that the more deeply a concept is processed, the better memory performance becomes. *E.g. When memorizing "car" on a print advertisement, a shallow level would be remembering that the word was spelled in capital letters (CAR). A deeper level would be to understand the word in a context, such as "The Lexus in that ad is driving on a highway similar to the ones my grandfather used to drive home on". The latter level of processing allows the individual to make more connections to the material and remember it better. Overall, the better a concept is organized and understood, the easier it is to memorize and recall. (Memory)*

Low-Ball Technique: An escalation of the terms of an agreement after someone has already agreed. Compliance is secured at a smaller cost, only to later reveal additional costs, making the initial decision seem irreversible. *E.g. An individual may ask their friend to help them carry some groceries. Once they agree to help, they may be asked to help grocery shop, help pay for the groceries, as well as help put them away. (Influence of Others II)*

M

Mean: The average value of the data set, calculated by adding together all of the points in a data set and dividing by the number of items in the set. *E.g. You can calculate your tutorial's mean age by adding up everybody's age and dividing by the number of students in your tutorial. (Research Methods II)*

Measures of Central Tendency: Measures that tell us where a data set is centered, using the mean, median, and mode. *E.g. To determine what value age is centered around in your tutorial, you collect all the ages in your tutorial and find that the mean is 18.4, median is 18 and mode is 18. (Research Methods II)*

Measures of Variability: Measures that tell us how other values within a data set fall around the centre of the data. *E.g. Both you and your friend may have a mean grade in all university courses of B+ but you may have a larger standard deviation than your friend, meaning your grades are more spread out from the mean while your friend tends to consistently get grades around B+. (Research Methods II)*

Median: The centre value in a data set when the set is arranged numerically from smallest to largest. *E.g. If there were 27 students in your tutorial, then the 14th student's age (after age is put in order) would represent the median. If there were 28 students, then the average of the 14 and 15th students' age represents the median. (Research Methods II)*

Message: The facts used by a communicator to persuade listeners, and a contributing factor in persuasion. They can be framed from multiple perspectives to effectively persuade multiple audiences. *(Influence of Others II)*

Milgram Experiment: An experiment conducted at Yale University in which a subject was required to shock a confederate learner if they answered a question incorrectly, and progressively increase the shock for each incorrect answer. The experiment measured the willingness of a subject to obey an authority figure when the actions conflicted with their personal conscience. *(Influence of Others II)*

Mode: The value that appears most frequently in a data set. *E.g. If the majority of students in your tutorial are 18 years old, or if 18 is the most frequently appearing age in your tutorial, then the mode for this data set is 18. (Research Methods II)*

Morpheme: The smallest unit of sound that contains information. A word can contain one or multiple morphemes. *E.g. In the word horseshoes, there are three morphemes. The word is divided as (horse)(shoe)(s), where one morpheme refers to the animal, the next to what goes on its feet, and the last to the fact that there are more than one. (Language)*

Multi-Store Model: The assumption that memory is composed of both short-term and long-term storage systems. In this model, incoming information is first stored in a short-term memory buffer. Information is then transferred into long term memory following active rehearsal of that information. *E.g. When learning lecture material, it is first processed by your short-term memory. Because this only acts as a buffer for that information, it will either be lost or, if rehearsed, transferred into long-term memory for later retrieval. (Memory)*

Multiple Intelligences: A theory, proposed by Gardner, arguing that there are separate and independent intelligences for different purposes. Therefore, one could be brilliant in one area while lacking in another. The eight intelligences that he specified were verbal, mathematical, musical, spatial, kinaesthetic, interpersonal, intrapersonal, and naturalistic. *(Problem Solving)*

N

Normative Function: The role of others in setting norms or standards of conduct based on fear of rejection. *E.g. If an individual doesn't enjoy eating pizza but the rest of the group wants to order pizza, they may conform by expressing the desire to have a few slices to avoid rejection. (Influence of Others I)*

Normal Distribution: A frequency distribution with a characteristic smooth, bell-shaped, and symmetrical-curve around a single peak. Many everyday measures are normally distributed. *E.g. Height is normally distributed, with individuals of an average height being the most frequent (creating a central peak) and the shortest and tallest individuals being the least frequent. (Research Methods II)*

O

Object Permanence: The understanding of infants that objects continue to exist even when they are no longer visible. *E.g. In a game of peek-a-boo with their father, an infant has not achieved object permanence if they are continuously surprised every time they see their dad's face again. This is because the baby thinks that their father stops existing when he hides his face behind his hands. (Problem Solving)*

Observational Studies: Studies in which the researchers observe the effect of variables they are interested in without performing any manipulation, allowing them to infer correlational relationships but not causation. *E.g. Researchers may compare the number of students who ride the bus and height of snow fallen in meters. This may help researchers determine how to organize the bus schedule based on certain weather conditions without performing any explicit manipulation. (Research Methods II)*

Omission Training: The removal of a positive reinforcement following a behaviour in order to decrease the frequency of that behaviour. *E.g. Billy steals his sister's laptop, which causes their mom to take away his bike for* *a week. (Instrumental Conditioning)*

Others' Opinions: One of the factors influencing attraction. Individuals are more likely to be attracted to those who have already expressed that they like them. This is especially true of individuals with low self-esteem. *E.g. You may be more likely to like someone who has expressed their like for you, especially if it was right after you failed your driver's test. (Forming Impressions)*

Outliers: Extreme points distant from others in a data set which easily influence the mean. *E.g. Nine out of ten of your first year grades are between B+ and A+; however, you did not do so well in Chemistry and got one D-. This D- is an outlier in your grades data set and will disproportionately bring down the mean of this data set. (Research Methods II)*

Overdose: When an individual administers too much of a drug, which the body cannot compensate for. It often occurs when an individual takes a drug they have previously taken in a new environment. *E.g. If they have previously taken a drug repeatedly in one specific environment like their room, they may have increased their dosage over time as the drug became less effective due to compensatory responses triggered from their environment. As they moved to a new environment, their body no longer experiences the same compensatory responses, leading to a much stronger effect from the drug. (Classical Conditioning)*

Overextensions: When children apply language rules too broadly, leading to semantic and grammatical errors. *E.g. When a child learns that a TV has a screen that shows images, they may then address a computer, a smartphone, and any other device with a screen as a TV. (Language)*

Overjustification Effects: In order for cognitive dissonance to take place, there must be insufficient justification for the behaviour that is in conflict with the attitude. When overjustification occurs, cognitive dissonance does not happen because the behaviour that is in conflict with the attitude is justified by some external means. *E.g. Emma likes programming code for fun on the weekends. Her friend Jesse though, gets paid to program code and considers it to be very boring. Jesse's behaviour of writing code is overjustified by the fact that he gets paid to do so he does not need to change his attitude to match his behaviour. Meanwhile, Emma's attitude must be that she likes programming code because there is insufficient justification for her behaviour. (Influence of Others II)*

P

P-value: The value resulting from a t-test used to determine statistical significance. If the p-value is below a predetermined threshold (usually 0.05), then the data set is considered statistically significant. *E.g. If you perform a t-test and the resulting p-value is 0.035, you can conclude that your results are statistically significant, meaning there is only a 3.5% chance that you obtained this result by chance. (Research Methods II)*

Partial Reinforcement: A schedule of reinforcement in which a form of reinforcement does not follow every single time a particular behaviour is performed. *E.g. If a young child has a bad habit of sucking his thumb, his mother may reward him with a chocolate for every five days that he does not suck his thumb. (Instrumental Conditioning)*

Participant Bias: When a participant's actions in an experiment influence the results apart from the experimental manipulations. *E.g. When testing the effects of caffeine on alertness, if the participant is aware of the purpose of the study, they may intentionally try to stay awake. (Research Methods I)*

Peripheral Appeal: Well-presented, easy to understand messages which are effective for unintelligent audiences. *E.g. When trying to persuade a less academic audience, quick decision-making techniques based on heuristics are more successful persuasion tactics. (Influence of Others II)*

Persuasion: The process of causing someone to believe an idea using reasoning or argument, which may affect their future thoughts, actions, and choices. *E.g. An individual may try to persuade their friends to join them on a trip to the Caribbean by talking about how much they all need the break after a hectic semester. (Influence of Others II)*

Phobia: An anxiety disorder, in which a person exhibits an exaggerated, intense, and persistent fear of certain situations, activities, things, or people, which is often disproportional to the danger that is posed. They are often the result of a specific traumatic experience involving the feared stimulus. *E.g. A common phobia is apiphobia (fear of bees). (Classical Conditioning)*

Phoneme: The smallest unit of sound in language, regardless of meaning. *E.g. The word happy can be broken down into four phonemes: /h/, /a/, /pp/, /y/, each of which has a sound but not necessarily meaning. (Language)*

Physical Attractiveness: One of the factors influencing attractiveness. Individuals are more likely to be attracted to someone they perceive as being physically attractive. This is used on the presumption that what is beautiful is also good. *E.g. People who are physically attractive are often judged as kinder, warmer and more intelligent. (Forming Impressions)*

Piaget's Stages of Development: A set of four basic stages that children actively partake in during cognitive development. The stages are called sensorimotor, preoperational, concrete operational, and formal operational. Each stage is characterized by different abilities and limitations. While different children progress through them at different rates, children must pass through them in the same sequential order. *(Problem Solving)*

Placebo Effect: An effect that occurs when an individual exhibits a response to a treatment that has no related therapeutic effect. *E.g. When testing the effects of caffeine on alertness, a participant may be provided decaffeinated coffee that tastes, smells and looks just like caffeinated coffee. If receiving decaf coffee, theoretically, participants should not have difficulties falling asleep; however, if they do experience difficulty, it may be due to the placebo effect. (Research Methods I)*

Population: The overall group of individuals that a researcher is seeking to study and that the results of an experiment apply to. *E.g. When testing the effects of caffeine on alertness, a select group of undergraduate students from diverse ethnic backgrounds in Toronto may be tested to represent the entire population of undergraduate coffee drinkers from universities in urban areas. (Research Methods I)*

Pop-Out Effect: A visual search task that is rapid regardless of set size. This occurs when there is a specific feature in the target that highly contrasts the features in the rest of the set. *E.g. A neon yellow square will pop-out in a set size full of red squares. Another example is how a flashing square may pop out in a set containing a large number of multi-coloured squares. (Attention)*

Practice Effect: Improved performance over the course of an experiment due to participants becoming more experienced. *E.g. When testing the effects of caffeine on alertness, with repeated trials, participants may develop strategies to help them fall asleep, independent of what kind of coffee they are drinking. (Research Methods I)*

Preoperational Stage: The second of Piaget's stages of development, from 2-7 years of age, where the child has mastered the tasks from the sensorymotor stage but is very egocentric and has difficulty seeing the world from the perspective of others. Children in this stage also begin to master seriation, reversible relationships, and conservation in this stage. *E.g. An egocentric child would think that if they were hungry and wanted to eat, everybody around them must also be hungry and want to eat as well. (Problem Solving)*

Primacy Effect: The finding that memory performance is better for items encoded earlier in a list because they are more likely to transfer to long-term memory. *E.g. If you were to repeat a list of words and add a successive* *word each time, the word at the beginning of the list will be repeated the most. The first few letters of the alphabet "ABC" are more easily remembered than the sequence of letters in the middle "KLO", because the earlier letters are repeatedly more frequently. (Memory)*

Prototype theory: The theory that suggests we categorize new objects by comparing them to *one* internal representation of the category called a "prototype", which is the "average" or "best" member of the category. *E.g. When viewing a new dog for the first time, you may compare it to one typical representation of what you consider a "dog", which is the average of every other dog you have seen before. (Categories and Concepts)*

Proximity: One of the factors influencing attractiveness. Individuals are more likely to be attracted to or become friends with people they work or live closely with. The important thing about proximity is that there is not only high proximity (physical closeness) but also low functional distance (higher probability of interaction). *E.g. You are more likely to be attracted to the friend you sit beside in class whom you talk to and study with than the person who sits directly in front of you to whom you've never spoken. (Forming Impressions)*

Punishment: The presentation of a negative reinforcer following a behaviour in order to decrease the frequency of that behaviour. *E.g. If Sally cheats on a test and is sent to detention (the presentation of a negative reinforcer), this is meant to decrease the frequency of the unwanted behaviour. (Instrumental Conditioning)*

Puzzle Box: A cat trapped in a box with a rope exhibits random behaviours. Its random behaviour would eventually lead it to find that when it pulls the rope, it can escape from the box. Over time, the number of behaviours before the cat finds the rope would decrease, suggesting the animal followed a stimulus-response process, or instrumental conditioning. *(Instrumental Conditioning)*

R

Random Assortment: Assigning participants to either the experimental or control group at random to avoid any biases that may cause differences between the groups of subjects. *E.g. When testing the effects of drinking coffee before bedtime compared to no coffee, the experimenter would randomly assign participants to either condition. (Research Methods I)*

Ratio Schedule of Reinforcement: A schedule of reinforcement in which reinforcement is provided once a predetermined number of responses has been provided. *E.g. If a salesperson sells 4 cars, he receives his pay check. (Instrumental Conditioning)*

Recall Test: A memory test in which a subject is asked to read a list of items, and after a time delay, to freely generate as many items as they can remember from the list. *E.g. A subject may be required to read a list of 10 animal words and two days later be asked to write down as many words as they can remember from the list. (Memory)*

Recency Effect: The finding that memory performance is better for items encoded later in a list because they remain in the short-term memory stores, since new items do not replace them. *E.g. When trying to memorize a new phone number, you may only be able to remember the last few numbers when you attempt to dial the number. (Memory)*

Recognition Test: A memory test in which a subject is asked to read a list of items and then after some time to read another list of items and determine whether each item is "new" or "old" (i.e. whether it was present in the initial list). *E.g. A subject may be required to read a list of 14 names. After two days, they return and read a new list of 14 names and are required to determine whether these names were present in the list they read two days earlier. (Memory)*

Reliability: A measure of the extent to which repeated testing produces consistent results. *E.g. If an individual* *performs a certain fitness test multiple times and achieves similar results each time, then the test can be considered reliable. (Problem Solving)*

Representativeness Heuristic: The tendency to assume what that we see is representative of a larger category we have in our minds, and to classify people based on how well their behaviour fits with a certain prototype. *E.g. In the gambler's fallacy, individuals believe that previous results influence later games, such as a game of roulette. However, what they do not consider is that each game is completely independent of any past or future games. Therefore, they may assume that a win on one game may represent a larger "winning streak". (Problem Solving)*

Research Method: An experimental method used to test a hypothesis. *E.g. When testing the effects of caffeine on alertness, the research method would involve an experiment that compared the time required to fall asleep between a group of individuals drinking coffee and a group of individuals drinking decaf coffee. (Research Methods I)*

Reversible Relationships: The ability to understand relationships from multiple perspectives. *E.g. If a preoperational child is asked if he has a mother, he may say, "Yes, I do! That's my mommy!" If he is asked if mommy has a son, he might say, "Mommy has no son!" (Problem Solving)*

Reward Training: The presentation of a positive reinforcement following a behaviour in order to increase the frequency of that behaviour. *E.g. If a dog is rewarded with a treat for rolling over, he is most likely to repeat that behaviour to obtain the reward. (Instrumental Conditioning I)*

Risky Shift: A theory proposed by Stoner, stating that group decisions tend to be riskier than the mean decisions of the individuals within that group. *E.g. An individual may not want to go cliff jumping on his or her own. However, as a group, everyone may want to. (Influence of Others I)*

S

S-delta: In instrumental conditioning, it is a stimulus that cues when a contingency between a particular response and reinforcement is no longer valid. *E.g. When a dog is asked to roll over by its owners' guests, it will not be rewarded with a treat and therefore, over time will learn not to roll over for guests because the guests (S-delta) indicate the contingency is not valid. (Instrumental Conditioning)*

Sampling: Selecting a subgroup representative of the underlying population to study. *E.g. When testing the effects of caffeine on the alertness of all university students in urban areas, the experimenter cannot perform a test on the entire population and therefore should ensure to select a participant group of university students which is representative of as many ages, genders, and ethnicities as possible. (Research Methods I)*

Scientific Method: A series of steps used to design studies that allow researchers to objectively and consistently find answers to specific research questions. The steps are as follows: theory, hypothesis, selecting a research method, collecting data, analyzing data, reporting findings, and revising theories. *(Research Methods I)*

Scatter-Plot: A graph used to display the relationship between two variables in a data set. Scatter-plots are used to determine the correlation between two variables in a data set. *E.g. If you wanted to illustrate the relationship between age and height, you would plot age on the x-axis and height on the y-axis. (Research Methods II)*

Segmentation: In spoken language, the process of determining when one word ends and the next begins. Segmentation is the process of naturally spacing the sentence into individual words to improve comprehension. *E.g. In this sentence, "Itisdifficulttoreadthisifeverythingisbunchedtogether." (Language)*

Segmentation Problem: The difficulty in segmenting words when hearing an unfamiliar language. *E.g. If you do* *not speak Polish, it will be very difficult to segment a Polish sentence if listening to someone speaking the language. (Language)*

Self-Serving Bias: The tendency to perceive yourself favourably. *E.g. Even if everybody in a class gets an 80% or higher on a midterm, you are more likely to attribute your success to your own intelligence, instead of simply saying the test was easy. (Forming Impressions)*

Semantics: The meaning of each individual word used in a sentence. While a sentence may follow syntactic rules, it can potentially carry no semantic meaning. *E.g. The sentence "Amazing colourless pink flowers jump inside banks" contains no semantic meaning. (Language)*

Sensorimotor Stage: The first of Piaget's stages of development, from birth until 2 years of age. It is the stage at which a child realizes they can affect change on their environment. Object permanence is achieved at the end of this stage. *E.g. A child at this stage may realize that if they push a ball, it will roll across the floor, therefore affecting change on their environment. (Problem Solving)*

Seriation: The ability to logically order a series of objects. *E.g. If a preoperational child is asked to place a series of cones of increasing size order, they may have difficulty ordering them from smallest to largest. (Problem Solving)*

Serial Position Curve: A U shaped curve describing the recall performance of each item in an ordered list of words, indicating that recall is worst for items placed in the middle of the sequence. *E.g. When learning a new unit in a course, information at the beginning and end of the unit will be recalled more easily than information from the middle of the unit. (Memory)*

Set Size Effect: In a visual search, it is the phenomenon of increased difficulty in finding a target amongst distractors as the number of items in the set increase. *E.g. A visual search task in which you are required to find a green T amongst 200 green L's would be more difficult than finding a green T amongst 10 green L's. (Attention)*

Shaping: When a behaviour is too complex for a subject to discover on their own, an experimenter can use shaping by successive approximation. This orders a complex behaviour into a series of smaller, more feasible steps, which when put together, lead to the final complex behaviour. *E.g. An animal trainer may train a dog to carry a toy across the room. First, the dog would be rewarded when they make any movement toward the toy. Once this is reinforced, the dog must pick up the toy in order to be rewarded. Once this behaviour is reinforced, the dog is then rewarded when it crosses the room with the toy. (Instrumental Conditioning)*

Social Facilitation: The increased performance that occurs in the presence of co-actors or an audience. *E.g. A basketball player may score more baskets when playing a real game than when practicing alone. (Influence of Others I)*

Social Learning Theory: Popularized by Bandura, this theory suggests that children learn language imitation and operant condition of adults. *For example, if a baby is babbling and stumbles upon the phonemes to say "mama", they will be praised for it with positive reinforcement, encouraging the child to repeat it again. Parents may also then start repeating this word so that the child will imitate them. (Language)* More broadly, the theory suggests that you learn behaviours by imitating the behaviours of others. *E.g. A child may learn to exhibit aggressive behaviours simply by observing adults acting aggressively. This would not require any explicit reinforcing of the behaviour. (Influence of Others I)*

Social Loafing: The finding that individuals are less motivated when working in a group than when working alone. *E.g. An individual working on a chemistry group project may not work as hard among four other students compared to if they were working alone. (Influence of Others I)*

Spearman's G: Spearman's measure of generalized intelligence, which demonstrates that individuals with a high level of "G" would perform well on a variety of classical intelligence tasks and tests. The use of G became controversial when Spearman advocated that only individuals with a minimum level of "G" should be allowed to reproduce. *(Problem Solving)*

Spontaneous Recovery: When a CS again elicits a CR after a rest period takes place following extinction in which the CS is repeatedly presented without the US. *E.g. Sarah is afraid (CR) of bees (CS) after being stung (US) which caused fear (UR). This fear (CR) is gradually extinguished by repeatedly presenting Sarah with bees (CS) without being stung (US). However, the following spring, after long winter of seeing no bees, she suddenly experiences fear (CR) again when she sees a bee (CS). (Classical Conditioning)*

Spotlight Model: A model of attention which suggests that an attentional spotlight enhances processing of objects within the spotlight. *E.g. When searching for your friend in a large lecture hall, you would move your attentional spotlight around the visual scene, enhancing whatever is in your spotlight at that time. You will find your friend when your spotlight reaches her. (Attention)*

Standard Deviation: A measure of the average of the variance of each data point from the mean. Data sets with a larger standard deviation are typically more "spread out" than data sets with a smaller standard deviation. *E.g. A population of 30 whose minimum height is 4'8" and tallest height is 6'2" will have a larger standard deviation than one with a minimum height of 5'3" and maximum height of 5'11". (Research Methods II)*

Stanford-Binet Intelligence Test: An intelligence test, developed in the early 1900s, involving 30 short tasks related to everyday life using all types of reasoning. The test is still used in some forms today. *(Problem Solving)*

Stanford Prison Experiment: An experiment conducted at Stanford University to study the behaviour of normal people under situations of authority. Twenty-four male subjects were divided into either prison guards or prisoners. What was supposed to last two weeks was cancelled in six days, because of sadistic behaviour demonstrated by the guards. The experiment demonstrated the issues of authority, assignments of control, as well as the ethical concerns of conducting experiments with humans. *(Influence of Others II)*

Statistical Significance: When the difference between two groups is due to some true difference between the two groups and not due to a random variation. *E.g. When comparing mineral content in water found in Hamilton compared to water found in Vancouver, statistically significant data suggests there is actually a difference in the fluoride concentrations, rather than a difference found by random variation or chance. (Research Methods II)*

Stroop Task: A task in which participants are presented with colour words and are asked to name the ink-colour in which the word is presented. Congruent items contain matching word and colour dimensions, such as RED written in ink-colour red. Incongruent items contain mismatched word and colour dimensions, such as BLUE written in ink-colour red. *(Attention)*

Subject/Participant: The individual taking part in an experiment. It may be a human or an animal, depending on the nature of the experiment. *E.g. When testing the effects of caffeine on alertness, a participant will be required to drink either decaffeinated or caffeinated coffee and attempt to fall asleep. (Research Methods I)*

Syntax: Refers to the rules that govern how sentences are put together; also known as grammar. Differences in syntactic rules vary according to where the languages originate. *E.g. In French, gender is assigned to all nouns while in English, gender is only assigned to those of biological gender. A table would be referred to as "it" in English, not "she". (Language)*

Systematic Desensitization: A mechanism used to treat phobias, in which the individual is presented with gradual exposure to the feared CS. An individual would initially be presented with stimuli that are closer to the end of the generalization gradient. *E.g. An individual with a fear of dogs may initially be presented with four-legged animals that do not quite resemble dogs, with each successive step involving conditional stimuli that are more similar to dogs. (Classical Conditioning)*

T

t-Test: A statistical test that determines statistical significance. It considers each data point from both groups being tested to calculate the probability of obtaining differences by chance if there is in fact only one distribution underlying both groups in the experiment. *E.g. A t-test can calculate the probability of finding a difference in height between members of a basketball team and members of a general population. If the results of a t-test are not statistically significant, this would mean that the members of the basketball team are not statistically different from the underlying population in terms of height. (Research Methods II)*

Taste Aversion: A rapid form of acquisition in classical conditioning specifically related taste. *E.g. Often, it only takes one trial of eating spoiled food and experience of sickness to learn to avoid the food. The CS is taste, the US is sickness, and the UR and CR are aversion. (Classical Conditioning)*

Triesman's Dual Filter Model: A model of attention in which there are two filters involved in attention. The early filter is a physical filter that evaluates information based on physical cues such as pitch or intensity. Relevant information is then passed through to the second filter, the semantic filter, which considers the deeper meaning when choosing what stimulus to attend to. *E.g. When listening to multiple musical parts in a song, the early filter may process each musical line. However, the semantic filter will process the meaning taken from the melody. (Attention)*

Theory: A general set of ideas about the way the world works. *E.g. A researcher may theorize that certain substances may affect human cognitive abilities (Research Methods I)*

U

Unconditioned Response (UR): A response, which is automatically triggered by a stimulus in the absence of learning. *E.g. If James is exposed to a cold environment (US), he will automatically shiver (UR). (Classical Conditioning)*

Unconditioned Stimulus (US): A stimulus, which automatically triggers a response in the absence of learning. *E.g. If James receives an allergy shot (US), he will automatically experience pain (UR). (Classical Conditioning)*

Underextensions: When children only apply a language rule to a specific context, and do not generalize it to other situations in which they should generalize it. *E.g. A child may use the word car to refer only to his or her family's car, and to no other cars. (Language)*

Understanding: The ability to evaluate a situation and act appropriately based on prior experiences. *E.g. If we categorize this scene of two people shouting as a private conflict, based on our prior experiences, we immediately understand that they probably do not need our opinion. (Categories and Concepts)*

Universal Phoneme Sensitivity: The ability of infants to discriminate between speech sounds in any language, including those from non-native languages. *E.g. Infants in English-speaking families are able to discriminate Hindi speech sounds almost as well as Hindi-speaking adults while English-speaking adults are unable to accurately discriminate these speech sounds. (Language)*

V

Validity: Measures the extent to which a test is actually measuring what it is supposed to be measuring. *E.g.*

Conventional eye charts that test vision at different distances may not always produce valid results. A person may have difficulty reading aloud the letters on these charts, despite being able to see the letters perfectly fine, because English may not be their native language or they may have dyslexia. (Problem Solving)

Variable Interval: An instrumental conditioning schedule of reinforcement in which reinforcement is delivered after some variable period of time around a characteristic mean. *E.g. In the case of an employee's bonus, they will receive it at random times during some point of the year regardless of how much work they have done. (Instrumental Conditioning)*

Variable Ratio: An instrumental conditioning schedule of reinforcement in which reinforcement is delivered after some variable number of responses around a characteristic mean. *E.g. In the case of slot machines, the payout occurs after a random number of plays around a pre-set mean. Behaviour is reinforced randomly which causes people to play for hours. (Instrumental Conditioning)*

W

Waggle Dance: A form of bee communication that uses physical movement to convey the distance and direction of food away from the hive. *(Language)*

Weschler Scales: Scales standardized to produce an intelligence quotient for every individual. They consist of the Weschler Adult Intelligence Scale (WAIS) and Weschler Intelligence Scale for Children (WISC). An individual who achieves the mean score will be assigned an IQ of 100. Scores around the mean fall along a perfect normal distribution with a standard deviation of 15. *(Problem Solving & Intelligence)*

Whorf-Sapir Hypothesis: The hypothesis that says that language influences our thoughts and the way we perceive and experience the world. *E.g. In a culture whose language does not have a word for war, they do not participate in war or understand the concept of war. (Language)*

Withdrawal: A group of symptoms that occur following the discontinuation of a medication or drug. These symptoms occur most often when an individual is in the environment in which they previously took drugs. These symptoms are internal compensatory responses that would normally oppose the drug effect. But without the presence of a drug, these symptoms would bring the body to levels away from homeostasis (and lead to discomfort). *(Classical Conditioning)*

Within-Subjects Design: An experimental design in which one group of subjects receives the manipulation of the independent variable to observe the effect of this manipulation on the dependent variable. In this design, one group acts as both the experimental and control groups. *E.g. When testing the effects of caffeine on alertness, there would be two conditions, which involve drinking caffeinated coffee or decaffeinated coffee. One participant would take part in both conditions on separate days. (Research Methods I)*

Z

Zajonc's Resolution: The presence of co-actors or an audience will improve performance in a task in which the individual finds simple or has experience with. It will decrease performance in a task in which the individual is unfamiliar or finds difficult. *E.g. A child may tie his shoes more quickly when his parents are watching but may have trouble completing his math homework that he finds challenging when they are watching. (Influence of Others I)*

A Final Word

With the semester drawing to a close, it's time to reflect: what have you learned?

The overarching theme throughout our Introduction to Psychology, Neuroscience & Behaviour has been how to apply the scientific method to understand such wide-ranging problems as learning, cognition, social psychology, personality and psychopathology. I hope you have learned to appreciate that the scientific investigation of these problems involves much more than "pop psychology" or even "common sense." In this process, it's important to realize that science does not necessarily seek to prove things to be true. While most people (including scientists) tend to operate as if it did, in fact, what the scientific method does is strongly suggest that things are *not* true. As summarized by Bertold Brecht, "The aim of science is not to open a door to infinite wisdom, but to set a limit on infinite error." Like other sciences, psychology is self-correcting because researchers put forth testable hypotheses that refine our theories of human thought and behaviour.

This means that although many of the core "facts" will be constant in the foreseeable future, some of what you have just learned will undoubtedly change next year! This is the heart of the self-correcting nature of the scientific enterprise. If you have been diligently following throughout this course, the skills you have gained in critical thinking, research methods and evaluating new information will go on with you into the next term and beyond. In PSYCH 1XX3: Foundations of Psychology, Neuroscience & Behaviour, we will build on these skills as we explore processes that guide the behaviours critical to our survival.

As a closing exercise, I would like you to estimate your final grade for this course. Was it above a B or perhaps an A? I doubt that many of you estimated anything in the C or D range. Like the residents of the fictional town of Lake Wobegon where "all the women are strong, all the men are good-looking, and all the children are above average", most of us feel that we are above average on many of the things that we do–above average intelligence, popularity and driving skills, to name a few, not you of course, but perhaps some of your colleagues. However, based on our statistical understanding of average, only part of the population can be above average. Can you think of a good psychological explanation for this effect on our judgment?

Dr. Joe Kim

Degree Programs

McMaster Undergraduate Degrees offered in the Dept. of Psychology, Neuroscience & Behaviour (PNB)
For students wishing to pursue further study in **P**sychology, **N**euroscience & **B**ehaviour here are some programs for you!

RESEARCH LOVERS: PNB offers research-intensive degrees in **Honours PNB (B.A. or B.Sc.)**
APPLIED APPROACH: Applied Science is offered in **Honours Human Behaviour (B.A.Sc.)**.

All the following programs require **Psych 1XX3** for admission and some also require **Psych 1X03** for admission or completion by the end of year 2.

<u>**Honours PNB (B.Sc. or B.A.)**</u>
This program prepares students for graduate studies (both clinical and experimental); for professional studies such as medicine and teaching; for research positions in government, university or industry, and for careers in health sciences, community services, education and government. **Within this degree there are two Specializations:**

(1) **Mental Health** – prepares students for graduate and professional training in Mental Health.
(2) **Music Cognition** – requires Advanced Rudiments in music to be admitted – brings together science and arts in a unique and innovative way.

PNB B.Sc. and the B.A. programs are identical, with the exception of required courses in Year 1.

<u>**Combined Honours Programs offered by PNB and Biology Departments**</u>
Honours B.Sc. Biology & PNB: A double major merging leading-edge knowledge from both fields, with an option to do a thesis in Biology or Psychology.
Honours B.Sc. Neuroscience: Interdisciplinary study, comprising all research related to neurons and nervous system. For students interested in a career in neuroscience research.

<u>**Combined Honours Programs offered by PNB and Social Sciences or Humanities**</u>
Honours B.A. PNB with Another Subject (in Social Sciences or Humanities): Double major merging knowledge in multiple fields: Examples - Hons B.A. Economics & PNB; Hons B.A. PNB & Sociology; Hons B.A. Philosophy & PNB; Hons B.A. Linguistics & PNB etc.)

<u>**Honours B.A.Sc. Human Behaviour**</u>
Prepares students to enter any work environment that requires understanding the determinants of human behaviour; continue their education in non-research related fields such as law, human resources, journalism, rehabilitation sciences, counselling, advertising, and education; or pursue a range of applied certificate/diploma training.
Within this degree there are two specializations offered jointly by PNB and Mohawk College. Students graduate with an Honours B.A.Sc. degree from McMaster University, and a Graduate Certificate/Diploma from Mohawk College.
Field placements occur during the Spring/Summer sessions

(1) **Autism & Behavioural Sciences** – leads to opportunities in Behaviour or ABA therapy in community treatment agencies, hospital/clinical settings, private agencies and school boards.
(2) **Early Childhood Education** – leads to opportunities in full-day kindergarten, child care and early learning agencies, parent-child drop-in programs and professional resource sites.

<u>**B.A. Psychology**</u>: A 3-year degree requiring Psych 1X03 (or 1F03) for admission. Prepares students for entry-level positions in human services, business, criminal justice, health and recreation, and education.